SORT OF A SHAMAN

MARK J. HOWARTH

SORT OF A SHAMAN

MARK J. HOWARTH

Copyright © 2018 by Mark J. Howarth
1st Edition published in 2018
2nd Edition published in 2022

ISBN: 0692984399
ISBN-13: 978-0692984390

Mark Howarth Publishing

All rights reserved. No portion of this book may be copied and distributed without permission from the author.
Website: www.markhowarth.com

The names of some of the people in this book have been changed to protect their privacy.

Dedication

This book is dedicated to my grandmother Mercedes, who seemed to believe I should be a writer. She died in 2004, at 101 years of age.

It is also dedicated to the young international travelers in our world who are searching for truth. May you find some in these pages.

Acknowledgments

Many thanks to Jeffrey, Tracy, and Dhara for periodic assistance with the editing. Your timely feedback was invaluable. Thank you Wesley for creating the cover, my website, and other digital matters. Thanks Pete for formatting the second edition.

Reuben, your early and enthusiastic support and networking skills were key. Your idea of using the Mayan image on the cover was perfect. Little did I realize the face of the shaman emerging from the serpent's mouth would eventually become mine.

Thank you so much Marti for your help in various ways and on numerous levels. I also wish to express my appreciation to Julia and Ginger for your early belief in me and this project. Thank you Conrad, Kaijah and Mira for your proof reading contributions.

With infinite gratitude, I wish to honor my parents for your unending support over the years; this book would never have occurred without you.

Contents

Introduction	1
Part 1: Early Life Searches	5
Chapter 1	7
Chapter 2	14
Chapter 3	18
Chapter 4	28
Chapter 5	37
Intermission # 1 – Climbing the Volcano	48
Part 2: Wrestling With Fears	65
Chapter 6	67
Chapter 7	77
Chapter 8	83
Chapter 9	90
Chapter 10	103
Chapter 11	112
Chapter 12	115
Chapter 13	123
Chapter 14	128
Chapter 15	134
Intermission #2 – South America Trip	143
Part 3: Deep and Intense	163
Chapter 16	165
Chapter 17	171
Chapter 18	178

Chapter 19	182
Chapter 20	188
Chapter 21	198
Chapter 22	204
Chapter 23	212
Chapter 24	215
Chapter 25	222
Chapter 26	229
Chapter 27	232
Chapter 28	239
Epilogue	240
Special Features	247
Traveling in Latin America	249
Amazon Herb Company	254
Ayahuasca Journeys in Colombia	257

Introduction

"The shaman goes into the darkness and transforms it. He is not afraid of the dark side." Those words flew from my mouth on the day my life shifted gears – again. A small group of us were in a circle around a medicine wheel on my land. We had gathered for a ceremony and unbeknownst to everyone, including myself, I was in the process of dramatically changing its direction. Unexpectedly, my spontaneous words became a challenge that rocked this group to its core. They were also the seed from which this book was born.

That experience happened in the fall of 2014. For close to twenty years, I had been aware of at least one shamanic presence who assisted me in the healing work I offered people. I also seemed to have access to his profound understanding of the nature of reality. Yet the repercussions stemming from the day around the medicine circle led to several more powerful realizations. This shamanic presence not only guided and protected me, he actively trained me from within.

The training I received took several forms. The foundational aspect of this unconventional teaching method was also the most important: I was consistently challenged to pursue and overcome all of my fears. I met a lot of them traveling internationally, others while hiking or backpacking in forests, mountains, and jungles from Alaska and Canada to the countries of South America.

These experiences can best be told in story form. I have seldom, if ever, shared the following stories with anyone, yet they are integral to this book and quite powerful when viewed as a whole. The reader might have difficulty accepting some of the subjects and conclusions addressed in latter chapters without vicariously experiencing some of the things I've gone through.

Over a three-year period, I lived, worked, and studied at a healing arts school run by a community of people in a remote area of northern California. I was intimately involved with running the school while immersed in its transformative environment. Since

1988, I've been practicing holistic forms of massage and trading sessions with other therapists. Although my classes at the school offered technical and philosophical information, I probably learned more about healing by actually experiencing it.

For many years, I was intensely focused on personal growth. Holistic healing, gaining insights into Creation, and exploring altered states of consciousness became my passions. I learned a great deal through inner teachings, which included self-study, meditation, and contemplation. I also regularly discussed spiritual and metaphysical principles with other people.

As I overcame fears, studied, practiced, and healed, I became an able vehicle for deep transformational experiences with clients that were open to this kind of work. Sometimes a person would show up for a massage or energy session while in the midst of suffering from past trauma. Some shared their story with me, others did not.

Magical transformations occurred when the person was willing to trust me enough to allow me to go deep into their darkness with them. With my support, they had enough courage to dive into their pain and in most instances we re-emerged into the light, into a joyfully connected state of being. "My Shaman," as I've come to call the shamanic presence, was intimately involved in those experiences.

It seems an integral aspect of transformation is a strong desire for change because this facilitates inner shifts. I've supported hundreds of clients in this journey, which culminates in a sort of inner celebration. Gratitude appears to be another important part of the process and I often experience a person's breakthrough into love and light nearly as strongly as they do.

Yet most people spend their lives avoiding these types of experiences. Even those committed to their spiritual paths regularly resist them. Either they don't feel they are necessary, don't want to deeply feel repressed emotions, or are too afraid of the really ugly stuff. Some people claim they don't want to "feed" the dark by focusing on it. The problem with this approach is that negativity tends to remain unchanged, often in the unconscious and always within a person's energy bodies.

We co-create our lives through the law of attraction – like attracts like. Each of us draws life experiences to ourselves with our entire energy field. Unhealed trauma will continue to attract similar situations indefinitely, despite thoughts to the contrary. We often manifest our fears and re-create inner pain, rather than the desires we actively focus on creating.

No matter what people want to believe, positive thinking cannot effectively compete with deep-seated trauma connected to unhealed wounds. Simply stated, we cannot create the lives and world we desire unless we continue to heal that which is dark and hidden, individually and collectively.

The vast majority of people on our planet don't know how to constructively deal with darkness. They spend their lives reacting to it and virtually all of us do this at least some of the time. Reaction takes form within the polar extremes of avoidance and obsession.

Avoidance is common in overly busy societies when negative thoughts, feelings, and behavior may become an issue. "I don't want to hear about it" is an avoidance type of statement. Denial is one of its expressions and is especially prevalent around extremely controversial subjects. It has become so normal in American society, I would venture to say that we in the States have become a culture of denial.

Obsession, on the other hand, looks like corporate news broadcasts. Obsessing shows up as the mind's excessive focus on drama and darkness, often in the form of worry and fear. Both of these reactionary states, avoidance and obsession, are not only flip sides of the same coin, they are dis-empowering and tend to directly or indirectly feed dark energies.

In contrast, taking a proactive approach to negative life experiences and realities is very empowering. It is the ideal stance for transforming manifestations of darkness. This book offers you the tools required to respond, rather than react, to the dark side. Ongoing transformation of the dark can be developed into an art and a spiritual practice. It can be utilized to serve all forms of life on our planet and is an integral aspect of mastering oneself.

The shaman has overcome his or her fears of the dark side and developed a relationship with it. He has created a much deeper and more meaningful relationship with the light. From this solid foundation, he is able to transmute darkness with a Tai Chi type of strategy. A fully evolved shaman doesn't need to fight the forces of darkness, rather he reveals the light within them.

One of the deepest truths I've seen is that duality is essential for Creation to exist. It's the polarity between light and dark, the extreme tension and contrast between these opposites that allows intention and energy to coalesce and express within all dimensional realities. Thus, the dark side is a necessary component of Creation. This is a key realization as it opens the door for us to begin to understand and work with it.

What the darker realities need is our attention – and ideally our love – not avoidance and judgment. Darkness is more or less the same whether it shows up inside oneself or within the global power structures. My personal experiences of the shadow are that it is extremely wounded. Rarely, if ever, would I refer to it as evil.

On our planet, the dark side wallows in self-inflicted suffering, which results in grief, inner turmoil, and rage. At the core of this pitiful reality is the pain of feeling separate from our Source. It exists in a reactionary reality and expresses its pain in anti-life and destructive behavior patterns. Therefore, transforming darkness is key to our survival and integral to our evolution as a species.

Join me on a journey of awakening. My search for truth began at an early age and became a lifelong quest for meaning. By sharing intimate details, from childhood onward, you can observe my growth and healing process on a very personal level. In addition, we will explore the concept of transformation, look at the experiences of some of my clients, and address the issue of what it will take for humanity to make foundational shifts as a species. It will certainly require a deep desire for change, healing, and unity.

Part 1

Early Life Searches

Sort of a Shaman

Chapter 1

The first stage of my life lasted twenty years, until the summer I escaped my birthplace, San Diego, California. People have idealistic images of southern California, its warm weather and Hollywood reality. I found it to be boring, shallow, and painful, so much so that I couldn't wait to leave by the end of my time there.

Possibly most difficult of all was my unending confusion, as life in suburbia USA never made any sense to me. There was absolutely nothing inspiring or creative about the way people around me were living. People lived methodically uninteresting lives. Looking back, it felt as if I lived in a perpetual daze, although it wasn't drug induced. Rather I've come to believe parts of my soul were not present; most of myself simply wasn't there.

The most significant trauma of my childhood stems from racism. My mother was born in Calexico, a small California border town in the desert east of San Diego. Her mother was from a rural Mexican-American community in west-central Texas, where she experienced deeply ingrained racism. Her father and stepfather were both born in northern Mexico.

From my mom's side of the family, my siblings and I inherited genes from Spain, Mexico (indigenous), Ireland, and probably France. From my dad, who was born in New Jersey, we inherited Hungarian, German, and Austrian. One can view my bloodline as a union of opposites; it can also be seen as balanced and complementary.

I was born in 1959 and suffered under the anti-Mexican sentiments prevalent in the Southwest, especially as the drama of the civil rights movement escalated in the Deep South. When I was five or six, my parents decided to move our family further east, towards the outskirts of San Diego's suburbs. Although I loved the neighborhood my siblings and I were growing up in, my mother wanted to live in a safer area.

Our three closest neighbors were older couples who drank too much alcohol and exhibited racist tendencies. There was always the fear that one of them would fly into uncontrolled fits of rage if my parents invited an African exchange student to our house or my grandparents crossed the border with their Mexican license plates. It got so bad, my parents finally had to take the worst offending couple to court. Mostly unaware of these problems, I was focused on my friendships, our two beautiful tomcats, and the canyon behind our home.

The move out of that neighborhood set the tone for the rest of my childhood. From that point on, I never felt accepted and was constantly on the defensive. Where my brother was more than willing to engage in fistfights with those who slandered us, I was passive and tended to hold my pain within. As a result, my self-confidence plummeted and I grew ever more shy and introverted. I was deeply unhappy as a child, trapped in a reality I could not understand, from overt racism, to the isolating tendencies of a nuclear family structure, to the strangeness of American culture.

My parents are good people and probably more loving than most. Actually, they must be saints – somehow they've managed to believe in me for all of these years. The love and character of my parents, plus the time I spent in nature and playing sports were the saving graces of my childhood. As a family, we would go hiking, camping and backpacking. We also ventured south of the border on a regular basis to visit my grandparents in the tourist community of Rosarito Beach, twenty miles south of Tijuana.

They owned a restaurant called "El Pinocho." Grandpa Louie taught us to ride his horses from a young age and we never tired of playing at the beach. My love of the outdoors grew steadily into adulthood and I became proficient in numerous sports. Although not competitive by nature, I persevered, especially in tennis, the sport I spent the most time playing. Yet my self-confidence was so low, it was hard to garner much athletic success until after my teenage years.

My father had a master's degree in engineering and mostly worked on military contracts, because those were the available jobs.

He worked for the University of California for many years, then as a civilian with the navy for many more.

My mother occasionally worked part-time as a registered nurse when we were growing up. But her true passion arose when, as she says, her issues really started coming up and she went to therapy. Deeply inspired by the process and results, my mom decided to go back to college and become a psychotherapist. She graduated with a master's degree in social work the same year I graduated from high school.

During my two years at our local junior college, it was not uncommon to find my mother and I awake at one or two in the morning discussing family dynamics or her clients' processes. This time was invaluable to me because I was able to absorb the best of what the system had to offer in the field of psychology, in a truly organic manner. Furthermore, this was the beginning of my personal growth, which gradually evolved into a lifelong devotion to the healing arts and transformation.

Here is a brief description of our family dynamics when I was growing up. I am the oldest of four children. Similar to my father, who was the oldest of five, I was rather serious about the responsibilities inherent in that position of birth. I could be so serious at times, my mother would tell me to stop studying and go outside to play. My brother was a year younger than me and also a lot more carefree. My mother needed to tell him to go inside and study. Notwithstanding our opposing natures, we were best friends during most of our childhood. I have two sisters and the elder is three years younger than me. She desperately wanted to be best friends with her two older brothers: unsurprisingly we didn't cooperate very well. My other sister is nearly six years younger and was very much the baby of the family.

My dad supported us adequately and was generally willing to leave most of the family challenges to my supermom mother. The main complaint I remember my mother making towards my father was that he was always "trying to save the world." In other words, my mother felt he wasn't showing up enough for her and his family, but instead prioritizing everyone else.

Despite their differences, both of them instilled in us a deep concern for the plight of humanity, especially social injustices. I remember boycotting Safeway and their grapes by toting signs in front of their grocery stores in support of Cezar Chavez and the migrant Mexican farm workers. As a family, we revered people such as Martin Luther King, John F. Kennedy, and Mahatma Gandhi.

My parents raised us as good Catholics, taking us to church every Sunday. We hated this and rebelled enough that my parents finally relented. They decided to let us choose whether or not we wanted to go and much to their disappointment, we mostly stopped. The only church services we were willing to attend were those led by Father Davis.

Along with my parents, Fr. Davis was the other person who had a major impact on my development. He was the only extraordinarily interesting person in my entire childhood. An Irish rebel, he was true to his bloodlines. My parents had originally met in a group Fr. Davis was facilitating. The focus of the "Young Christian Workers" was to live the teachings of Christ, rather than preach or idealize them. It was on a trip to Rome, for an international conference, that my father proposed to my mother.

Father Davis was a unique character, in a truly Irish manner. He went out of his way to demonstrate what he felt was important in life: loving people, Christ, and God were at the top of his list, while pilfering a wine glass or cloth napkin from restaurants he frequented was his way of showing us what was more or less irrelevant. At times, he would stand on a chair in these same restaurants and recite poetry to everyone present.

He celebrated me and my brother being boys and promoted naughtiness. We heard our share of dirty jokes from him and often played poker after dinner when he visited our family. Dinner itself was always a bit of a ritual. It usually started with a glass of bourbon and water plus an appetizer. The main course usually featured a meat dish, often steak and potatoes, plus a glass of wine. This was followed by a cup of coffee with dessert and occasionally a small glass of after-dinner liquor to top it all off.

Early Life Searches

After Fr. Davis had his first heart attack, he spent several months at my family's home recuperating. He definitely had a hard time adjusting to the diet his doctor prescribed. Leo Davis was loved to the extreme by nearly everyone, even though he was somewhat controversial. At his funeral, there were over 700 people from all walks of life, including the mayor of San Diego.

The summer before leaving San Diego for college in northern California, I, a young man of twenty, engaged in my first vision quest of sorts. Since the beginning of the summer, I had been talking with my brother and two friends about going on a major backpacking trip. We wanted to hike the entire John Muir Trail, which is in the middle of the Sierra Nevada mountain range of California. Unsurprisingly, our two friends came up with excuses to back out of the trip. Then my brother said he could only hike the last nine days because of a job. This left me on my own for the first fifteen days. Although I had never backpacked alone, I was determined to go.

Stepping off the bus into the desert approximately fifty miles west of Death Valley, I managed to hitch a ride to the edge of the mountains where my hike would begin. Since I was unable to get a permit from the forest service for my preferred trailhead just east of Mt. Whitney, I had to begin about forty miles south. The top of Mt. Whitney, which is the highest point in the continental United States, is the southern end of the John Muir Trail.

I started my hike at an elevation of 5,000 ft. with 72 lbs. on my back. Considering I only weighed 145 lbs., this was a large load. It was August 1st, 102 degrees in the shade, and I was sweating profusely. By the time I crossed over the pass that led into the high country, I was desperate to lighten my load.

Two weeks of food was the majority of weight in my pack and it was definitely non-negotiable. I finally chose to leave my book by a tree, which felt like leaving a friend behind. Throughout my childhood, books had not only been an escape, they had regularly replaced a lack of close friendships. As I continued my hike to Mt. Whitney, it seemed as if every muscle in my body were sore. Even worse were the huge blisters on the backs of my feet.

On the fourth day, I reached the peak at an elevation of 14,494 feet. I was elated to have finally reached the official beginning of the trail, yet the realization that over 200 miles remained – through some of the toughest, rockiest, and highest terrain in those mountains – was daunting. As it turned out, the physical challenge was not as difficult as the psychological.

Over the next eleven days, I continued to spend the vast majority of my time alone. Although the John Muir Trail is popular, the forest service dramatically limited the number of people with access to it. I never found anyone to hike with and only passed a handful or two of people each day going in the opposite direction.

More often than not, I seemed to camp alone. Struggling with intense loneliness, I would usually join hikers at their campfires when I did camp near others. Not only did I enjoy their company, they often offered me extra food. Since I never seemed to have enough to eat and had an insatiable appetite during the hike, I always accepted.

Having been relatively introverted, I was still unprepared for the depths of loneliness I would experience in those fifteen days. I have no idea how many times I looked at the map and saw a trail heading east or west out of the mountains, then contemplated taking it. Those deliberations would go on for an entire day or two until I walked past the trail, somehow having found enough inner strength to persevere yet again.

Fears arose as I slept alone miles from another human being, hung my food in trees to keep it from bears, and constantly risked possible injury. The tiny diary I wrote in, the breathtaking scenery, the constant connection to nature, and the certainty that I would meet my brother all kept my momentum moving in a forward direction. Every couple of days, I meticulously calculated the mileage to go and continued to push myself, hiking eight to ten hours a day.

I arrived at Duck Lake the afternoon before my brother and I were to meet. The following morning, he hiked in four miles to our meeting spot with a lot of food. After that the last nine days of my journey were easy. Upon arriving in Yosemite Valley, the northern end of the John Muir Trail, I certainly felt a sense of pride and accomplishment. I had hiked 277 miles in 24 days, lost fifteen pounds of body weight, overcome my inner demons, and probably proved to myself that I wasn't a coward.

After the hike, my brother and I hitchhiked back to his car and drove home. Actually, it wasn't going to be "home" for much longer. A week later, I left for the University of California at Santa Cruz (UCSC) – I was heading north to finish my bachelor's degree. I view my initiation on the John Muir Trail as the transition period leading into the next stage of my life.

Chapter 2

The second stage started with a bang – I fell in love for the first time! Not only that, I experienced my very first orgasm – with my new love. It practically blew my mind. When I arrived at the university, I was assigned to an Arts College dorm even though I was enrolled in the Environmental Studies College. The hall I lived in was co-ed, which I had chosen given it was an option. This was a very liberal university; our dorm hall was equipped with a co-ed toilet and shower facility with a minimal amount of privacy.

Jim was my roommate and we rapidly became good friends. Directly across the hall, two female art students shared a room. One of them became my lady and playmate for the next two years. Lolita was born in Cuba, but left the country with her parents at the age of two when they fled the Castro regime. She was sexy, radical, and pretty darn bold.

From what I can remember, she told me that her parents were extremely conservative Castro and communist haters; luckily I only met them once. In contrast, her older brother had introduced her to Ram Dass' book, *Be Here Now,* along with much of the alternative-minded Sixties culture. Lolita was a talented artist, and she ended up being good enough to make a career of art after college.

We had an incredibly fun time together that first year. Living in the dorms felt like living with family, and sometimes like a never-ending party. Halfway through the first quarter, Jim moved out of my room and Lolita moved in.

The experience of falling in love hit me square in the chest one afternoon. I was saying goodbye to Lolita while passionately kissing her outside of the building to my next class. She walked off and I just stood there leaning against the wall. The feelings coursing through me were completely overwhelming and I was at a loss as to what they were.

Romantic love is such a high. I felt indescribable joy mixed with other emotions. One of them was fear – of losing something I had only just found, which felt so tenuous. Little did I realize I had stumbled on what would become my main addiction in life: falling in love. I've never experienced another high that is so all-encompassing and attractive. Of course, the problem with any addiction comes when you lose your "fix," as the withdrawals can be incredibly painful.

There were so many firsts that year: eating Szechuan Chinese food, which I came to crave, watching *Harold and Maude* at the theater, which became my favorite movie, a new richly textured laugh, which people all of a sudden started commenting on, and eating magic mushrooms. Now there's a story worth telling: my first psychedelic experience.

Lolita and I ate mushrooms with two friends and we all went to the amusement park by the beach. The rides, the love, and the fungus combined in the most spectacular fashion. After leaving, we drove north to an isolated beach. It was night and the phytoplankton were in full bloom, shining their fluorescent green colors in the waves and wet sand whenever we shuffled our feet. We simply couldn't get enough of it. That was undoubtedly the most magical day I had ever experienced.

Our university was situated in a redwood forest on a hill overlooking Santa Cruz and the Pacific Ocean several miles below. The setting was incredible and distractions were everywhere. One of my favorites was the intramural sports teams I regularly played on. I remember going to a counselor the first quarter concerned with my inability to focus on studying. He actually had some good suggestions. The strategy that paid the best dividends was to isolate myself in the library for extended periods of time and force myself to study.

During a break, Lolita and I rode our bicycles from Santa Cruz down the coast to southern California. We managed to tie enough supplies to our bikes and camped along the way. The dramatic up-and-down coastline provided us with endless views. We parted ways in Malibu: Lolita rode to her parents' home in the San Fernando Valley and I continued south, passing through the never-ending city of Los Angeles. Towards the end of the day it began to rain, so I found a restaurant and enjoyed a well-deserved dinner. While contemplating where I would sleep for the night, a man at a neighboring table offered to drive me to my parents' home fifty miles further south. I was very surprised, but could hardly say no.

That summer, Lolita and I traveled to Casper, Wyoming to stay with her brother and some of his friends. They told us we would easily find work, which turned out to be true. While there, I got caught up in a dream of going to Colorado and working in a ski resort for the winter. As much as I loved the university, I disliked the classes and was sick of the unending school reality.

Lolita went back to Santa Cruz, but I chose to stay and work for another month before heading south to Colorado. Although there was snow in the mountains, I was much too early. The more ski resorts I drove to, the more jobs I applied for, and the longer I waited, the more I missed Lolita and our friends.

Therefore, I drove back to Santa Cruz and re-enrolled for the following quarter. I mostly took art classes upon returning – as a way to extend my break from the science courses I was used to. Although most of my biology classes had been bearable and occasionally interesting, the chemistry courses were awful. Mathematics had always been easy for me and I found calculus to be a curious challenge. As for physics, well how could they have possibly made a potentially interesting subject so boring?

The American schooling system did its best to destroy my love of learning. Although it failed to do so, it has managed to achieve that goal with countless numbers of other people. If I had been more aware at the time, I would have chosen environmental studies for my degree since it would have been a much better fit for me. But I was enamored with the idea of becoming a marine biologist and had illusions of getting a master's degree in marine biology at UCSC.

The following year, I spent the first quarter doing research at a marine lab in Bodega Bay, north of San Francisco. I'll never forget snorkeling with my friends for abalone, which we grilled and feasted on. Not only was it incredibly rich and tasty, it was also abundant in those days. But similar to all sea life, its numbers were rapidly declining. Thus my main research project at the marine lab focused on the growth of baby abalone when fed different types of diets, for commercial aqua-culture potential.

I took my first and only pre-med class during the last quarter of college. It was on the development of the human fetus, which I found to be interesting. But the teacher ruined it by demanding we memorize hundreds of ridiculous words for the different body parts as they changed and evolved. I rebelled at this stupidity and got terrible scores on my first two tests, without a doubt the worst performances of my entire schooling career. I remember one of the students standing up in class offering an all-night study group at her home and talking about stress management. That was definitely not my cup of tea! I finally gave up and dropped the class.

I still managed to graduate with a B.A. in Biology by the slimmest of margins. I needed 200 course credits to qualify for my degree. I had 199.6 credits and was amazed when the school official told me she needed to round this number up to 200. I knew it was going to be close when I dropped the pre-med class, but didn't know it would be that close!

My idea of obtaining a master's degree in marine biology ended because I couldn't stand to be in school any longer. During the final quarter, I constantly thought of traveling and couldn't concentrate on classes anymore. I had also stopped thinking about a professional job as a biologist because the word was out at my Environmental Studies College: very few graduates could expect a job, the pay was really shitty should we manage to get a "good" job, and we would likely be stuck in a laboratory living the 9 to 5, 40-hour per week hell reality. That spring, I instead took a plane to Alaska to work in a salmon processing facility.

Chapter 3

I went to Alaska four summers in a row, from 1982 – 1985, and worked all types of jobs. Starting out in Anchorage, I can still claim this as the largest city I've lived in since leaving San Diego. I traveled and worked throughout the entire southern coast of Alaska, from the southeast panhandle to Bristol Bay.

I backpacked the Klondike trail north of Skagway. A century earlier, it had seen thousands of gold miners hiking north hoping to strike it rich. I backpacked in the Kenai Peninsula and camped near Mt. McKinley, maybe 30 to 40 miles from the mountain. I had heard many people spend a week or more in the park and never see the peak because of cloud cover.

It was cloudy in the afternoon when I arrived, but the next morning was crystal clear. I crawled out of my tent not knowing this and there before me was the mountain – it was mind-bogglingly huge! I had seen Mt. McKinley several times from an impressive 175 miles away while on an Anchorage overpass, but its majesty was truly stunning as I visually took in the mountain from my campsite.

The first year, I stayed past the salmon season into November to work the king crab season on Kodiak Island. I camped out with two Israeli medical students who were taking a break from their studies and the military. I would visit them in Jerusalem a year and a half later.

During the second and third summers, I ended up on the west side of the Aleutian Islands for the red salmon run and worked at a cold storage plant in Dillingham. The first time, I was flown to a salmon processing ship in a helicopter and worked there for several weeks. I rapidly got involved with an attractive rather exotic looking woman named Cynthia. She was the only woman I ever got sexually involved with in Alaska, the land of minimal women.

The week after we met, she discovered Bob Dylan had just released a song inspired by her at a party they had both attended in Duluth, MN. Her friend sent her a letter describing the situation, along with a cassette tape. Of course, Cynthia couldn't stop listening to it. The song was titled: *What's A Girl Like You Doing In A Place Like This?* I visited her in Minnesota that fall and saw a video of the song on MTV some years later.

In between my trips to Alaska, I traveled all over the place. I flew to Europe twice and made two trips to Mexico. On the first trip to Mexico, my college friend John and I drove his VW bus down the west coast to Puerto Escondido before heading inland to the city of Oaxaca. We eventually made it to the Yucatan peninsula and from there drove north back up the east coast to Texas.

We brought scuba equipment and surf boards, camped out on isolated beaches and visited tourist towns. We ate way too many chilies and probably drank too much beer and tequila. John had grown up in southern California by the ocean; he was a good-looking surfer and a womanizer. Despite his obsession, he was a very heartfelt person. Two experiences on that trip stand out.

In the city of Oaxaca, John and I stayed at a great little hostel where we met lots of backpack travelers. We ran into this young international hippie backpacker crowd regularly as we kept tapping in to the circuit of cool places to visit. Traveling with a backpack instead of a suitcase has obvious benefits and allows for maximum flexibility. Travelers are very different from tourists, people with suitcases on vacation from their jobs.

From this point onward, the following distinctions will be used. "Backpackers" travel with backpacks and regularly stay in hostels on the beaten path. They tend to party a lot. "Travelers" desire to experience and understand the local culture and language and are into personal and/or spiritual growth. "Backpack travelers" are a combination of the two terms, those who are evolving from the first to the second. "Trekkers" hike in the mountains and sleep in tents, huts, or hostels. I define "backpacking" as hiking with a large pack and camping in nature.

At the hostel in Oaxaca, I was attracted to an American woman named Sonya. This progressed to infatuation while listening to her play her guitar and sing her angelic melodies. She told us about a wonderful beach on the Pacific coast in the area we had just left. She had stayed in Zipolite for several weeks and absolutely loved it. I kept in touch with Sonya by mail, visiting her in Switzerland the following year. Two years later, I visited Zipolite and it changed my life.

The second experience occurred on the day we arrived in Palenque to visit the famous Mayan ruins. At the main campground, our neighbors offered us tea made from magic mushrooms they had harvested in the surrounding pastures. We definitely weren't going to pass up their offer and gladly accepted. The moon was full and the two Swiss guys who gave us the tea suggested we join them on an adventure. John stayed behind, but I went off into the jungle with them.

Their route took us on a thirty-minute walk along a stream, bypassing the guard booth at the entrance and right into the ruins. We proceeded to spend the entire night playing and drumming among the pyramids. This was the first night I had ever heard howler monkeys and they sounded to me like nightmarish monsters. If you've never heard them, their howl is extremely loud and eerie.

To spend the night in a place like this sounds magical and sacred. I suppose it was, but considering we were little more than kids, our "cool fort" just happened to be an ancient Mayan temple complex. It is probably the most important and famous of the Mayan sites in Mexico.

The next morning, just before sunrise, a guard saw us on top of one of the pyramids. He was an older man with an old-fashioned military rifle that had a saber sticking out of the end. He yelled at us to come down and as we stood before him, one of us had the audacity to laugh at the situation.

A moment later, the guard was yelling and chasing us towards the entrance. I got jabbed in the back by his saber and started running even faster. As we burst through the entrance of the ruins, the guard stopped his pursuit since he probably just wanted to teach us a lesson.

After the second summer in Alaska, I made my way to Vancouver, spent a few days on Vancouver Island, then hitchhiked to the Rocky Mountains, spending an afternoon at a Canadian rodeo along the way. Except for the Molson beer and hearing "eh" at the end of every other sentence, it felt like I was somewhere out west in the United States.

Upon reaching the mountains, I spent several weeks hitchhiking and backpacking around Banff, Jasper, and Mt. Robson National Parks. It was beyond beautiful and the fall colors simply added to the splendor.

In one spot, I was camping about eight miles from the road when it started snowing. No one else was camping at the campground and as the snow continued to fall I got nervous. I remembered seeing a ranger's cabin a short walk away and decided to move my tent to its large porch. As I lay in my sleeping bag, a ranger clad in snow shoes suddenly walked up and smiled, quickly ascertaining my situation. He invited me in, we started a fire in the wood stove, and he shared his dinner with me.

The Canadian Rockies are incredibly rugged and I was in total awe the entire time. Yet it was time to head south and meet my dad in Glacier National Park, Montana. He had been working in Seattle the previous week and was only a short train ride away. It meant a lot to me, camping and hiking together.

I then continued hitchhiking and backpacking through Montana and into Wyoming, keeping just ahead of the snow. All in all, I spent six weeks of the fall like this, mostly by myself.

Leaving the Rocky Mountains, I went to visit Cynthia in Minnesota. We proceeded to spend a very romantic night together at her home. The next morning, Cynthia embarrassingly confessed she was obsessed with Bob Dylan and the song. So that was that – she dumped me for Bob, even if he was just in her head!

Continuing east to Maine, I spent the coldest months of winter with a friend, drawn by the prospect of making money scuba diving for scallops. Connie and I had done research together at the Bodega Bay marine lab. She had a fishing boat and we went diving when the seas were calm enough, but mostly for sea urchins since the scallops were becoming scarce.

Sometimes heavy ice ringed the edge of the harbor where the boat was stored, with daytime temperatures barely reaching ten degrees Fahrenheit. We would dive two consecutive tanks of air and be underwater for up to four hours. It was exhausting work, yet our dry suits kept us surprisingly warm. We only dove once or twice a week and occasionally worked odd jobs around town.

In between, I regularly went ice skating on the lake behind Connie and her boyfriend's home or cross-country skiing with their two large dogs. As it turned out, many things were surprisingly different in rural New England. Relating to the locals could often be frustrating because I didn't know what anyone was talking about.

Come March, I flew to Europe and spent several months traveling around. I started out by visiting Sonya, who was working as a nanny in Switzerland. I really wanted her to take a break from her job and go traveling with me, but she wasn't able to.

After a few special days together, I went skiing at the ultra-famous Matterhorn in the Swiss Alps. Although I enjoyed the experience, I kept wishing Sonya was with me. She actually visited me a year later in San Diego and we connected another time at Mammoth Lakes in northern California. I really thought we would stay together at some point, but that never happened.

From Switzerland, I proceeded south to Venice, Italy. I had timed my trip to Europe to coincide with the Venice Carnival since it was supposed to be a big deal. Sadly, it was snowing and I was informed all the hotels were full. I ended up sleeping at the train station where I met a couple who lived in Rome. Confused and uncertain what to do, I decided to join them on their way home the next morning. I was hoping they would invite me to stay at their place and show me around the city, but that was wishful thinking.

Although I visited a few of the most famous sites in Rome, I spent much of the time totally miserable, sick with a stomach flu in my hotel room bed. The thing I remember most clearly about the city was how fast and seemingly crazy everyone drove on the narrow curvy roads. There was an incredible abundance of mopeds and somehow they managed to survive the apparent chaos.

Since Italy wasn't being very kind to me, I went further south to the warmth of Greece. I avoided all of the cities and tourist sites and instead spent my time in rural areas. The food and wine were great, but it was the Greek people and their culture that really touched me. They lived slow paced traditional farming lives.

The older men were often playing board games outdoors, discussing politics and drinking traditional beverages. Considering the simplicity of their lives, they had a considerable knowledge of international events. While exploring the southern coast of the island of Crete, I finally found what felt like family – a group of very cool European travelers living in a small fishing village known for the caves along its beach.

After six weeks in Greece, I crossed the Mediterranean Sea on a passenger ship to Israel and went to Jerusalem to visit the medical students. It is a fascinating city and I thoroughly enjoyed being there with them. I spent many days walking around the old and new cities, getting a feel for the place.

Delicious falafel sandwiches could be found at almost every street stand and I would return just to eat more of them. Through my friends I discovered that Israeli politics were as varied as its multi-national populace. A local saying summed things up rather well: if there are twelve Israelis debating a subject, they will present at least thirteen different perspectives.

After leaving Jerusalem, I spent a few days at a kibbutz harvesting bananas, which turned out to be hard work. The most interesting part of this experience was the manner in which I was invited to stay there. I was visiting an area with caves along the Mediterranean Sea and saw young people jumping off cliffs into the water. I like doing that sort of thing and quickly joined them. We were jumping and sometimes diving off of progressively higher spots. Only one man jumped from the highest ledge, at least thirty and possibly forty feet above the water. I went to the same spot and dove! A wild cheer ensued; everyone was so impressed, they invited me back to their kibbutz.

For those of you who don't know, a kibbutz is an agriculturally-based intentional community whose origins date back to the founding of Israel. They fluctuated between being idealistic communes and a practical political method of holding on to the land Israel had acquired through either the United Nations or their occasional wars.

Compared to Israel, my nine days in the Sinai desert along the Red Sea were a vacation. Two years prior, Israel had returned the area to Egypt as part of an historic peace accord. Israel was such an intense country in every way imaginable: the religions and history, its stark, severe deserts, constant contention, and fear of bombings all contributed to the tension.

In contrast, the Sinai was extremely laid back. Additionally, the Red Sea featured a world-class diving region. I found myself on a beach about half way down the peninsula in a classic traveler's scene, a traditional Bedouin village with simple, cheap accommodations. All day long most of the travelers hung out in cafés, usually sitting on the sandy beach drinking some kind of caffeinated tea, smoking hashish, and playing backgammon.

Every morning I would wake up and walk down the beach in one direction or the other, then jump in the water and spend an hour or two snorkeling the entire way back. The coral reefs were definitely first rate and I thoroughly enjoyed my time alone. After breakfast, I would usually join the other travelers in the cafés.

They were fascinating people, many being true world travelers. Most people's visas lasted only a week, mine included. But I didn't feel ready to return and had heard that people weren't usually hassled when they showed up at the border a few days late. I tested my luck – and got away with it. After a few more weeks in Israel, I headed back to the States.

On my fourth trip to Alaska, I decided to work in a new area. Since I couldn't find a job on the mainland in Ketchikan, I took a ferry to Prince of Wales Island. I hitchhiked from the east to the west shore, but couldn't find work on either side. Not only was it still early in the salmon season, this region's proximity to Seattle and the lower forty-eight created a situation where there were too many workers and not enough jobs.

After camping for a few too many days, I was feeling extremely impatient. While hanging out with two of my fellow campers, we met some "tree thinners" who were earning $200 or more per day working in the forests. We signed a sub-contract deal with them, bought some of their used chainsaws, and found a crab fisherman to take us to Heceta Island, the place we would work.

We purchased and loaded a month's worth of supplies onto the fishing boat in between the crab cages. Leaving early the next morning, our captain slowly felt his way through a heavy fog that was periodically broken up by patches of light mist. After several hours of ocean and islands, we arrived at our destination and proceeded to haul our supplies to shore in the fisherman's dingy. The area appeared to be completely isolated, but the acreage we had agreed to work was supposed to be close by. It was all so incredibly surreal, the stuff of movies.

We found our parcel, set up camp, and began to cut down spruce trees. After a week with those two guys, I knew the situation was simply not going to work out. Not only did they spend more time playing chess than tree thinning, I found out we might not even get paid for our work. I had met another tree thinner who was living with his family and working near the logging camp on the other side of the island. He told me that the men we sub-contracted with had a reputation for not paying people who worked for them.

Recalling their rude and crude behavior, I felt gullible as I realized our mistake in trusting them. Since I had a good feeling about this man, I decided to work for him. I encouraged my previous partners to join me, but they wouldn't hear of it. So I cut my losses and left the rest of my supplies with them. I found out later one of them cut himself deeply enough with his saw that they gave up and left the island.

The temperate rainforests of southeast Alaska grow thick with spruce trees. Much of it had been logged in large scattered sections through contracts with the forest service, because it's mostly Tongass National Forest. Since there is an abundance of rain, young spruce immediately start to grow in the clear-cut areas. After about ten years, tree thinners come to work the parcels of re-growth.

There were usually 1,000 – 4,000 young trees (1 – 10 in. wide) per acre. We cut down the vast majority and left the largest ones spaced in a loose grid (14 – 16 ft. apart). The dead trees would eventually decompose and feed the ones left to grow, thus creating a new forest to harvest in the future.

I proceeded to thin nine acres over about three weeks, a reasonably successful achievement for a first-timer. Working with a chainsaw for at least six hours a day in those conditions was exhausting. Not only did it rain often, I was always keeping an eye out for grizzly bears, which were a favorite topic of conversation in the logging camp.

Some memories stick out from my time there. I'll never forget winning an arm-wrestling contest with one of the young loggers who was bigger than me. Nor will I forget the eight stitches I received over my right eye after holding the scope of a rifle too close to my face. I had never used a scope before and my impatient companions urged me to shoot a bird before I had it in focus. But one of the least interesting of the various experiences became the most significant: I lost a small bag of chainsaw tools in the forest while I was working.

Although I appreciated the loggers and some of their families who lived in the camp, I was vastly different than them. The conversation was limited and I quickly got bored. The tree thinner I worked with gave me a few buds, so after work I occasionally went into the forest alone.

When I smoked and got high, I could see everything from a different perspective. In this state, my cannabis self could have interesting and insightful conversations with my normal self. That was exactly how I experienced it at that time, age, and maturity level. Now I would venture to say the cannabis opened me up to a higher aspect of myself. These may have been the first times I actively received information from My Shaman.

When the rangers came to check our work, my acreage failed because I had left a few too many trees. The truth is that I didn't feel good about cutting them down in the first place. The ranger who checked my plot went through a short process. She pointed in a random direction and said a random number to count off the number of steps she would walk. Then she placed a long stake in the ground and counted the trees within a certain radius. After repeating this process, she decided I flunked my test.

She returned and informed me that I needed to go over the entire nine acres and cut down more trees. She handed me the small bag of chainsaw tools that I had lost ten days earlier and said she nearly pierced it with the long stake on her second sampling. I could scarcely believe my luck and felt like that spot where she placed the stake was cursed. While lying in bed that night, totally and completely depressed, I intuitively knew it was time to leave the island before I cut myself, or something even worse happened.

I flew on a small prop plane to Ketchikan with my backpack and chainsaw, then took a ferry to Juneau to stay with a friend. Juneau is the capital of Alaska, but it took less than an hour to walk out of the city and find myself in relative wilderness.

On several day hikes, I struggled intensely with feelings of failure. I constantly reviewed my disappointing summer and kept coming back to that damn stake. As I began to realize the odds of it nearly skewering my bag of tools in a nine-acre parcel must be a million to one, I shifted from perceiving the situation as negative to one of amazement over the extreme coincidence.

This shift in perspective led to a deep inner knowing that there must be a profound message for me. What initially felt like a curse prompted me to revise the plans for my next adventure, one that would change the direction of my life.

Originally my plan was to go to South America with plenty of money and travel around the continent. Instead, I decided to take a suggestion my mother had made months earlier: I would help a Catholic priest who was working with the poor in Peru.

Chapter 4

I had met Leah somewhere in Alaska and she decided to join me for the first part of my trip. I was planning to go by bus and train all the way to Peru. We started our journey by camping on a beach along the Gulf of California. From there, we traveled southeast to the Copper Canyon area in northern Mexico.

At the bottom of one of its many canyons, we met an American living in the village of Creel. He took us to his home and showed us a map of the region. We were interested in a trail that led to another village in the next canyon over, passing through the high country and pine forests in between. The hike was supposed to take two days.

I copied the map by hand on a piece of paper, bought some food, and we started walking up the side of the canyon. When we reached the forested area on top, the trail kept splitting and we followed our intuition until periodically running into indigenous Tarahumara indians, at which point I would ask for directions. Since none of them spoke Spanish, the only viable solution was to use body language and pronounce the name of our destination.

The next day, Leah and I stumbled upon a ranch in the early afternoon and were invited to take a break. Since some of the men spoke Spanish and offered us their homemade liquor, we drank and laughed with them for several hours. Leaving this most enjoyable encounter, we got back on the trail and walked until sunset. After another cold night camping, we found a canyon that led to the river. We spent the entire afternoon trying to get down, but the terrain was much too steep and I finally had to admit this was not the correct way. We had run out of food and I was simply trying to force a solution. By the time we stopped for the night, we were near the place we had started in the morning and went to bed hungry.

Around noon the following day, we saw a little cabin with smoke coming from it. As we approached the humble abode, we met a very nervous Tarahumara woman who was home alone. She smiled and relaxed after we pointed to our mouths and stomachs, then proceeded to feed us beans and corn tortillas. We were undeniably grateful for the simple fare. Afterwards, she pointed us in the right direction and by late afternoon we reached our destination, found a restaurant, and then a shower and bed at a little hospedaje in town.

The next morning, I went for a walk along the river and ran into some local men. They had been drinking mescal all night and asked me to join them for a drink. Mescal is a less refined version of tequila and the cheap stuff usually tastes terrible. I still accepted their offer and after an hour realized I had probably overdone it. I was totally caught by surprise; after all, they had been drinking all night and I figured I could keep up with them for at least a little while. It turned out I underestimated their capacity to drink and overestimated mine. I managed to find my way back to our hospedaje, then slept the entire afternoon and all through the night.

Making our way south by bus, we eventually arrived in the city of Oaxaca. Remembering my desire to visit Zipolite, we headed west to the coast and made our way to a little village. The scene was truly idyllic: a beautiful crescent-moon-shaped white sand beach, while off to one side in the ocean stood a large guano-covered rock. We walked to the opposite end where we found a wonderful, inexpensive hotel set on the side of a hill boasting beautiful views of the entire beach.

Within a few days, we heard about and visited a place called "La Escuela Pina Palmera," translated as "The School of the Pineapples and Coconut Palm Trees." I sensed almost immediately that the Pina Palmera, here in the south of Mexico, was what I had hoped to find in Peru. I ended up staying for a long time, but Leah left soon after to return to her home in the States.

Arriving one year after its founding, I never found out how they came up with the name. There weren't any pineapples and it wasn't much of a school, but there were about 200 coconut palms. Many of them were full grown and some rose at least eighty-feet above our heads. There were also several large mango and guanabana trees, plus a fair-sized banana patch. The five-acre property featured several buildings, all with thatched palm roofs that shed the rain very efficiently. It was situated a long stone's throw from the beach, with a neighboring coconut grove in between.

Frank and Anna ran the Pina Palmera. Frank, who was in his late fifties, was from the States. Anna, in her late twenties, was from Sweden. Frank's vision for the place was one of a clinic integrating both Western medicine and natural remedies. But Anna, who just happened to show up several months after he started, changed its direction. Although single, she had an extremely strong mothering energy. By the time I arrived, Pina Palmera was already becoming a home for handicapped and orphaned children.

Most of the children at the Palmera were pure blood Zapotec indians. Our cook, a single Mexican woman who was probably mestizo (a mix of indigenous and European blood) had three young boys who lived with us. There were another five children plus several teenage boys who did most of the labor-intensive work around the property, including climbing the palms to collect coconuts. The two older ones were in their mid-to-late teens; watching them climb the tallest palms was incredible and frightening, especially since there was always the chance they would run into a wasp nest in the canopy. Within a week, I was welcomed into their community – or should I say, family.

Frank was a true healer. In Zipolite, they called him Panchito. In the San Francisco healing circles where he developed his talents, they called him Sashwa. Prior to that, he had worked in a high management position for a major oil company in the States. I remember him telling me that at some point in his life, everything started turning inside out. Strange metaphysical experiences started happening without him doing anything to initiate them. He was so preoccupied during this period that he often forgot to fill his car with gas. In one instance his car kept going for months despite not being filled. Finally accepting that he was being guided to radically change his life, he quit his job with the petroleum company.

This was in the 1960s and it was then that he became involved with a community of healers in San Francisco. He also became a follower of Sri Aurobindo, a yogi from India. Frank first started visiting Zipolite in the '70s and often did healing work with the native people.

He once told me about a Zapotec woman with a large tumor on her body whom he helped to heal. He placed his hands on the tumor and after a short while, it gradually receded beneath his palms until it was gone. When I asked how this was possible, he replied: "With enough love, anything is possible!" That is the most powerful statement I've ever heard anyone say.

Zipolite consisted of a mile-long beach, broken up by several clusters of traditionally constructed wood and thatched roof cafés. Being one of only two overtly nude beaches in all of Mexico, it was frequented by backpack travelers from all over the world. Everyone seemed to smoke pot, including most of the locals and some of the Mexican women – it was part of their culture. A half to one-ounce sized baggie, grown in the local rainforests, cost about five dollars. Travelers smoked openly in the cafés, drank beer and hung out. All the cafés doubled as restaurants and hospedajes. Renting a hammock and a space to hang it cost about two dollars a day. They operated on an honor system, with each traveler writing down their ongoing expenses.

Zipolite means "Beach of the Dead" in the Zapotec language. Although people regularly drowned from strong rip currents, that isn't how it obtained its name. It is a "power spot" and has been recognized as such for hundreds, if not thousands of years. Zapotec natives from the jungles and coastal areas had traditionally brought their dead to Zipolite to bury the bodies and send their souls to the spiritual realms. I've lived in several extremely powerful locations such as this and visited others. Depending on one's level of sensitivity, they may or may not be very obvious.

Power spots are areas where energetic ley lines cross, which allows for other dimensions to be more easily accessed. Planetary ley lines are analogous to acupuncture meridians in the human body. The veil between the worlds is thinner in these locations, the light and dark are both amplified, and everything is much more intense. One of the unique aspects of Zipolite is its location. The coastline runs directly east to west for several hundred miles in the region. In the winter, when the sun is over the southern hemisphere, one can watch both the sun rise and set over the Pacific Ocean on the same day. It's quite remarkable.

It was the combination of Zipolite, Frank, and some mystical experiences that opened my mind to other dimensions and realities. Over the next year and a half, I was thrust onto my spiritual path. Frank had a strong metaphysical background and he helped me understand what was happening.

Although I didn't realize it until much later, this was during the time frame of the Harmonic Convergence, a very significant cosmic event. For those of you who know a bit about astrology, this was also during the time of my Saturn return. Because I'm very grounded, due to a lot of earth signs in my chart, I don't have metaphysical types of experiences very easily. Nonetheless, there were a lot of forces at work and they opened me up. Here are two experiences I remember.

I was watching a friend swinging on a wooden board and then suddenly, she was a little girl! After a short period of time, she was my adult friend once again. On another occasion, I had just returned from a trip to Central America and opened a gate leading into Pina Palmera. The change in energy as I crossed the boundary was so obvious, my eyes flooded with tears. I had never experienced energy or an energetic shift in such a palpable manner. The tears came as I instantly realized how much I loved and missed this place that had become my home.

In our community I did anything and everything I could to help keep the place together and growing. I usually worked the entire day doing things I mostly enjoyed, while pacing myself in a typically Mexican manner. I was very involved with the children, even periodically feeding the two young ones with cerebral palsy.

I regularly took the kids to the beach and on three occasions someone got caught in a rip current and was being pulled out to sea. The first time it happened to one of our children, the second to a large German man who was helping us at the Palmera, and the third to a stranger. Thankfully I was able to rescue each one of them.

None of those experiences seemed like a big deal at the time since they were just another unusual event for me in Zipolite.

I fixed equipment, drove our old truck to Pochutla for food and supplies, engaged in construction projects, and helped keep the peace by communicating with others when tensions ran high. It moved my heart deeply to live what I believed in. I wasn't paid anything and in fact twice gave Frank several hundred dollars when the Palmera was broke.

The place was mostly supported by Frank's healing community in San Francisco, but the donations were irregular – although the timing was often uncanny. I once asked if he was worried about us living on the edge. Panchito sincerely replied that it was all in the hands of his guru, who had guided him to start the project in the first place.

Zipolite and the Palmera were filled with animals, children, and laughter. I absolutely loved living in community and was very happy. At least once a week I connected with our teenage workers and any of their friends who were visiting, by joining them in their morning ritual. One of them would roll a joint, which started making its way around the circle. Another did the same so that there were two joints being passed around. A third was rolled and it followed the other two. This continued until everyone had their own joint, at which point each person finished smoking whichever one was in their hand.

I left the Palmera three times for extended breaks, spending eighteen months total in Mexico and Central America. In my first excursion, I traveled north to the city of Zacatecas to study Spanish for several weeks. Although I grew up hearing it and the accent has always come easily, I never learned to speak as a child. My other two trips were to Central America, in order to obtain a new six-month visa. Generally speaking, the simplest way to get a new visa in most countries is to cross a border and then return. Both of my trips to Central America ended up being much longer than planned.

During the first, I ran into a friend from San Diego while traveling in Guatemala. It was an amazing country, despite the guerrilla warfare in isolated pockets of the mountains. My friend was on his way to Nicaragua, so I decided to join him. We quickly passed through Honduras, but spent more time in El Salvador. I have never been to a country, before or since, where the entire population was depressed – no one was smiling.

Government supported "death squads" were shooting indigenous villagers, often singling out those who chose to take a leadership role. The same thing was happening in Guatemala, yet it was more extreme in El Salvador. They were intimidating the locals, hoping to stop them from supporting the guerrillas. When they decided to make an example, the death squads had no problem lining up a group of men in the center of a village and shooting every one of them. The guerrillas were fighting for their land and rights, an all-too-common theme for indigenous people.

The United Fruit Company and other American corporations dominated Central America. Although it wasn't officially called a colony, they treated it as such, placing the indians at the bottom of the pecking order and corporate interests at the top. The indigenous people suffered (and still suffer) many abuses as local power structures exploited the land and people in order to get their share of the "rewards" of Western economic endeavors.

Despite the violence, we were relatively safe because the governments and guerrillas were reluctant to hurt or kill foreigners. There was a public relations battle raging on an international level and neither side wanted to appear to be the "bad guys."

The topic of ongoing U.S. government support of right-wing dictators in those countries had been at the center of numerous and often intense conversations at my Environmental Studies College at UCSC. Those conversations, more than anything else, led to my disillusionment with the American government. I had grown up hearing cold war propaganda – the USA was the good-guy police of the world – even the horrors of the Vietnam War had made minimal impact in suburbia.

Nicaragua was in a different situation since they had successfully revolted against their dictator several years earlier, yet its people were also suffering. The American sponsored blockade was most certainly making things difficult on a number of fronts.

Around the same time the Nicaraguans revolted, a major earthquake severely damaged the capital city of Managua. Because of the blockade, rebuilding efforts from both the war and earthquake were progressing extremely slowly, if at all. Politically speaking, the people were not generally for or against their new Sandanista government, which was socialist. They just wanted things to work.

I've continued to return to those countries over the years, watching them develop after the American government stopped its aggressive support of their heinous dictators. International pressure towards U.S. policy finally paid off several years after my initial trips to the region. With the worst dictators gone, the Central American governments gradually changed for the better.

The most difficult situation I experienced during this period of my life was driving Frank from the Pina Palmera to the hospital in Miahuatlan. Anna came to me one morning saying that Panchito was very sick, so we drove him to the tiny hospital in Pochutla. They said his colon had burst and we had no choice but to drive him over the coastal range to a much larger hospital.

Thus ensued a five-hour pain filled venture on incredibly windy mountain roads. Anna was in the back seat supporting Frank while I drove. Although he managed to stay more or less conscious until we reached the hospital, Panchito died the following morning. I've always thought of him as the person who inspired me to open my mind and heart to a spiritual path. Most everyone in Zipolite mourned with our Palmera family as he was well loved by the locals.

We managed to keep the Palmera together after Frank's death. On the surface, not much had changed. Yet on a deeper level, everything was different. I felt his absence very acutely, especially the spiritual focus he had brought to the Palmera. Because of him, it had been like an ashram for me. Anna also struggled with Panchito not being physically present and threw herself ever more deeply into her work, continuing to accept children. It felt to me as if she wanted to save every needy child in Mexico. As much as I loved giving to the children, my newly awakened spiritual identity needed my attention as well. The tension around this dynamic grew as time passed.

A couple of months after Panchito's passing my visa was about to expire. I planned a short trip to Guatemala and Belize, which turned into two months. Needing time away to do some soul searching, I didn't rush back. When I finally returned, Melinda was living there as a volunteer. She was tall, slender, and had long brown hair. Melinda, like Anna, was a Paramahansa Yogananda devotee. It wasn't long before she became the second woman I fell in love with, but our magical time together at the Palmera lasted only a month or two.

Three situations conspired to pull me back to the States even though I hadn't considered returning prior to Frank's death. First, my heart wasn't into working at the Palmera anymore; instead it quickly became focused on my new love. Then Melinda told me she was returning to the States and asked if I would join her. She flew back on her own before a third event occurred, which brought me back as well. My brother was going to get married and wanted me to be his best man.

I visited Pina Palmera seven years later and found Anna with her own child, married to a Mexican doctor from Pochutla. There were over thirty children living at the Palmera and some were accompanied by their single mothers, who were now also part of the organization's mission. Anna is an incredibly dedicated, resourceful, and talented person. Not only did she create a regular flow of donations from Sweden, but she also managed to develop meaningful relations with wealthy Mexicans in Mexico City.

The latter turned into personal donations and governmental support, which was no small achievement considering the mentality of the Mexican upper class. Pina Palmera has flourished over the years, eventually developing an extensive outreach program supporting handicapped children throughout the region. According to their website, it continues to serve and evolve. I've always felt it was an honor to be so intimately involved in its humble beginnings.

Chapter 5

I've fallen in love eight times; I managed to stay in six of those relationships for at least eighteen months. Being the main loves of my life, they are gradually being introduced. In between the fifth and last long-term partnership, I was involved with three women for several months each. Since I was in the process of falling in love with two of them, I consider those to be the sixth and seventh women I fell in love with – but barely.

In my frame of reality, falling in love is a process, not something that happens at first sight or because of one night. It takes time to build deep connection and trust. This is what allows us to access deeper spaces in our hearts.

I did not fall in love with Cynthia or Leah or Sonya or any other woman with whom I spent a few nights or weeks. I was with each of them only long enough to begin to know them. I was constantly moving on and so were some of them – we were like ships passing in the night. There was certainly attraction and potential, but simply not enough time to genuinely fall in love. Still, each of them was a gift for which I felt extreme gratitude.

In between my time at UCSC with Lolita and meeting Melinda at the Palmera, intimate experiences with women were quite rare. Considering the amount of time I spent alone, my desire for connection was always strong. Nevertheless, I would wait for attractions to be mutual. The concepts of picking-up or chasing a woman were completely foreign to me.

In that line of thought, it felt as if Pina Palmera was the matchmaker, Melinda and I its recipients. The fact that we chose to remain in each other's lives for well over a year felt incredible, especially because I had never before experienced such depths of intimacy and love.

After I returned to the States, Melinda joined me for my brother's wedding in the spring of 1987; it was a multi-day event and certainly a lot of fun. Afterwards, we went to live with her mom in the sparsely populated canyon area southeast of Los Angeles. Melinda and her mother were into health foods, dietary supplements, and healthy living in general, so we grew a large garden. I eventually started working temporary jobs through an agency before finally staying with a company for several months. It became the only 9 to 5 job I've ever worked at in my life.

Alas, this brief exploration of normality was not destined to continue as I was feeling pulled north to live and work in another community. While in Zipolite, I met a Canadian woman who had just finished studying massage at a school in northern California. She litup while telling me about it and I intuitively knew while she spoke that I would someday live at this place.

Well, the future had arrived since the school had accepted our applications for a ten-week volunteer trial period. If all went well and there were openings, we could then become full time staff members. Melinda and I packed my recently purchased VW camper van and headed north towards Heartwood Institute.

We stopped near Monterrey for the only Grateful Dead concert I've ever attended and camped out with the Deadheads for a few days. Though many people assume their culture to be centered around drugs, I found it to be much more about love and community. From there we drove 200 miles north of San Francisco to the town of Garberville, in Humboldt County. Twenty miles east, on a slow windy road into the foothills, was Heartwood.

I ended up spending three years there, but not with Melinda. The morning after we arrived, she informed me she was going to be celibate for an undetermined amount of time to focus on her spiritual growth. This news came as a surprise and shook me to my core. My excitement with Heartwood quickly vanished as my world came crashing down. I reacted in an immature fashion and our relationship came to an abrupt end.

This exceedingly painful experience had the effect of unearthing deep-seated abandonment issues, which I had not even known existed. Over the next several months, I dove into my healing journey, willingly accepting sessions from students who needed to practice their developing skills.

Heartwood Healing Arts Institute was founded by Bruce and his wife Chela in Santa Cruz, around the same time I was there studying. For years, Bruce had loved nothing more than hanging out with the yogis in India. He became an expert in polarity therapy, a form of bodywork based in Ayurvedic medicine. I'm not sure what inspired Bruce to start the school, but he and Chela took a major leap of faith when they purchased a deserted 200-acre hunting and fishing resort facility in the Humboldt hills. Although they were able to buy the property with its perfect assortment of buildings, they never had enough money for improvements and expansion.

Heartwood was eventually sold to a gay couple from Chicago, who resonated with the challenge it offered. Bob and Roy had been attending personal growth workshops for many years and were committed to healing. Bob was a successful corporate lawyer, while Roy was a marketing wiz. Their talents matched Heartwood's needs and they had money to invest in its infrastructure. Bruce continued to teach and offer his unique spiritual depth, while Chela worked closely with Bob and Roy managing and developing the school towards its potential.

I arrived several months after Bob and Roy bought Heartwood, during a time of transition. Things were fairly rustic and funky when I arrived. Most of the staff smoked marijuana since the majority of our widely scattered neighbors made their living growing it. At that time, Humboldt County was infamous for being at the center of the cannabis revolution, the region where the first high grade THC hybrids were being created. Heartwood evolved in a very positive manner during my three years at the school. The marijuana culture naturally found a healthier balance and a deeper sense of mission, inspiration, and professionalism grew in its place.

When I lived at Heartwood Institute, it was the only massage school in the country operated by a community that provided residential quarters to its students. Heartwood offered two separate programs, which were intertwined. The "transformational therapy" path was a 750-hour commitment and so was the massage therapy certification. Each of them required nine months of studies, separated into three quarters. Students who committed to either full length program were required to take classes from both, but most people weren't that ambitious. The majority of students only studied for one quarter or attended a one-to-three-week intensive course in between the quarters.

The term "healer heal thyself" was fully integrated into the classes. Although most students came for the vocational possibilities, nearly everyone realized at some point that their personal healing was the main reason they were there. It was often humbling for students to realize that even the "healthiest" of us had innumerable issues and deep inner pain to resolve.

In any given quarter, there were between 80 – 100 people living at the school, with approximately half being students and the other half being teachers, permanent staff, and volunteers. I was assigned to the maintenance department and after the first quarter became a staff member working at least thirty-two hours/week with a salary of $200/month. Room and board were included, as well as a specific number of classes. During my time there, I was one of only two staff members who worked full time and consistently took as many free classes as possible. By the end, I earned my 750-hour massage therapy certification.

After several quarters, the maintenance manager left and I was asked to replace him as head of the department. I went to weekly managerial meetings and became intimately involved in the functional aspects, yet the task I enjoyed most was cutting up dead trees around the property for firewood. We could get a fair amount of snow in the winter and many of our buildings were heated with wood stoves. Our water supply came from a spring on the property and it supplied all of our needs.

Along with repairs, our maintenance staff was usually engaged in at least one small construction project at any given time. I developed deep friendships with several of the men: we were an unusually sensitive and caring group considering we were "maintenance men." Yet the fact is we were all taking holistic courses and receiving healing sessions.

It wasn't long before I developed an extreme passion for the healing arts. One of Heartwood's strengths was emphasizing the artistic component of healing. We are all so different and what each person needs at any given moment is constantly changing. The overall focus was extremely holistic, honoring all four bodies, which include the physical, emotional, mental (psychological), and spiritual.

An extra focus was placed on emotional release work, based in holotropic breath-work, primal therapy, and other foundational modalities. Hands on bodywork greatly facilitates the release and processing of repressed emotions. Most people are unable to understand the significance of our emotional body or how to increase their "emotional intelligence." Negative emotions are one of humanity's greatest stumbling blocks.

The majority of our teachers loved what they practiced and taught – some of them were also extremely adept. After suffering under conventional schooling systems for way too many years, the classes at Heartwood were truly a breath of fresh air. We usually sat in circles, often on the floor. Our teachers encouraged participation and hugging was a usual occurrence, before, during and after classes. In fact, hugging was one of the main constants at the school with almost everyone including faculty and staff members.

Heartwood was a place of extreme intimacy! In our courses, the person receiving was nude if it was an oil massage or deep tissue class. They were usually covered by a sheet, but not always. Although we avoided massaging a woman's breasts, we massaged her chest by working around the breasts, which were usually uncovered. Our school had a pool, hot tub, and an amazing wood heated sauna, all overlooking a large, visually stunning valley. Most of us used these facilities in the nude, day or night. In our transformation classes, we regularly looked deep into each other's eyes and just as often shared intimate secrets. We cried on our partner's shoulders and learned to openly express our emotions in class settings.

The depth of healing that occurred at Heartwood was extremely inspiring. Imagine being surrounded by nature and living with a supportive community of people who have your best interests in mind. Imagine there is almost no exchange of money going on, few cars other than those sitting in the parking lot, relaxed attitudes about schedules one is supposed to keep, and lots of laughing and crying. Imagine three healthy vegetarian buffet meals every day and yoga, Tai Chi, and other movement classes available within walking distance. Imagine you are surrounded by therapists who are skilled at different types of healing modalities and desire to serve your healing process.

Furthermore, this situation continues for weeks, months, or potentially years on end. After experiencing this, I believe such an environment is the best way to facilitate the depth of healing almost every human being needs and deserves. Taking an hour from one's busy schedule in a city to go to an occasional class or therapist is obviously a far inferior substitute. If human societies were designed similar to Heartwood, humanity would surely evolve rapidly.

As a part of our communal life, I experienced my first sweat lodge ceremonies, along with my first and only Native American prayer meeting. I coincidentally arrived at Heartwood a day after the death of Rutherford, a medicine man who had been a spiritual foundation at the school. In his honor, they offered one final full night ceremony of peyote and prayers. I also experienced my first Hindu chanting with a harmonium, led by Bruce. I was always amazed at how high and happy I became by simply chanting simple mantras in a group.

In my enthusiasm, I managed to take my work and classes too seriously and occasionally burned out. So I took breaks and traveled. I went camping, hiking and backpacking in the region with various friends from Heartwood. We checked out other communities and went on two trips to Mexico. It was a joy to be in a community again, as opposed to being alone so much.

One of the most enjoyable parts of my job was promoting our school at a variety of events and festivals. It all started with organizing Heartwood people to staff the refreshment booths at Garberville's biggest event, the Reggae on the River music festival. Approximately fifty students and staff members each worked a four-hour shift during the three-day event and received free tickets in exchange. I also got a backstage pass all three years.

Soon after I started managing the festival's soft drink booths, our school began to promote itself through university, environmental, and holistic events. I was responsible for getting everything to and from those venues, in addition to setting up and dismantling everything. Several students would join another staff member and myself to disseminate literature and give paid mini-massages to people visiting our table.

Around the beginning of my third year at Heartwood, I fell in love for the third time. Mia was from Switzerland and had been an international model for ten years. She quit the year before we met while still at the top of her profession, having become disenchanted with modeling for reasons she only hinted at.

I remember noticing Mia for the first time in our hydrotherapy workshop. It was a small class and we were practicing "salt rubs." We were nude and yes Mia and I were partners. My first impression of her was that she was so thin. But it wasn't long before I discovered Mia was beautiful inside and out, had a good heart, and was an intelligent Virgo who spoke four or five languages.

We were both in Bruce's polarity therapy class, a course focused on transformation. His wife Chela had led the hydrotherapy workshop and it was she who initially paired us up for the salt rubs. Mia and I started trading healing sessions, some of which were exceedingly intense. Then we started nurturing each other in the evenings and spending nights together. It was very romantic, especially since we slept together for many nights before becoming sexual. We basically fell in love while healing one another.

Mia's visa was due to expire soon after she finished her ten-week quarter of classes, so we decided to go on a trip together. We flew to Mexico City and from there went south by bus to the states of Oaxaca and Chiapas, the most magical region in the country. On a previous trip, I had heard of a river in southern Chiapas that flows into Guatemala, bypassing seldom visited Mayan ruins. We made our way to the river, hired a guide with a boat, and camped out for several nights along the way. At one of the ruins, Mia took a photo of me, a side pose against a large rock carving of a Mayan man's face. The similarity was quite striking.

We returned after several weeks and upon arriving in San Francisco passed through customs. They asked Mia a lot of questions and finally let her pass. Afterwards, we asked each other what we would have done if they had refused her entry. She would not have been able to continue her studies and our relationship may have come to an end.

It's not so simple being in a relationship with someone from another country, but there are certainly options. After much discussion, we decided the most practical solution was to get married since we clearly wanted to be together. So that's what we did several weeks later, before a magistrate judge and two friends from the school.

Mia finished her final quarter of classes and flew back to Europe to visit family and friends. It seemed to be time for me to leave as well. I was beginning to realize I craved a deeper sense of community than what Heartwood had to offer. For obvious reasons, the school's needs always came first while the community's needs were secondary. I was also tired of maintenance work and wanted to practice the healing arts as my primary focus. Plus, Mia wasn't interested in working at Heartwood. We eventually decided to meet at the San Francisco airport upon her return and begin our new life together.

Everything was off from the beginning. While in Europe, Mia's family and friends questioned her marriage to an alternative California, New Age, hippie, whatever. They most certainly got into her head, so much so that she almost skipped the flight back to San Francisco. After reuniting, we began to discuss our future plans.

Living a free-spirit lifestyle was my undeniable preference, especially since I had always dreamed of having a steady partner to travel with. But Mia was tired of traveling because her modeling profession had required her to be constantly on the move. She wanted to settle down and create a home together. Frustrated and unsure how to proceed, we decided to check out the Nevada City/Grass Valley area because a couple we knew from Heartwood had invited us to visit.

After staying with them for a few weeks, we moved in with a friend of theirs who was looking for housemates. Our goal was to either work in a chiropractor's office as massage therapists or start private practices of our own. Unfortunately, we had trouble finding jobs and the idea of starting my own business freaked me out.

Even worse, some of our unhealed issues began to dominate our lives. Her Swiss pride and superiority were constantly triggering my extreme lack of self-worth from childhood, which I had obviously not healed. This dynamic started the day she returned from Europe, which was perplexing to me as it had not been the least bit evident at Heartwood. The situation got so bad, I left for a ten-day backpacking trip to Mt. Shasta.

Nothing seemed to improve after my return. I was petrified of fitting into the system and living a boring domestic type of lifestyle. I could travel through war torn third world countries and hike alone almost anywhere mountains existed, but to live like other Americans? I didn't think I could do it. Or more accurately, I knew on an unconscious level that if I had to live a "normal" life, I would hate it and self-destruct in one way or another. So I was in constant reaction to the life we were starting to live and Mia unwittingly fed the fire with regular doses of criticism.

Whenever I managed to start building up my confidence, there she was to pull me down. It felt like I was in a vortex and couldn't pull myself out. We stopped making love and started sleeping apart. But one night we slept together and sure enough, Mia became pregnant. After being together for eighteen months, what a time for this to happen! We didn't know what to do. Finally realizing I was in no condition to make a clear-headed choice, I left the decision entirely up to her. Several weeks later, she decided to give up on both our marriage and the pregnancy.

Many years and relationships later, I've come to realize she made the correct choice. Mia, similar to most women, was wanting and needing a stable man to help her raise a child. I could not fill that role, which she came to understand. Living a conventional sort of life has never been my destiny path. I've tried to do it and I'm simply not able to feel happy, content, or fulfilled. Four out of the eight times I've fallen in love, my relationship ended because of this dynamic. Either my partner or the circumstances were pushing me to live a life that wasn't my truth.

Soon after we had arrived in Nevada City, our friends introduced us to an acupuncturist with a successful private practice. We kept running into him over the next several months in a variety of locations. We even ran into him walking his dogs in the area where we were living. Around the time Mia got pregnant, his dogs actually came to the front door of our house. The strange thing is that I knew they had come for her. We had to call the acupuncturist and ask him to come retrieve his dogs.

Unsurprisingly, it was only a few weeks after our marriage ended and I moved out that they got involved. He was the stable sort of man I couldn't be. It was obvious they had some sort of soul connection, but that didn't make the situation any easier.

For the first and only time in my life, I became exceedingly jealous and almost got into a fight with the acupuncturist when we ran into each other in a parking lot. I struggled for months with incredibly painful emotions, all of them connected to the complexity and intensity of the circumstances. Everything considered, this was possibly the most painful experience of my life. I not only relived the zero-confidence reality of my childhood, I had lost – no, given up – what appeared to be the perfect woman.

That experience concluded the second stage of my life, which lasted thirteen years and was obviously one of constant change. After Mia and I split up, I started making good friendships, most of them through a group of spiritually-inclined people. My self-confidence also returned, partly through the sessions I traded with several massage therapists. I worked through an enormous amount of old pain, which had been triggered by my experience with Mia.

I eventually started a private practice with a massage therapist with whom I traded intense healing work. We set up our space in a spare room at the residence of an amazing artist who painted interdimensional masterpieces.

Daniel's home was the focal hub for a group of free-thinking metaphysically inclined seekers. The monthly gatherings that occurred at his house are the stuff of legend – well almost. During this period, a newly released book, *Bringers of the Dawn*, radically shifted my view of reality. The over-all transformation I experienced during this period was incredible. As far down as I had fallen in the previous months, I rose much higher in the ensuing year.

During this time, Mia and I healed the painful ending of our relationship. Soon after we separated, she got into Buddhism and meditation and over the years committed ever more deeply to the Buddhist path. She eventually married the acupuncturist and they had a child together. Nevertheless, Mia and I have managed to maintain a close friendship, albeit mostly at a distance.

Intermission # 1 – Climbing the Volcano

I wrote the following account when I was 26 years old, soon after having this adventure. Despite being edited, it leaves intact a relatively accurate perspective of me at that age. While taking my first break from the Pina Palmera to study Spanish, I saw Citlaltepetl on my map as I gradually headed back to Zipolite. The last time this volcano erupted was in 1687. Pico de Orizaba (Orizaba Peak) is its common name and Citlaltepetl (Star Mountain) is its indigenous name.

Volcan Citlaltepetl (5,640 meters)

I knew nothing about this mountain other than it being a spot on the map with a name and an elevation. It was apparently the highest volcano in Mexico and the goal of climbing it was a great excuse to explore another region. A week after my decision on the train, I jumped out of a pick-up truck and continued the momentum on foot up the hill that led into Coscomatepec. A medium sized town, "Cosco" appeared as close to Citlaltepetl as any city on the map.

I happened to arrive on market day and the zócalo (central plaza) was packed full of people and activity. It was hot, so I bought an ice cream cone from a street vendor. Leaning against my backpack on the grass behind several women with their children, I rather tiredly, yet intently, took in the entire scene. Another vendor was yelling "Four melons for 100 pesos" in Spanish through a loud speaker. The local men were always found beneath their sombreros. The indigenous women, who were draped in colorful dresses and shawls, were always busy: making, carrying, and selling while keeping an eye on their children.

I eventually rose to my feet to search for a hotel. Asking two young men seemed as smart a start as any. Not only did they point out the direction of what was apparently the only hotel in town, they soon became my friends. In the ensuing conversation, I asked them about Citlaltepetl. "Qué?" came their reply. So I repeated myself: "El Volcan, puedo ir alla de aqui?" "Ah, El Volcan de Orizaba, no sabemos," they replied. Despite their uncertainty about whether or not I could reach the volcano from there, I obtained more information about the mountain. It's called Volcan de Orizaba or Pico de Orizaba by the locals. The city of Orizaba is located at its base on the other side of the mountain.

Carlos and Sebastian appeared at my room an hour later with two friends and their English homework. This wasn't the first time I made a friend simply by knowing English. I had spent the past week with Hector, a university student in Jalapa, with the base of our friendship being each other's desire to learn the other's language. Carlos and Sebastian were renting a room at the hotel for eight dollars each per month while attending preparatory school. They ate dinners with a local family who made extra income by feeding students and I was invited to come along for a meal.

While in Cosco, I did some informal research on the volcano and focused on letting my body recover. After three months of virtually perfect health in Mexico, the past ten days had humbled me. I exhausted myself on peyote and rural family life in a desert village to the north, got my first bad case of diarrhea, then caught a cold. The diarrhea situation had much improved by the time I'd reached Jalapa, only to reappear as a worse case, probably from bacteria in the fresh milk and cheese I ate with Hector. My bowels were also continually aggravated by the hot spicy food I over-indulged in. This culture is in my blood and I find its food irresistible. Furthermore, the later stages of poison ivy rashes, acquired in the hills above Jalapa, continued to itch. Added to these ailments were scratches on my chest and leg from rocks I'd scraped while diving into the Apazapan River. Fortunately, all of the above had more or less healed by the time I reached Cosco and I nearly felt new by the time I left two days later.

My hike began at an elevation of about 1,800 meters (5,700 ft.), after a ride in a truck to the cement mine near San Nicholas.

The mining was very interesting to watch. Men were on cliffs attached to trees above by ropes, digging out a ledge wide enough to stand and work on as they picked and shoveled their way down. Much of the construction in Mexico is still done by hand and lots of grunts. The campesinos work very hard, but at a pace and with an attitude that seems very humane to me. Even the women, who nearly fit the definition of slaves, pace themselves wisely, adding humor to a job in an environment that is incessantly routine. This attitude towards work seems to be unjustly interpreted as laziness by Americans, who bestow an unfair stereotype on a people who deserve much more respect.

From the mine, I crossed several more valleys, stopping for lunch above the pleasant enough pueblo named Titlocinco. Pico de Orizaba, still in the distance, brazenly overwhelmed the scene. Below and around me, the multitude of fields were being busily attended to by their owners and hired helpers. The maize season had begun; those fields that didn't contain freshly sprouted corn stalks were in the process of being plowed and planted by hand. Closer to Coscomatapec, where it is lower and warmer, the stalks were already a foot or more high despite it being a full month before the rainy season officially began. None of the farms were irrigated, but as one farmer explained to me, the light preseason rains were enough to get things rolling. Months later at the end of the rainy season, the ears of corn would be harvested.

Walking around the outskirts of Titlocinco, I happened upon a rather humorous scene. As I approached the last few houses on the edge of town, I heard yelling and screaming. Was the commotion a family squabble? No! It was a family on the death march and having a blast in the process. "Ya, dos ratones," shouted one of the boys. As more screams emerged from inside the house, another mouse rushed out of a hole in the side of the wooden building, only to be chased down by a club in the hand of one of the men outside. Everyone was joyfully involved in the event: to call it anything less would only serve to shortchange the affair.

Taking my leave as the excitement began to dissipate and another mouse had met the same fate as its siblings, I continued on to the town of Chayuamacan. Passing a relatively large school, I was approached by multitudes of students on break. "What are you doing? Where are you going?" The usual questions came, along with the accompanying high degree of curiosity. And then with widely opened eyes and dilated pupils, the inevitable question always flowed forth: "Estás solito?" Yes, only me, myself, and I. Mexicans, being family oriented and extremely social, constantly had trouble ingesting the fact that I was traveling alone. "Well, aren't you afraid of coyotes? What about the bulls?" Now this was the second time in the past few hours I had been warned about coyotes. "They must be awfully brave coyotes to bother a man," I replied. "Well, if you are alone," said one of the older girls, "they might attack, kill, and eat you. Don't you have a pistol?"

Earlier in the day, another man had asked the same question. Once again, having discovered I was defenseless, I was warmly wished good luck, along with a nod of amazement. "He is too much: alone, unprotected, and thinking of climbing the volcano" seemed to be the unspoken thoughts going through their heads. I would not have been surprised had I received haughty, self-righteous smirks, insinuating that I was a fool who would never make it. But contrary to expectations, I nearly always sensed a feeling of wonderment and respect emanating from these campesinos. This felt good because I don't feel crazy or brave; I'm just doing my thing.

After another town and some fresh water to fill up my water bottles, I began the last stretch of the day on a wide dirt trail to Potrero Nuevo, the highest outpost of constant human habitation on this side of Citlaltepetl. At least an hour out of Potrero Nuevo, I met a caballero riding a horse, bringing cooking oil up the mountain on his packhorse. After conversing awhile, we ran into his cousin, at which time they relieved me of my backpack and Oaxacan shoulder bag. We proceeded along the trail at a brisk pace, them talking and me panting. By the time we reached Potrero Nuevo in the late afternoon, I was totally worn out.

Rather than a pueblo or farm, this collection of buildings was called a rancho. At a height of over 3,000 meters (9,900 ft.), corn would not grow. It was replaced by cattle, horses, lumber, and potatoes, which formed the crux of the lifestyle for the hundred or so members of this family. As was explained to me, everyone living in the rancho was born there and furthermore they were all related by blood. Wow, what a contrast to the environment in which I grew up: California separatism and individualism.

The cousins guided me to a small school house and said I was welcome to sleep inside. Once again, it was not long before I became the center of curiosity, the main attraction. An older man with a cane and damaged foot was the first to approach. While the women and children peered around the sides of houses, he began to ask me the usual set of questions.

A younger man, who had previously summited Pico de Orizaba, joined in our discussion. It wasn't long before the conversation centered on the volcano, towering above the last few ridges that separated us. While we conversed, I offered Guadalupe some of my peanuts and tamarrindos. As the sun was setting, he proceeded to invite me to his home, followed by a meal and a place to sleep for the night.

Guadalupe and his attractive wife, Maria, had four children: the 10-year-old boy was attending the school I had passed in Chayuamacan. His two younger brothers and sister were rather shy, mischievous attention seekers. I enjoyed their smiles and inquisitive loving eyes. Love exuded from the entire family and my heart opened to these simple, caring people.

Since Guadalupe and Maria were interested in the outside world, I told them about some of my travels. As they responded and shared their thoughts with me, I realized how much their culture is under assault. The pressure on the land is great: too many people, too few acres. Mexican families are breaking apart at an unprecedented rate. Still, this mountain refuge, several hours from the nearest car, seemed to be resisting much of what modern civilization has to offer – and take.

Guadalupe was rounding up his horse the following morning when I awoke to the smell of smoke. I had slept in their cooking building while the family slept in their home next door. As poor as they are, wood is plentiful here and they could afford the luxury of two buildings. Drinking the weak coffee my hostess had offered me, we talked while she prepared breakfast. Upon Guadalupe's arrival, we ate another meal of tortillas, beans, chilies and coffee, the staple of much of the Mexican population, especially in rural areas. While saying goodbye, I was flustered by tears that flowed to my eyes as I described to Maria how much her family and my time with them had meant to me.

Guadalupe and his neighbor accompanied me on the trail that led to the volcano since this fit in with their wood cutting plans for the day. Upon reaching their destination, we veered off the main trail and followed a side one to their recently constructed cabin. To facilitate their weekly lumber cutting ventures and hunting trips, they had built this sweet-smelling edifice in a most becoming spot. Two creeks passed close by, one with splashingly fresh water. It was so incredibly peaceful, so tranquilo; I could certainly enjoy staying here for a while. Guadalupe's offer to stop at his home or this cabin on my way back was followed by smiles, clasped hands, and a parting of ways.

Continuing my ascent through the pines and an occasional fir, I happened upon two men cutting lumber boards with a huge two-man hand saw. Also from Potrero Nuevo, they took advantage of my presence and used it for a nicely timed break. Leaving this joyfully light atmosphere, I walked two more hours to "Las Casas" at 13,800 feet. I had learned from Guadalupe that these two huts set above the tree line on the north side of the mountain were used by mountaineers attempting to ascend the peak. Guadalupe also told me about a road that runs up the western Orizaba side to Las Casas.

The chances appeared good that some trekkers might be staying there, providing company and a chance to borrow or buy gear for the glacier that I would need to ascend. I hadn't spoken with any foreigners in nearly three weeks and I found the prospect of meeting American or European climbers exciting.

Upon my arrival, I found the huts depressingly vacant. "Well heck," I thought as the afternoon drew to a close, "I'll head on up tomorrow and give the glacier a go anyways." I tried not to fool myself about my chances of reaching the top; they did not appear good. Yet the peak had never been my main objective. The extreme friendliness of the campesinos, along with the beauty of the forests and farm lands had already made this hike well worthwhile. If I happened to accomplish the feat of making it to the top of the mountain, that would be a bonus.

Sipping the lone beer I had so gallantly (or foolishly) carried this far, the sound of a motor invaded my awareness. Having already been fooled several times in the intense silence, I rather doubted newcomers would be arriving so late. But startlingly enough, the noise continued to increase, terminating in the presence of a truck at the larger building below. Not knowing what to expect or get prematurely excited, I watched five figures emerge and begin to unload supplies. Before long the Americans offered me the use of their gear without any prompting on my part, since they needed to spend a day or two acclimating to the altitude.

Quickly, so very rapidly, my chances of reaching the peak increased many times over. I soon discovered that this 18,851-foot high volcano was the third highest mountain in North America. Only Mt. Mckinley in Alaska (20,321 ft.) and Mt. Logan in Canada (19,521 ft.) are higher. John, Todd, Tully, and Dee had been planning this hike for a year and they were admittedly excited.

They moved into the smaller upper hut with me, making quarters a little cramped, but just right for heat retention and partying. Breaking out a six-pack of Tecate, they continued to pull out all sorts of stuff, including a huge papaya. Well, I suppose there are some advantages to "cheating" and driving most of the way up the mountain.

Eating and talking until after dark, I found out a few things about my new hut-mates. They had arrived in Mexico City two days earlier and planned to spend the remainder of their two-week vacation in Oaxaca and the Yucatan. Being from Oregon and Washington, they had climbed several peaks together in the Cascades and even had a group name and caps to go with it: "The Blue Ice Ramblers."

The hiker who stood out was Todd; he had backpacked over 11,000 miles in the States! Only thirty years old, he had hiked the Appalachian Trail twice, the Pacific Crest Trail, and the little-known Continental Divide Trail. Each of them extends from the Canadian border to the Mexican border or the Gulf of Mexico. Hiking all three with his former girlfriend, they were among the first ten people to complete the newly forming Continental Divide Trail through the Rocky Mountains. He wrote newspaper articles, lectured, and gave slide shows about the eight-month adventure.

Inspired by the situation and my new friends, I decided to hang out the following day. Awake at first light, I found myself itching for something to do. Rising quietly and setting off for a nearby ridge, I watched the sun rise through yellow tinted haze, which was much darker on the smoggy Mexico City side. My day was relaxing: talking, eating, and hiking down the nearby canyon back into the trees. I spent much of the afternoon in the company of a pine tree, drawing and writing in my journal. The fire that evening was most welcome, although everyone went to bed early due to lingering headaches from the altitude.

Having lived at higher elevations for much of the previous six weeks, I felt fine. Although they planned to rest for another day, eager anticipation filled my being. My equipment was ready, including John's heavy hiking boots that fit me perfectly. His glacial gear was the main reason I wouldn't wait any longer; their one set per person would leave me with nothing but my light hiking boots if I went with them.

For some time, the question surrounding a solo attempt at the peak had frequented my mind. I obviously knew one's safety is dramatically increased when accompanied by competent companions. The more difficult or dangerous the endeavor, the more important the teamwork. But past experiences had proven to me that help is seldom required if one is careful and skillful enough. Honestly, I didn't know if my abilities could match the challenges of the mountain. In the end, the deciding factor in my decision to go alone came down to confidence: I simply believed I would succeed.

Sleeping more soundly that night, I awoke at 4:30 am, taking care not to disturb the others. Leaving soon after my snack of bread and jam, I found the trail with my flashlight. Lacking a moon, the star filled sky helped light the way. Rising steeply, the trail went up a ravine, winding around rocks of various sizes. Close to an hour passed before tinges of light appeared in the eastern sky. Fading stars accompanied the illumination of the trail, which could be seen rising to the glacier.

Reaching it before sunrise, I was able to discern the shape of its lower extremities. Attempting to keep my breathing at a level where I wasn't gasping for breath felt like a safe pace. Stopping occasionally for water, food, clothing and equipment changes gave me the much-needed breaks I found difficult to take without a reason. My body seemed to have a mind of its own; it was so pumped up, so high, it desired nothing less than constant movement – it wanted that peak!

As the sun rose, I reached a point where I was forced to continue my ascent on the glacier, which had melted extremely unevenly. It continued to rise up the valley, then widened into a large basin, with the peak rising beyond the opposite side. By this point I had covered perhaps half of the 5,000 ft. elevation gain between the huts and the top.

Studying the glacial face rising above the opposite side of the basin, I attempted to visualize a route up the final stretch of the glacier. The map on the wall of the hut showed it veering off towards the left and coming back towards the middle as one approached the peak. But the driver said that way had been rather dangerous of late. He recommended hiking up the right side and coming back towards the middle several hundred meters below the top. Since he worked for a small company that specialized in driving mountaineers to the cabins, I took his advice, but only some of it. He had also warned me to not go alone.

Crossing the basin with its gradual gradient, I contemplated the usefulness of the crampons and ice axe. Although the glacier's irregular surface continued to be a pain, it certainly prevented me from sliding very far. Later, on the steeper and scarier sections, I was very grateful for John's generosity.

As I began the final steep climb up the northern face, I stopped frequently to catch my breath, yet I was surprised the thin air was satisfying my needs so well. Despite my sunglasses, the glaring sunlight felt intense. Light photons bombarded my environment, forming wavelengths of sharply contrasting colors. A cloudless sky filled half of my view in blue, bordered by the shimmering whiteness of the glacier, while below the haze of air pollution floated above the valleys, plateaus, and forests in the distance. I couldn't help but contrast the awful brown haze to the gloriously clear air I had experienced in Alaska, where I could see mountains 150 to 200 miles distant with startling clarity.

Continuing up, up, up, I began encountering cracks of varying sizes, which served to increase my concentration. Since my glacial experience was so limited, I'm not sure when those increasingly large cracks could be termed "crevasses." Leaping over the narrow ones and skirting those that were wider, my plodding steps continued to be broken by frequent stops.

On any difficult peak, there always seems to be at least one point where distances seem unending, one's willpower to continue comes into question, and the mountain's unmerciful omnipresence becomes overwhelming. I reached such a point less than an hour from my destination. The growing number and size of the crevasses eventually formed what appeared to be an impassable web. Off in the distance to either side, the situation looked little better. As my confidence and determination ebbed, frustration and fear mounted.

Since hearing the Americans drive up, then offer their equipment and information, my desire to "conquer that mountain" had risen with the odds. But now as my efforts began to appear in vain, my entire perspective changed. Suddenly "that peak" lost its importance and my safety became the major issue. My mind and emotions were overwhelmed with a realization that the most important goal is not to reach the top of the mountain, but rather to make it back down.

As fate would have it, while seriously considering descending the glacier and possibly trying again the next day with my friends, I discovered a relatively safe route through that mess of crevasses. Taking some deep breaths and calming myself, I hardly stopped long enough to realize what had happened. From there to the top became a matter of nothing more than slow determined steps, yet not as slow or difficult as I had expected. The elevation proved to affect me less than I had feared: there was no headache, dizziness, or any other sign of oxygen deprivation.

I traversed the final broadly rounded ridge and saw the cross that capped the peak, just a few minutes ahead on the higher western edge of the volcano. Calm down Mark – take your time! Trampling over several ice-free spots, I fell to my knees on the dry sand that comprised the apex of this surprisingly hospitable peak. I felt wonderful, except for the fact I couldn't stop gasping for air. For the first time, I actually feared I might pass out, more from excitement than anything else. Energy – nervous energy – filled my being, threatening to carry me off – to where I couldn't imagine.

A lack of wind and surprisingly warm temperature caressed me into remaining on top for an hour. Walking in a southern direction, I once again noticed the steep cliffs on the eastern side. Strangely, this face had not looked so dramatic during my hike up the mountain. Suddenly a grand, tension releasing laugh emerged from the bowels of my body as the irony of the situation struck me.

This is a volcano! Every child knows a hole tops these creations, the place where lava spews out in waves of grandeur. These cliffs were the sides of such a pit, a caldera I believe it's called. Inching up towards the edge, I was better able to perceive its steepness and shallowness. Laughing again, I realized the altitude might be affecting my brain after all.

Bidding farewell to that safe little area at the top, I marveled at the distances one would have to travel to find a higher peak. Not until Mt. Logan in northwestern Canada or who knows what peak in the South American Andes could one ascend to such a height. Putting aside such ego masturbation, I began my nerve-wracking descent. Reaching the crevasses before regaining my concentration,

I made what could have been a fatal mistake. Drifting to the right of the route I had taken up, my advancing leg found one of the hidden crevasses Todd had warned me about. His fears concerning the mountain almost manifested at this moment.

Quickly jerking my entire leg out of the hole, I managed to catch a view of the cavern I'd nearly found myself inhabiting. It was twenty to thirty feet deep and straight down. Shaken, I crawled away from the danger, gathered my wits and reviewed the situation. Since my ascent had been safe, it made sense to apply myself fully to the task of retracing my steps. Checking the landscape, I frustratingly backtracked up towards the left and found what seemed to be familiar territory.

Before long, I threaded my way down through the intricate section of crevasses that had given me second and third doubts on the ascent. Negotiating these, I continued to encounter more and more. "Damn, which way did I come up? There couldn't have been so many before!" The temptation to look further down the glacier to safe territory was overpowering. Struggling to focus and keep my pace slow enough to prevent stumbling on the icy ridges, I continued downwards.

Having sensed for some time that a problem existed with my left boot, the lack of a red boot strap broke through into my conscious awareness as the terrain improved and I was able to process such information. My first thought was that I'd be damned if I would backtrack to look for that crampon. I'm sure John wouldn't expect me to, especially since they seemed to fit his boots so poorly. Although I could pay for the crampons, and John would still have one for the glacier, the loss ignited a series of negative thoughts. I had broken my sunglasses, lost John's crampon, and nearly spent an undetermined amount of time in a crevasse.

"What in the hell was I doing here alone anyways? What right did I have to endanger my life when so many people would dearly miss me? Who did I think I was and what was I trying to prove?" On and on these thoughts continued, filling my mind with a sense of loss, frustration, and self-hatred.

By this point I had reached relatively safe ice. Thus my lack of concentration and judgment – due to this indulgence in self-criticism and abuse – were not terribly detrimental to my safety. Reaching the basin, I sloshed through the melting ice. Then I stumbled, bounced, and crashed my way down the last steep icy section – putting that treacherous glacier behind me was all that mattered. I'd had enough! My growing headache, due to the jarring tense descent signaled as much.

Reaching rocks and gravel, the terrain that is my forte, I put those heavy boots to the test. Jumping, hopping, and rapidly sliding ever downwards, the huts appeared before long. The feeling of well-being and elation that grew with the size of Las Casas surprised me. Bounding into camp, I was first greeted by Todd and his grand smile. In response to the questions of the gathering group, my story gushed forth, releasing bottled-up emotions in a strangely anti-climatic, yet orgasmic manner. Comprehending more fully the extent of emotional strain encountered on the climb, I felt more impressed than ever with the relatively cool, collected self I had witnessed on that volcano.

Drinking the beer my pals had so thoughtfully cooled off for me, I gradually calmed down. As the wind picked up and we retired to the hut for a rest, one of them mentioned how quickly I had completed the journey. Since their book estimated six to nine hours for the ascent alone, five hours up and less than half that on the return did seem rather quick.

I was not eager to spend another cold night in the hut or be awakened at four in the morning by my departing hut-mates. Instead, I felt the beckoning call of a calm pleasant cabin set in the woods an hour or two down the mountain. Since my present exhaustion felt more emotional than physical, I felt I could reach it before dark. So, while they cooked an early dinner, I packed my belongings and said my good-byes.

Nearly drooling over my proposed indulgence in relaxation, I felt rather flustered upon realizing I had passed the two trails that led to Guadalupe's cabin. Refusing to quit, I backtracked up hill in frustration. Disappointment felt like an understatement as it quickly got dark and the mysterious cabin had yet to be found.

Mumbling my sour grapes verdict, I told that uncooperative edifice it would simply have to spend a cold, lonely night without me. Grabbing my flashlight and discovering the batteries were dead, I couldn't help but mutter a few insulting curses into the enveloping darkness. My goodness how luck and fate can shift about.

Stumbling through dark brush towards the sound of flowing water, I arrived at a nondescript stream. To be sure, that was not the flattest nor most pleasant of camps. But the stream was the real disappointment since it was colored a deep gray. Incredibly unappealing in appearance, my dry throat cringed in disgust. With the final couple sips of water in my canteen, I managed to swallow the last of my stale tortillas and a can of sardines in tomato sauce.

I couldn't help but shake my head in amazement: this was one heck of a way to end my most victorious of days. It seems as if this universe keeps an eye on us insignificant beings. It makes sure nothing worthwhile comes too easily, thus preventing us from becoming too prideful.

Rising early the following morning, I half-heartedly continued searching for the cabin, eventually arriving in Potrero Nuevo instead. Heading for Guadalupe's place, I found Maria and their children at home. She cheerfully invited me to breakfast, proudly serving stewed meat that perfectly complemented the usual fare. Guadalupe arrived several minutes later, walking into the room with a huge smile on his face followed by an enthusiastic "Mi amigo!" and a warmly extended hand.

Several visitors and conversations later, I took my leave, continuing the hike that carried me out of the mountains. La Cumbre, where one could catch a ride to Orizaba, was only a half day walk away. Of the numerous ranchos and pueblos I passed that day, Potrero Nuevo's neighbor was the most attractive. From there I ambled on down the well-used trail, stopping often.

Watching the changing vegetation, I was fascinated by a prominent pine tree that had long thin needles in irregular groups of three, four, and five. Exchanging oaks for pines, the terrain continued on downwards. An hour short of La Cumbre, I was treated to an absolutely enchanting valley while skirting its northern rim. Two streams flowed down the valley, one along each of its sides forming a plateau in the middle covered with fields of crops. Completing the collage of varying shades of green, the valley walls were covered in jungle green. I eventually descended the lower end of the valley into stifling humidity, only to ascend the other steep and curvy side. As easily as that, or maybe as difficult considering my semi-depleted state, I found myself at the end of my hike.

Catching the first truck out of La Cumbre, in what amounts to a bus service, we bumped our way ever downwards. Once again fields of corn planted on hills steep enough to make challenging ski slopes astonished me. Sadly enough, many of these slopes eventually become unsightly, unhealthy erosion problems. As the population of Mexico continues to grow unrelentingly, people are forced to till land that is borderline in usefulness.

I began chatting with the fellow next to me as we sat on bags of potatoes in the back of the truck and soon discovered that he worked for the driver, who was driving the truck not only to Orizaba, but all the way to Oaxaca. Claiming that bags of potatoes make a comfortable enough bed, he saw no reason why I couldn't join them to their destination. Wow what a surprise, a ride south to my subsequent destination of Oaxaca without even trying. It was at this point, once again marveling at the flow of life, that the idea of writing this story was born.

But for the second day in a row, I was mercilessly shocked out of my euphoria, relieved of my petty plans, and forced to marvel even further at the human experience, consisting of its unlimited variety: its highs, lows, and never-ending challenges to the spirit. Reaching the small town of La Perla, on the outskirts of Orizaba, the driver stopped the truck, opened the back door, and ordered me to get out.

I was flustered, to say the least, especially as events unfolded. My protests that we had failed to reach Orizaba went unheeded, my questioning assertion concerning their trip to Oaxaca denied, and my desire to continue on to their destination and willingness to pay, ignored. It wasn't until disembarking from the back of the truck and noticing the other five passengers still sitting that I realized the extent to which I had been singled out.

I could think of nothing I had done to anger this man. Yet he was making a public spectacle at my expense and furthermore holding out his hand asking to be paid. Saying I owed him nothing since we had failed to reach Orizaba, I began to walk away. Grabbing my backpack, he threatened to hit me. While listening to his ensuing curses, I thrust a bill in his hand and left. Jumping into his vehicle, he then proceeded on down the road towards Orizaba.

Watching the truck disappear, my mind wandered to the volcano, which had for a short time been the focus of my existence. "So why did you leave the mountains Mark? Was it to get thrown out of a truck, ride an all-night bus, deal with grumpy people and closed hotels upon an early morning arrival at my destination, and then finally to plant myself on a park bench in the zócalo of Oaxaca below fading stars?" So why does anyone do anything anyways? I suppose writing this story is as good an answer as any: the description of an event that flows forth from the heart of Mexico, with its campos, campesinos, and their lands, the forest, mountain streams, and that glacier – and then finally the volcano, Citlaltepetl (5,640 meters).

Sort of a Shaman

Part 2

Wrestling With Fears

Sort of a Shaman

Chapter 6

Fear can paralyze people. It can keep someone from realizing a higher destiny in life. How a person responds to fears associated with the physical world, as well as the metaphysical realms, strongly determines the direction their life will take. Furthermore, a person's relationship to fear significantly impacts their personal and spiritual growth process.

In the following chapters, we will explore the various types of fears I have confronted during my life. This will include stories and commentary, starting with "mundane" types of fears. We will conclude with those I refer to as "core" fears. These include the fears of: death, going insane, demonic possession, the dark side and its hellish realms.

One of the most interesting patterns to emerge in the following stories concerns the fact that the fears I felt were valid, yet seldom did they materialize. I may have felt fears traveling in war torn countries, but I was never shot. I was never mugged, robbed, or beaten. I never broke a bone or had a terrible accident – and I certainly have not yet died in this lifetime. In my ongoing relationship to fear, I see it usually proves to be a toothless, clawless tiger. It has a vicious snarl, yet it seldom lives up to its reputation.

There is a fine line between listening to one's fears to avoid trouble and obsessing on them to the point of actually creating them. Developing a keen sense of intuition seems to be the key. It is always best to fully feel our emotions, including fear. By applying one's intuitive faculties to the fear, it is possible to discern whether or not it should be acted upon. Action may entail something as simple as increased awareness or stepping back from the edge of a cliff. Engaging and challenging your fears is about taking calculated risks, not about being foolish. If it doesn't feel right today, then maybe tomorrow. Wrestling with your fears allows you to gradually free yourself from their grasp.

Fear is a tricky, slippery sort of thing since all humans have a fight or flight response built into their DNA. This mechanism utilizes our endocrine system, mainly adrenaline. From a biological perspective, the body's reaction to fear is designed to ensure an individual's survival, as well as the survival of our species. For various reasons, this fear response has become counterproductive.

At this point in our evolution, survival doesn't usually depend on outer threats such as lions and tigers and bears. Instead, it is more closely linked to inner challenges associated with humanity's various addictions. These cover a broad spectrum including, but certainly not limited to, legal and illegal drugs, repressed emotions, non-stop activity, dysfunctional thoughts and belief systems. Those are the types of threats that are killing us. On a deeper level, they are all coping mechanisms based in fear.

Generally speaking, individuals and human societies are self-destructing from within. The fact that we are in the process of self-destructing as a species is becoming more obvious to more people every year. Our fear of the dark side, the power structures, foundational change, and finally, fear of our potential have held us hostage and rendered us incapable of shifting our course. To evolve forward and indeed survive, humans must learn to overcome their natural fear response much more effectively. Furthermore, this must occur in the face of a global system that promotes fear and separation on all levels.

In order to move beyond living a fear-based life, building a new framework of understanding is essential. What we were taught does not serve us anymore and it's highly questionable if it ever did. The perspectives I will present are a platform from which you can move forward towards new possibilities. They are aligned with cutting edge teachings and based in a highly metaphysical and spiritual view of reality. They are a synthesis of years of study and experience coupled with what I've seen through My Shaman's consciousness. It is an attempt to understand and explain the nature of reality.

Taoist masters assert that reality cannot be fully comprehended by our minds. I agree and am therefore walking a fine line in my desire to not ignore their eternal wisdom. Yet the reality system promoted by Western power structures and cultures is so distorted and destructive, it begs to be challenged and ultimately transcended.

All perspectives on reality have at least some validity, simply because they exist. Thus, the question you may want to ask yourself is: does your belief system serve you? Is it based in deeper truths viewed from numerous angles and sources – or is it just another commodity designed for mass consumption? Is its philosophy limiting or expansive?

The perspective I present facilitates your ability to overcome all fears. It promotes more freedom, which inevitably results in taking more risks, thus allowing you to live a more interesting, enjoyable, and powerful life. It also supports you in developing a mature relationship with the dark side, one that can lead to complete mastery over it.

To begin, All is ONE. The Creator and the Creation are ONE. There is nothing outside of ONENESS; no separation exists. This seems to be the foundational experience of all masters, mystics, and enlightened people on our planet, whether past or present. It also appears to be the core realization shared by many who have had a "near-death experience" (NDE), as well as people who have had enlightenment types of experiences.

Yet this deepest of truths, in and of itself, is not very useful. For a functional understanding of reality, one that can serve us, it is helpful to view the Creator and the Creation as separate. Science and our educational system consistently separate in order to understand things, especially in a logical manner: thus our brains have been taught to think in this way. Ironically, separation is the core issue humanity is facing.

My favorite name for the Creator is "Great Mystery," borrowed from our Native American brothers and sisters. I regularly use the term "Source." I find the Christian words "God" and "Divine" to be perfectly acceptable as well, although I seldom use them due to unavoidable religious connotations. Pure awareness and infinite creative potential might be descriptive of this greatest of all mysteries. The Creator exists in a state of no form, simply Is.

From my understanding, this is what the Buddhists refer to as the "Void." In its state of pure potentiality, the Creator has no ability to experience anything.

There are many Creation stories and myths. Some say the Creator chose to experience itself by creating a Creation. These Creation stories usually have a beginning. But, does time exist? Since Einstein and his theory of relativity, there seems to be agreement across the spectrum that time is a relative phenomenon. It has been referred to as the fourth dimension. There are legitimate logical reasons for this, so I will tend to refer to it as such.

Apparently, the deeper metaphysical truth is that everything happens in the eternal now, in no-time. If this is true, there never was a beginning. Creation has always existed! There never could have been a Creator without its Creation. There appears to have been a beginning to our universe (the Big Bang), but that which our eyes and telescopes are able to perceive is only a tiny fraction of the totality of Creation.

For the sake of clarity, our Milky Way Galaxy exists within a 14 billion-year-old universe. There are at least one trillion galaxies within this universe! Our sun and its solar system reside towards the edge of the Milky Way. The star we call our sun is one of approximately 250 billion stars in our galaxy. These terms: universe, galaxy, star, and solar system are very specific and not interchangeable. They are finite phenomena that exist within a potentially infinite Creation.

It is important to address the issue of scale as I proceed with this presentation on the nature of reality. Some of the descriptions that follow might only apply to the Milky Way Galaxy, since galaxies are semi-autonomous units and each may have their own unique reality. The same could be said for our universe. Nevertheless, considering the starkly blatant reality of Oneness, I've chosen to present the following concepts as applicable to all of Creation.

Creation is divided into various levels, which are usually referred to as dimensions or realms. Each dimension vibrates at a different frequency and contains its own unique reality. Different dimensions fill the same space in a manner similar to television, radio, and light frequencies.

Souls have the ability to visit any dimension and incarnate into all of them in a potentially infinite number of forms. This is referred to as "multidimensionality." Humans are multidimensional beings! Over the past several decades, quantum physics has begun to confirm the existence of other dimensions. The potential exists for an infinite number of universes, dimensions, and parallel realities within the totality of Creation.

Creation exists because of duality: light/dark, yin/yang. Duality and polarity are needed to manifest all of the dimensions within Creation. The extreme tension between polar opposites allows intention, thought, and emotion to coalesce and express in form. We are able to experience this form as solid in the physical realm. It is more subtle and dream-like in other dimensions.

Love is the glue that holds Creator/Creation together. Love is Connection. Total and complete connection is Oneness. Think about this. You can have an experience of love just as easily with an animal as you can with a person. In fact, you can have an experience of love with a plant or a stone or anything. Let's say you are focused on a flower, fully appreciating its beauty and magnificence. Your heart starts opening and you begin to realize you are feeling love – not so much for the flower – you are simply having an experience of love – because of your connection with the flower.

Creation is imbued with love! It is all connected, totally and completely intertwined. Understanding love in this way is vital and it will serve humanity in discovering new abilities fueled by the power-of-love. People presently understand aspects of love, but fail to grasp it in its entirety. We tend to view love as types of love, such as: a mother's love, a child's love, a lover's love, or even one's love for a type of food. Maybe we need a new word for love, one that clearly states "Love is Connection." Its opposite is the experience of separation. Feelings of separation potentially lead to fear.

As the Chinese have graphically shown with their yin/yang symbol, Creation is made of the light and the dark. Yet nothing is totally dark or totally light, as there is at least a little light in the dark, and vice versa. The core attribute of the light is connection. The core issue of the dark is separation. In the highest dimensions of Creation, those of incredible love and light, any sense of individuality could be interpreted as a little bit of darkness.

On planet Earth, the dark side feels abandoned, vulnerable, and hurt. It feels hatred towards its condition and because of this it's angry. It is also very good at denying all of this and aggressively acting out its pain in egotistic and destructive ways. This happens just as much on an individual level as it does with humanity as a collective. It could be argued that a person's dark side is a result of pain and trauma.

Feelings of separation define the dark. Darkness and fear are like twins of the same mother; they both rely on a sense of separation in order to exist. Yet ironically, the experience of feeling separate allows us to have an individualized soul experience within Creation. So maybe separation and darkness are a good thing!

Another important aspect of Creation is "maya," the illusion of it all. It is a fact that each and every atom is nearly pure space, with only the tiniest bits of proton, neutron, and electron. Yet to our five senses, this third dimensional reality seems real and appears very solid. But these apparently "solid" objects are more than 99.999999999999% space! It is a true miracle we can experience them as solid.

But are they real? This question has been debated for millennia by mystics of various cultures. Nothing in the physical world is permanent: everything is constantly changing and every living thing dies sooner or later and is recycled back into its component atoms. So is any of this actually real, or is it just a fantastic movie we are temporarily acting in? The truth, as far as I can discern, is that Creation is both real and unreal. This is the ultimate paradox, in a Creation full of paradox.

Creation is an illusion, simply a play of energies designed to offer souls a potentially infinite variety of experiences. The duality of light and dark is also illusion. Yet, our experiences are real. They are real simply because we experience them as real. In other words, perception is reality.

There is a Buddhist story that goes something like this: the teacher asks his students if this reality we live in is real. Evidently, they had been discussing this topic among themselves and had decided that no, it's not real. So the teacher hit one of the students on the head with his stick. After a scream, the teacher asks "Was that real?" The slightly offended student didn't know what to say, but answered "Well, it felt real" – to which the teacher replied "Then it is real."

Archetypes are the building blocks of Creation. Archetypal concepts and thought forms are similar to the ABCs of our alphabet. The reason astrology, tarot, and other types of divination tools are often so accurate is because they tap into these base energies. A highly intuitive person can interpret their symbolism extremely effectively. Archetypal images and experiences come to us in our dreams and waking life. If we are perceptible, they can provide us with a continuous stream of profound information.

The law of attraction (like attracts like) may be the most basic law in Creation. It is also the foundation for karma, the law of "cause and effect." An example of karma would be that if I help or hurt someone, in the same life (or another), the same soul (or another) will offer me a similar experience. Let's say I steal something and later someone steals from me. It is the same experience (like attracts like), just the other side of it.

However, karma is not just an eye-for-an-eye sort of mechanism: it is much more complex than that. A potential "pay back" depends on many factors, including the amount of repressed emotional energy attached to an action. Karma can be healed, forgiven, or simply released. It can result when impinging on the freewill of others, even if it is for their own good. Karma is a super-complex system that operates in all dimensions and enables duality. On a macro-cosmic level, karma keeps the polarities balanced so that everything holds together, continues to create and express.

Humanity was created by souls from higher dimensions. Beings with vast creative abilities started by creating simple carbon-based organisms and gradually evolved their creations into more complex forms, such as mammals and humans.

Reality is a hologram. Due to its holographic nature, it consistently mirrors itself on all levels. Thus, creating in other dimensions has similarities to creating in the physical realm. For instance, a modern-day fighter jet was gradually developed from much simpler designs through a process of trial and error. The human DNA genome was created in a similar manner.

Life on our planet has the ability to continue to evolve, more or less on its own, because of its DNA blueprint. DNA exists on multiple levels and the information that allows life forms to replicate is in higher dimensions, not in the physical realm. Genes that comprise physical DNA are a type of code, which mirrors the information contained within the higher realms.

This view of reality is what I see. It is also what I choose to believe. The reality system presented above was developed over time as I grappled with understanding, accepting, and embracing darkness within and without. I am not a good liar and I am not able to live a lie. I am completely devoted to understanding and living truth. This is apparently how I'm designed as an individual.

In my process of trying to understand what is happening on our planet, I had to look ever more deeply into the darkness so prevalent within the global power structures and their systems. Yet, as I progressed in my healing process, I became ever more committed to living a joy-filled life imbued with spiritual awareness and inner peace. The reality system I developed over time allowed me to fully embrace the light I desired, as well as intense levels of darkness, which can be so difficult to come to terms with.

We each have the Creator given right to believe whatever we choose to believe. Our belief systems are not just philosophies or ideas to debate with other people. Instead, they constantly influence us and strongly impact the quality of our life experience.

Here are some extremely important questions for you to consider. Is the Creator/Creation love? Are you intrinsically loved simply because you exist? Or do you fear God's judgment – either consciously or unconsciously? Are you Spirit, first and foremost? Are you a soul, a semi-autonomous consciousness, a presence of awareness? Do you believe you are eternal?

These fundamental questions dramatically impact how safe you feel in life. People who have had near-death experiences (NDEs) consistently say "Yes" to these types of questions. Enlightened masters and the channeled beings I've listened to say "Yes" as well. You have free will and the ability to choose yes or no to these questions. It's your choice and they are the most important choices you can make when dealing with fear, especially core fears.

If you can honestly say "Yes" to these questions, you can overcome all fears. Yet if you say "Yes" and are serious about developing mastery over your fears, you will be tested. Your faith in Love and belief in the indestructibility of you as a soul will be tested. That's OK since this is the process of remembering and claiming your Oneness with the Divine.

Resistance to negativity and darkness compels people to live extremely reactive and dis-empowered lives. As a person overcomes their fears, they can live life more proactively. At that point, developing mastery over the dark side simply requires time, energy, practice and some creativity.

I once had a client who told me she didn't think she had any fears. My response is that she probably wasn't challenging herself enough to bring up her fears. In the following chapters, you will see how I relentlessly pushed myself in every area of life in an attempt to unearth all of my fears. At the time, I didn't know why I was doing this. I just did it – and I'm still doing it!

This type of behavior is in extreme contrast to how most people live, which is to constantly avoid their fears. In this manner, their fears actually run their lives, dictating their day-to-day choices. Living a normal modern life enmeshed in the system is completely foreign to me. Yet this type of life is assumed to be safe and sensible by the majority of humans, so that's probably why they do it.

Ironically, a life of avoiding fears actually feeds that which we do not desire. This ultimately makes a person's life experience less safe and more difficult. This dynamic occurs on an energetic level, which I will attempt to explain more clearly.

By denying and resisting fears, we retain those frequencies within our energy fields. This results in their vibratory qualities strongly radiating outwards. These frequencies will inevitably attract complementary experiences. This tends to produce situations in our lives that create more things to fear, which ultimately results in a vicious cycle of negative manifestation.

By sharing my stories, I hope to inspire others to wrestle with and eventually overcome their own fears. I feel it is impossible to overstate the importance of human fear and the manner in which we interact with it. How we deal with our fears as individuals will strongly impact our collective future as a species.

Chapter 7

The experience of feeling isolated is the first fear we will address since it is the most basic. It is the fear most closely associated with the dark side's core issue of separation. But is it really even possible to be alone? If Creator/Creation is all One and everything is connected, then no, it's not possible. Yet we can certainly feel lonely and experience a sense of separateness.

When I was a child, I felt huge amounts of pain when one of our cats died. I bonded very deeply with several of them. Sometimes they slept on my bed and came under the covers at night. Except for sleeping with my parents when very young, I was alone at night – similar to the majority of us. My cats were the exception to this sense of isolation.

Every time I fell in love and my relationship ended, I went through extreme loneliness. As with my cats, I struggled when I lost my partner, the woman I held on to at night and with whom I felt such a strong sense of connection. Most of us have fallen in love and lost it and many have lost a beloved pet, so nearly everyone can relate. When something like this happens, we can feel excruciatingly alone, even in the company of people who care about us.

From my experiences, the best healing salve is the one called mourning. When we lose someone, we can go through many different emotions throughout the day, which is very positive. Traditional Chinese medicine claims that every human emotion has two separate two-hour periods each day when it is most prevalent. Therefore, the ideal is to allow movement and not stay stuck in one emotion for more than two hours.

Many people have discovered that the more they opened their heart, the greater was the pain and grief from a loss. This is a perfect opportunity to heal core unresolved trauma and to assess one's belief systems about love. In general, the more issues a person processes and the deeper they go, the longer they need. It is imperative to give ourselves time to process a loss.

Yet, at some point, it is also vital for a person to let go and move on. Over-attachment creates unnecessary suffering and energetic stagnation. This will eventually impact our health and well-being in a strongly negative manner.

As I traveled and hiked alone throughout the years, I gradually became more comfortable with the feelings of loneliness that arose. I discovered that the more time I spent by myself, the easier it got. Over the years, I learned to like myself and the more time I spent alone, the more I seemed to like myself. After all, if you don't have anyone else to interact with, it's best if you are nice to yourself. The nicer you are to yourself, the nicer a person you become. The nicer you become, the easier it is to like yourself!

One of the main issues I'm aware of with most people is that they have not spent enough time alone. Spending time with oneself in a conscious manner is essential to one's spiritual awakening. Ideally, a person will be present with their fears around isolation and go into the feelings as fully as possible.

I found these were times when I made breakthroughs with spiritual beings who exist in higher realms. When I was deeply enough in the pain and fear of separation, which was unbearable at times, I often prayed for help. This created the opening needed for loving spirit beings to make their presence known. They have tremendous compassion for us struggling humans on Earth.

Bhagwan Shree Rajneesh (Osho) makes a clear distinction between being alone and loneliness. Being alone is meant to be an empowering experience, allowing us to go within and discover unlimited connection with the invisible realms. Loneliness is disempowering because it is a product of our egoic structure and its sense of separation from everything else.

Feeling lonely and dealing with what it brings up in oneself is critical. This is possibly the most important of all the fears to address. Taking appropriate time to process one's feelings and emotions in relation to any fear is crucial. "Processing" means that you take the amount of time needed, for the experience you need to go through, in order to heal and grow. "Processing one's emotions" refers to being present with the deeper feelings that arise and then somehow making peace with them.

You may, for instance, find appreciation for the experience of aliveness they offer in their intensity. You may experience love and compassion for the part of yourself that is suffering. You may cry and notice that you feel afraid. Or you might just give up and later find a deeper strength than you knew you had. Whatever you feel and do, it takes time and energy. It can be physically demanding. Fully feeling your fears and emotions can leave you totally exhausted, but in the long run, it's most certainly worth the effort.

Exploring loneliness was a way of unearthing the deepest issue in my life, although it took many years for me to understand the main cause. Feelings of abandonment have been my core issue. The racism I experienced as a youth certainly triggered this, but it was not the cause.

I had a birth memory arise during a session I received at Heartwood. Although it had a dramatic impact on my psyche, I discovered it still wasn't the main cause of my abandonment issue. In my birth memory, I saw myself screaming, just after birth, because the nurse was taking me away from my mother. I simply could not believe what was happening – it did not seem possible! I was being separated from my mother, in whose body I had been created and felt at one with. The separation we experience from our mother just after birth is analogous to the separation we suffer from in relation to our spiritual Source.

I discovered the root cause of my abandonment issue during the third stage of my life. I was in the midst of a two-year period where I allowed myself to express intense levels of rage at the Creator. I was angry about many things here on Earth, both personal and general. Very few people knew about this; if I told someone, they usually stared at me in semi-disbelief. Yet what better and more appropriate being is there to express our rage at? Expressing it at people in our lives is often inappropriate, hurtful, and damaging to our relationships. It is much better to go right to the Source!

During this time, I saw a vision of myself in another life while in the midst of dying. Later I tuned into other similar lives. Those experiences and my reactions to them were the main cause of my core issue. In them, I died feeling forsaken, isolated, and extremely angry at God. Sometimes it was because of suffering I had endured, the unfairness of it all. Other times I was furious because my entire family or community had been slaughtered. Since I died with this anger in my heart, it carried over very strongly into other lives.

Notice that I wrote "other" lives. When I speak of another life I've lived, I don't usually refer to it as a past life, since everything happens in the eternal now moment. As incomprehensible as this is for most humans, it is apparently true. Virtually all metaphysically inclined teachers seem to agree. All of our lives are happening simultaneously, influencing our "present" life much more than people realize.

I also wish to comment on visions and the third eye. I've had several experiences in my life that I refer to as "visions." A shaman would most likely call them "waking dreams." I see visions with my third eye (sixth chakra). I've also seen ethereal spirit beings, but I saw them with my physical eyes, not my third eye.

Visions are rare for me, but receiving images with my third eye is common. For instance, I regularly see images of where to place my hands on a client, or how to organize my gardens. I see them behind the front of my forehead, with the "mind's eye," a phrase that perfectly describes the pictures I see with my third eye. They are like snapshots, while the visions are more like a movie.

Due to the naturalness of seeing in this way, people often fail to realize they are seeing with their third eye. If you can't see in this manner, your pineal gland is probably calcified from the fluoride added to drinking water and toothpaste. Chlorine, bromine, and calcium also block its effectiveness. Third eye capabilities depend on the pineal gland.

Returning to the topic of isolation, I believe feelings of separation are the underlying reason for people's addictions. I define "addiction" in a very broad manner: consistently engaging in any activity in the outer world for the unconscious purpose of fulfilling a deep inner longing for Source connection. The yogis and mystics talk about "bliss consciousness" – joy far beyond circumstantial happiness or pleasure. Real bliss barely exists within the reality of duality. It seems to accompany experiences of Oneness, transcendence, and the higher dimensions.

Our higher selves exist in a state of bliss and humans ache to consciously experience this in their daily lives. Thus, we constantly look for it, hoping it can come from somewhere outside of ourselves. Corporate advertising preys on these tendencies. We unconsciously look for this because we feel a desire way down deep that we wish to fulfill. This is the root of addictions. They are definitely spiritual at their core.

The main overriding addiction I see Americans lost in is one of constant activity. As the saying goes "We are human beings, not human doings." Most people are stuck in constant doing-ness because they are so agitated and uncomfortable inside of themselves. They don't take the time to simply be, to sit with their deeper emotions, to work through their inner pain and heal it. Bliss exits beyond the pain of separation and ironically embodies it. Paradoxically, the concept of the Void, the emptiness Buddhism strives for, is the ultimate experience of being alone.

My addiction to falling in love was my attempt to satisfy this inner ache through a connection with a woman. I would not feel lonely when I was experiencing romantic love and feelings of separation were kept at bay. For me, it was an addiction because I relied on it to satisfy my desire for bliss consciousness, for union with Source.

The problem with any addiction is the focus of your obsession can be taken away – and then we tend to crash, sometimes miserably. The other problem is our addiction never seems to meet our real inner need no matter how much we indulge it. Addictions are dis-empowering because they depend on something outside of ourselves that we seldom have control over. Although addictions are spiritual at their core, they usually have psychological, emotional, and physical aspects connected to them.

This is why they can be so difficult to overcome; they tend to be a very complex phenomena.

Spiritual masters have been telling us for millennia to look within for that which we seek. Going within is the best way to connect with Creator. Time alone is the best way to find the peace and quiet necessary to go within, to connect to our higher selves and the transcendent state of being. We can certainly find the Creator in its Creation, but then again, worldly stuff can so easily distract. It seems virtually everyone must first find a deeper connection within, before consistently finding it outside and not getting caught in distractions and addictions.

Since the revelation concerning my core issue, I've been slowly rebuilding my relationship to Source. Having released much of my rage towards God, I opened the door for something new. I began to realize my anger had created a sense of separation, when in reality there wasn't any. Identifying with feelings of abandonment had left me feeling needy, which I habitually tried to address by falling in love.

At one point, I had to stop doing the addictive cycle of falling in romantic love with women. I slowly began to understand what self-love is really about. On a deeper level, loving oneself means loving One's-Self. This entails a process of releasing identification with the ego-self and starting to identify with the Soul-Self and/or one's expanded multidimensional selves. It's about relationship with the Divine – what the gurus and mystics have spoken about forever and ever. This Divine love affair was the focus of the incredibly eloquent prose written by the Sufi poet Rumi.

My process of opening to a deeply fulfilling Source connection continues today and I'm sure it will continue for the remainder of my life. It's subtle and challenging, but as I gradually rely on more help from higher spiritual realms, my endeavor seems to lighten and become more enjoyable.

Chapter 8

Modern societies usually teach their people to fear and dominate nature. Respect and cooperation would be far more sustainable and enjoyable. The natural world is always in harmony when undisturbed by man and resilient when human behavior interferes with its environment. I feel compassion for people raised in big cities, or children who spend the vast majority of their time with phones and computers.

I was thankfully raised connecting with Mother Nature on a regular basis. As a child, undeveloped canyon areas always seemed to be close at hand. My brother and I were constantly playing in them with any friends who might join us. Nature is most certainly an unending playground. Despite my comfort level, the natural world has challenged and humbled me to my core. Intense fear has surfaced on numerous occasions, especially in the ocean.

In my youth, I remember snorkeling with my brother and father and how scary it was the first several times, especially when the visibility was low. Then the movie *Jaws* hit the theaters and it created even more fear because I couldn't keep images of sharks attacking me out of my mind. That didn't stop me though; I just learned to deal with it.

The ocean is incredibly powerful; it simply demands our respect and at times leaves little room for error. Once while snorkeling near Rosarito Beach as teenagers, we got caught in the surf on our way back to shore. The waves were really big and we tried to get in between the sets, but didn't make it. Since I was last, I got smashed and tumbled more than the other two. After struggling back to the surface each time to catch a quick breath, another wave would slam down. Thankfully, the waves pushed me in as they threw me about and I managed to literally crawl onto the beach in total exhaustion and gratitude. Without a doubt, I gained a healthy respect for the ocean from that day on.

People regularly died along Zipolite's notoriously fickle beach. Strong rip currents would form without people noticing, especially since they didn't know what to look for. I spent a lot of time body-surfing when the waves had decent form. When they were choppy, I rode the rip currents out past the wave sets and swam parallel to the beach. I would even swim on overcast winter days.

Sometimes when I went to the beach to go for a swim, a deep intense fear would wash over and through me as I watched the waves. I could literally feel hungry spirits who wanted to devour me. It's always difficult to know the truth behind such a feeling, but after regularly swimming without fear, I was relatively certain those spirits were real and would indeed take my life. I never swam outside of the waves at those times, but often compromised by staying in shallow water.

The most dramatic experience I ever encountered in the ocean was on the island of Kauai. I spent six months camping along the beaches of Kauai over the course of three winters, from 1999 to 2001. During this time, the most amazing experience was the two weeks I spent in Kalalau during the millennium change of 2000. The most difficult occurred twelve miles away in Polihale.

The last totally undeveloped coastline on Kauai encompasses this region and it is indeed very powerful. Traditionally, people who lived on Kauai, as well as royalty from other Hawaiian Islands, were taken to Polihale for their burials. From my understanding, Polihale served the exact same purpose as the beach in Zipolite – a place to send souls off to the higher realms.

While buying food for my upcoming camping trip to Polihale, a synchronicity came into play: I ran into an American woman I knew from Zipolite. Ruby had helped us occasionally at the Pina Palmera and even lived there for a while. Several months before running into her and Jack on Kauai, they had sailed his sailboat from Alaska to the island. Upon learning I was going to Polihale for a number of days, they decided to join me.

The day after we arrived, Jack and I were body-surfing. I was tired and heading in when I saw him off in the distance frantically waving his arms to get my attention. I swam out to him and discovered he was definitely in trouble. Since Jack was barely able to keep his head above water, I immediately started towing him in. He kept telling me he wasn't going to make it and I kept saying he was.

I was extremely exhausted by the time I flagged down Ruby on the beach and she came to help. Jack was probably unconscious when he was torn from our grips by more waves near the shore. Other people on the beach finally realized what was happening and came to help drag him out of the water. Then they gave him CPR while I lay on the sand completely spent.

After some minutes, I began to realize Jack may have been correct: he might not survive. As I gathered myself together, I knelt behind his head and silently communicated that it was all right if it was time for him to move on. I was surprised when I mentally received a clear response. He told me that he was indeed finished and most definitely ready to leave.

Several hours later, Ruby and I stood by his body at the hospital. The doctor told us she was fairly certain he had suffered a heart attack, since Ruby had confirmed he did in fact have a heart condition. Soon after, Jack once again communicated to me. He showed me a vision of another life we had lived together, yet that time he was the one standing over my dead body. We were friends and I died in a battle we had fought in together. Jack then let me know he felt incredibly honored to have died in Polihale; it had been his destiny to die there.

Ruby and I spent the next three days in Polihale as some of his family and friends began to arrive from the States. It was a perfect place to work through the avalanche of emotions that arose in each of us. She cried a lot and told me some stories about the two of them. One occurred the previous month when she and Jack were riding mountain bikes in a park above Polihale. They were heading for a point directly overlooking the beach when she got tired and stopped. He rode on to the lookout before returning to meet her for the ride back. It suddenly became obvious to both of us at the same time that some part of Jack had known he was going to die there.

Now we move on to a fear of heights and the prospect of falling to one's death. For me, it was minimal as a child; it seems my cats inspired me. I probably climbed nearly as many trees as they did. While camping with my family in Yosemite Valley, I remember looking down the face of Half Dome while my sister held my ankles. The 3,000 ft. sheer drop into the valley was both awesome and incredibly unsettling.

While I've only used ropes on a few shorter climbs, I've spent plenty of time on rocks over the years. I can't tell you how many times I've asked myself what the heck I was doing on a rock face with a sheer drop. The drop was usually only twenty to forty feet, but that's more than enough to maim or kill a person. The most powerful experience I've ever had on rocks was during my hike on Mt. Shasta.

I spent ten days camping out in Panther Meadows, several hours from the parking lot. It was fall and very few people were staying at this popular backpacking spot. I was trying to find clarity and healing in my relationship with Mia and had not bothered to go to the top of the mountain. But someone who was camping nearby loaned me his book and informed me of a possible route from there to the peak.

So on my last morning, I left at first light and followed the ridge-line above the meadow until it became exceedingly narrow, with sheer drops on both sides. Once I realized it was in fact passable, I stopped for a break and began to read the borrowed book. It was about the older less famous of the two Indian yogis named Sai Baba. Evidently Sai Baba regularly showed up to his devotees as different types of animals. As if on cue, I looked up and an eagle was flying straight at me from across the valley.

I made it to the peak a few hours later and went down another way. The route I took back to my camp was not a trail, similar in this respect to the one I had taken up. But it was more isolated in the sense that no one would ever have a reason to go that way. While on the scree near the top, I took another break to read the book. When I looked up, there was a hawk flying above me.

A little while later, I came to a gorge carved out of the mountain by the flow of water from a glacier. I made my way down and walked along the fast-flowing stream looking for a way up the other side. I knew it probably wouldn't be more than an hour or two to my campsite once I managed to get up the steep side of the gorge, but I kept walking down the river and couldn't see a way to the top.

Since it was getting late in the afternoon, I finally chose a route even though it looked highly questionable. It didn't get really steep until the last section, at which point it was a ninety-degree face of at least thirty feet. I managed to shimmy up a crack in the rock until I could go no further. As I looked for a possible way to the top, my arms started getting tired and I kept looking at the sheer drop below. Getting there hadn't been easy and I certainly didn't want to go back down, especially knowing daylight was an issue.

I was almost certain I would be able to reach the top of the canyon if I could get around a large rock bulging out just in front of me. The seconds ticked by and my arms started aching. All of a sudden, without making a conscious decision, I leaned out and stretched around the bulge, finding a handhold. I was moving along an exceedingly thin ledge in a sideways manner, not knowing exactly what was on the other side. The scariest part was that I was leaning outwards and if I lost my grip, I would fall backwards head first onto the rocks below. Somehow I got my body around the bulge without falling and there I was on the far side. It was only a short quick scramble to the top from there.

As I finished the hike, I kept asking myself why I had tried going around the bulge in the rock. Objectively, I would have given myself less than a 50% chance of making it. I virtually never risked my life on such poor odds, especially when no one in the world knew where I was. I couldn't decide if my action had been an act of faith or simply foolish. I eventually arrived at my campsite as darkness enveloped the mountain.

The first snow of the season started falling as I hiked out the next morning. I found out later that a foot of snow fell during the day. Looking back, I've come to believe I had spiritual assistance on the rock face. A part of me that exists in another dimension made the decision to go and something else helped me around the bulge in the rock. It felt kind of magical while it was happening.

Mt. Shasta has been considered a sacred mountain for millennia by native people in the region. After my time there, I certainly understood why.

Another basic human fear is claustrophobia, and it's one I've encountered on rare occasions. I remember as a kid crawling inside a very long and narrow metal culvert that was probably only two feet in diameter. Some friends and I wanted to see if we could reach the other end. I've never forgotten how unnerving it was to be deep inside that narrow pipe.

Years later at UCSC, I went into a cave with friends several different times. The cave was only a mile walk through the forest from my dorm. It took about forty minutes to crawl to the end with our flashlights and another five minutes to make it down the vertical shaft at the end. The second time I went into the cave, all of our flashlights stopped working for one reason or another by the time we reached the shaft.

This meant that we had to crawl out of the cave in total darkness by simply feeling our way along. At about the halfway point, we came to a small room and could not for the life of us find the hole on the other side. As we got more frustrated and our fears escalated, one of my friends started panicking. After calming him down, we spent more time calming ourselves as well. Soon afterwards, we found the opening we had been searching for. When we finally emerged from the mouth of the cave and saw the light of the setting sun, the feelings of relief were indescribable.

I've also felt claustrophobic while scuba diving when the visibility was low and the surface of the ocean was not visible. I've probably experienced this most strongly while diving for sea urchins in Maine. The visibility was usually minimal, sometimes as little as a few feet. After an hour underwater, I frequently found myself in an altered state of consciousness. Upon returning to normal awareness, I occasionally felt like I was trapped in a tiny sphere and had to strongly temper my initial reaction. Developing self-control is an important practice, however one does it.

Moving at high speeds can be both exhilarating and frightening. It's easy to see how people get addicted to the adrenaline rush that can accompany such experiences. I've ridden bicycles all of my life and even now I do most of my errands around town on a bike. My brother turned me on to mountain biking as an adult and I've fallen many times while making slow difficult turns. On the other hand, when going in a relatively straight line, I'm constantly amazed my bike stays upright and I virtually never fall while riding rapidly over extremely rocky and uneven terrain. The only other sport I've experienced that exceeds mountain biking in speed related intensity is downhill skiing.

I've often felt fear while skiing. Looking down a treacherous incline covered with powder, hard snow, ice, trees, and/or rocks can be extremely intimidating. Not only did I tear ligaments in both of my knees over the years, I ventured into places I shouldn't have gone. I've always been awed by really good skiers – their grace, courage, and ability to make it look so easy. It seemed to me that with enough determination, I might be able to ski like them. Having first skied at eighteen and not getting serious about it until I was in my thirties and forties, I discovered this was not a realistic goal.

Being high up on a mountain in the middle of winter is the most incredible feeling, especially when no one else is around. Since I usually skied alone, this was a way to spend quality time with myself and I often processed difficult and negative emotions. Sometimes I challenged my ability to focus and ski to my capabilities. Other times, I played and enjoyed myself to a degree seldom experienced in my other athletic endeavors. Maybe that was the most important objective – it seems to me one of the main reasons a Creator would create a Creation is to enjoy it. If we aren't doing our best to enjoy life, we might just be letting the entire process down.

Chapter 9

Sexuality is an arena filled with joy, indescribable pleasure, and deep intimacy. It is also full of fears, lack of clarity, and unending dysfunctional behavior. I've experienced my share of those extremes. Since I grew up Catholic, repressed sexuality was the norm throughout my childhood and teenage years. I certainly don't recommend suppression because sexual desires squeeze out one way or another.

Sexual energy and its related hormones are incredibly powerful in young people and modern societies offer few adequate solutions to this challenge. From what I'm able to ascertain, indigenous cultures groomed their youth in functional sexual behavior much more effectively.

In Nevada City, I participated in a weekend workshop focused on a Native American tribe's methods of teaching their teenagers about sexuality. It was very revealing in various ways and went far beyond anything taught in my schools, which in truth felt like a mockery. On the other side of our planet, many traditional societies in the Polynesian South Pacific were able to celebrate their sexuality freely and beautifully. This worked well because individuals were supported by their entire cultural fabric.

Possibly the best way to manage sexual energy is to learn pranayama techniques, such as those taught to spiritual aspirants in India. Pranayama focuses on the breath and energy field in a manner utilized by yogis for countless millennia. Working with sexual energy in support of one's spiritual growth is a high path, one that can be taught in the home by more enlightened parents.

I grew up in a Christian society whose sexual roots were being shaken to their foundation by the Sixties free-love culture. I discovered in my late teens that the level of confusion, crudeness, and sexual immaturity among my male peer group was phenomenal. As I navigated sexual desires and fears from my twenties through fifties, I desperately held on to some sense of integrity. My parents had instilled deep integrity within our family dynamic and my father did a great job modeling it.

Over the years, I gradually gained maturity in relation to my sexuality, although the process seemed nothing short of chaotic. I never dated or learned to pick-up women because the game-playing felt so deceitful. Instead, I forged my own unique path with women, sexuality, and love making.

For me, the core of sexuality is connection and intimacy. I crave deep intimacy and physical touch and believe these are core human needs, ones that are pure and holy. Sex is a way those needs can be expressed and thankfully that was my experience most of the time. Sexuality was often playful, sometimes passionate, and my addiction to falling in love was undeniably connected to a deep need for intimacy.

Let's begin a thorough exploration of this subject with the topic of nudity. It wasn't until I went to UCSC that I began to overcome inhibitions surrounding naked bodies. My fellow students and I would occasionally sun-bathe nude in the meadow alongside our dorm complex. Although people were discreet, it was common for us to stumble upon our friends hidden in the long grasses. "Streaking" had become popular in America and several students from another dorm had gone to lunch nude.

Thus, it wasn't completely out of the norm when Lolita, Bill, and I decided to be the first in our dorm facility to experiment with this idea. It was a huge challenge for me to walk around our large dining hall naked, with hundreds of other students present, but it was also a major breakthrough. Lolita was a bit of an exhibitionist; it may not have been as difficult for her.

Living at Heartwood and the Pina Palmera served the next phase of my process around nudity. Ironically, I was not sexual with a woman at either of those communities during the first year. Although there was a lot of nudity, there was also plenty of touch and intimacy. Most people naturally assume sex would follow. Yet this wasn't my experience since my need for connection and affection were being met. If modern societies had an abundance of those attributes, most of the sexual dysfunction we see in our world would probably disappear!

Working as a massage therapist at Ojo Caliente Hot Springs for eight years was a process that took nudity in my life to an entirely new level. I worked at "Ojo" between the years 1997 and 2009, with a three-year break in the middle. In my time there, I gave over 5,000 massages to people from all walks of life. Almost everyone had been in the springs before their massage and they nearly always slipped out of their wet bathing suits (while I waited outside) before crawling in between the sheets on the table.

At least two-thirds of my clients were women and a certain percentage of them were extremely attractive. Sometimes I was amazed at being paid to place my hands all over these women's naked bodies. At times I felt frustrated since the professional agreement certainly didn't include sex. I occasionally questioned my ability to stay in integrity. Many women have been damaged by inappropriate male behavior; I was determined to help heal their pain and confusion, not add to it.

At Heartwood Institute, the core philosophy of our school centered on opening to feelings and emotions, as well as all of our body's energies. For health purposes, energy must flow and sexual energy is no exception, especially since it's very connected to our overall life-force. I took two full-body oil massage classes at Heartwood and the teachers suggested we try to ignore or close down our sexual energy if we were strongly attracted to a client.

Not only was this type of repression relatively ineffective, it ran in opposition to the school's philosophy. But the fact is that these teachers were concerned with protecting our profession, our clients, and those of us who were becoming therapists. In those days, massage was still strongly associated with prostitution in the minds of the general public because prostitutes often offered massage as part of their business.

All of this touches on a core issue for humans. How much should we allow our animal nature to express itself, emotionally, sexually, or otherwise? People who completely suppress themselves can be like robots, or a bomb waiting to explode. Allowing expression of basic human energies is vital to our overall well-being, but if they start to run our lives in an uncontrolled fashion, this is problematic to say the least. Learning self-discipline as a means of tempering our natural urges is vitally important. Yet over control leads to repression. Finding the balance is an art form and one of our biggest challenges as human beings.

Because of a lack of clarity around this complex issue, I decided to make a practice of working with my sexual energy when I was giving an oil massage to a woman I couldn't help but desire. Since I was unwilling to repress myself in any manner, this felt like the only viable solution. Their bodies, body language, and openness on the massage table occasionally challenged my maleness to extreme degrees – talk about temptation!

I was originally attracted to this profession because it is multifaceted, tapping into time tested traditions of healers from cultures all over our planet. Innumerable modalities and alternative therapies were loosely tossed into the field of massage therapy. Sadly, in America, this extremely eclectic profession devoted to healing was gradually pushed by economic forces into a mold that felt safe and comfortable to people: an oil massage in a spa setting.

Thus, it became associated with pleasure and relaxation, rather than holistic healing. This is tragic and I found myself right in the middle of its development. Although a great massage is one of the most pleasurable experiences in life, the profession of massage therapy shouldn't be limited to that reality.

Since an oil massage is a highly sensual experience, it's normal for unfulfilled desires and associated emotions to arise in a client. The more physically and energetically attracted I was to a woman, the more challenging this dynamic was for me. Although I maintained a relatively high level of integrity, I wasn't a saint. Since I was willing to walk a fine line and work on the edge, I did cross over at times.

This line of integrity was arbitrary to a fair degree since I was the one drawing it. Having sex with a woman on the massage table was definitely way over the line, so I never allowed it to happen. Touching a woman's genitals was something I also avoided at all times. There was one exception and that was a massage therapist friend I traded deep healing work with for two years, but never got involved with sexually. At one point, she asked me to focus on the inside of her vagina to help release old trauma.

This is usually done by couples who delve into tantric sex and choose to heal deeper levels of their sexuality. Offering healing touch to the inside of a woman's vagina can be achieved by applying pressure to painful points along the inner walls. A woman can do this herself, but can't reach the deeper areas and will need help. Although this can be powerfully healing, I recommend women only do it with a trusted partner or woman therapist.

I've also worked on the inside of a person's anus with several men and women. This was taught to me in my "trigger-point therapy" class. We wore gloves and the people I worked with were either classmates or friends. This part of the body holds major trauma. Because the vaginal and anal areas are on either side of the first chakra, the issues addressed (foundation, survival, fears) would correspond to it. Second chakra issues connected to sexuality are also addressed. It would benefit almost every person on our planet to receive this type of bodywork from a massage therapist they trusted. Another area of similar intensity and importance is the inside of the mouth.

Breast massage can also be extremely beneficial since it increases circulation, which helps to prevent breast cancer. A female therapist at Ojo Caliente told me that she regularly asked her clients if they wanted their breasts massaged, partly to educate them so they could do it themselves. I started asking some of my clients the same question and received mixed responses. I rapidly began to question my motives and stopped soon afterwards.

If I found my mind obsessing on a woman's body, I was crossing the line. I knew on some level she could feel it. The session was about her, not me and my desires. Since women with nice bodies are often athletic, they usually have some really tight muscles. So I would focus on making the session more therapeutic with deep tissue work. If I was still obsessing, I might focus on a Hindu mantra. If that didn't work and I was irritated enough with my lack of discipline, I would intentionally close down my sexual energy as much as possible.

After all, it was one thing to enjoy massaging a beautiful woman's body; it was quite another to obsess on it. I became quite strict with myself concerning my mental focus and approached these situations as opportunities to develop mindfulness. If I noticed my mind obsessing on anything and I wasn't present for my client, I would pursue some type of solution.

When a woman whom I was attracted to opened up under my hands on the table, the sessions often took the form of a dance. It was similar to dancing with a person you recently met, where there is mutual attraction and sexual energy is flowing. In an ideal situation, both people are focused on enjoying the moment, not a sexual agenda.

In some of those massage sessions, I felt my client and myself flowing in our sexual energy exchange. Neither of us believed we would have sex, yet the sexual energy was extremely palpable. It was as if we were making love, but only on an energetic level. It was a balancing act for me to keep my client's needs as the priority, yet enjoy my work and honor my deep need for inner growth by challenging myself as a therapist.

Throughout the years, my experiences as a massage therapist brought sexual discipline into my life. I was able to spend the night with numerous women, while we were partly or fully nude, without becoming sexual. There was mutual attraction and respect. Two of the women were lesbians, or at least preferred women to men. It did not take long for me to realize how healing this could be for a woman, yet I wouldn't be surprised if most have never experienced it. Trusting a man in this manner must not be easy.

Sometimes we decided to not be sexual beforehand; other times we discussed it after we were already in bed. At times this subject was never even broached. Once in a while, I asked the woman if she was sure she wanted to be sexual when the situation was rapidly moving in that direction. Several times the answer was no, which was not always easy for me to honor, but I did. There was also one time where the woman I was with became angry at me for not being sexual with her.

But overall, our focus on touch, affection, sharing loving energy and healing was very rewarding. I encourage more men to explore this type of experience. I was amazed I could share with a woman in this manner, without the sexual fulfillment my body usually desired. Realizing I could discipline myself to this degree was extremely empowering for me as a man.

Before I became a massage therapist, life started to challenge me concerning whether or not I was bisexual. Since I was obviously attracted to women, I was relatively certain I was not homosexual. But I didn't know for sure since no one talked about this sort of thing in those days. Much less clear was the question of whether or not I was bisexual. Was I meant to love everyone, even sexually?

From the time this question started showing up in my life, I was open to finding the truth. I knew I didn't want to live a lie. If I didn't know the clear and certain truth concerning my sexuality, I might inadvertently do just that. Was I afraid of what I might discover? I certainly was, to the extreme! Homosexuality was highly frowned upon at the time; things have changed a lot for gay people in the past three decades. The Sixties may have opened up sexuality for heterosexuals in a major way, but not for homosexuals.

When I first started working at the Pina Palmera, a Mexican man named Rolando said I could sleep at his place – next to him as it turned out, although I was in my own sleeping bag. In my naïveté, I had no idea he was gay. I was totally surprised when his hand came on my bare chest that night. In a partial sleep, I swung my arm outwards and hit him. That was the end of him trying to seduce me, but it was just the beginning of a four-year period where gay men who were interested in me kept showing up in my life. When I finally gained total clarity that I was indeed heterosexual, gay men almost completely stopped approaching me.

At Heartwood, I developed a close friendship to Bob and Roy. Since they had recently purchased the school, they didn't have close friends. I had just broken up with Melinda and was looking for friendship as well. In the entire time I knew them, their long-term relationship seemed to be one of the happiest and most functional of any I had ever experienced.

As our friendship grew, the question of sex kept coming up. Since they were wonderful people in many ways, I was open to the idea. Although I was never totally nude with them, since I stayed within my comfort zone, we often kissed each other, sometimes passionately. I was more intimate with them than with any other man in my life. They were excellent chefs and appreciated good wine and friendship. Bob and Roy were also honorable and never tried to manipulate me into being sexual with them, despite their clear interest in a threesome.

They were amazed that a man who was apparently straight could be so open to sharing intimately with other men. For my part, I was able to talk honestly with them about my lack of clarity concerning my sexuality. Over the years I have found gay men to be more willing to speak of intimate subjects than heterosexual men; they often speak about topics of the heart, similar to women. This was very important to me, especially considering my classes. I was regularly massaging men and actively searching for clarity in my determination to not be homophobic. I simply had to deal with this fear as opposed to living my entire life with it.

I finally gained clarity on the matter just before I met Mia. A statement of apparent truth came up in my classes several different times: "the body never lies." I began to realize that I never got an erection when I shared intimate experiences with men; my body was clearly not sexually attracted to them. I never had sex with a man and found out it wasn't a necessary ingredient to knowing my truth. In fact, it may have created unnecessary confusion and pain.

Interestingly, all of this happened while I was exploring my inner feminine, the yin aspects of myself. At Pina Palmera, I cared for infants and handicapped children, while at Heartwood, I explored my emotions more deeply than most men could imagine. Although I very seldom cried during my childhood, I discovered a well of tears on the receiving end of healing work. I also found greater joy than I had known was possible.

I discovered that by opening more fully to one emotional extreme, the other side opened as well. This was a truly profound discovery for me – one based in personal experience. My willingness to explore the negative dark stuff within, allowed me to open more fully to the light – to deeper levels of love. If there is one thing I wish most for people, it is that they discover this for themselves.

Unwanted pregnancy is a very real fear connected to sexuality. As I previously shared, Mia became pregnant in the most difficult of circumstances. But she wasn't the only woman with whom I managed to create a pregnancy and not have a child. I'm certainly not proud of myself, especially for being too pushy when my partner was reluctant. With each pregnancy, I let my girlfriend choose what she felt was best.

Surprisingly, I was not even aware that I did not want children. For me, mostly on an unconscious level, children represented loss of freedom and enslavement to the system. I would be forced to make enough money to raise them "properly." I believe the ideal way to nurture healthy children is in a tribal sort of communal setting, but I wasn't searching for that and the right woman and community did not appear. My partners may have been more aware than I concerning my fear of having a child, which affected their decisions.

It seems clear that very few women want to have an abortion; the decision probably always comes down to circumstances. From a higher perspective, any soul considering an incarnation is fully aware. It understands the situation more deeply than we do and realizes it can simply incarnate at another time and place. There is no judgment towards the couple that could have given it a birth.

One of my original sources of information concerning this belief is the book, *Life Between Life*, which I read many years ago. The author, Joel L. Whitton, M.D., Ph.D., practiced "hypnotic regression" with numerous patients. A number of them went to past lives, and some even found themselves in between lives. Whitton offers us accounts of these other lives, along with the perspectives of various souls prior to incarnating into new bodies.

The various forms of contraception available on the market all seem to have significant drawbacks. It seems to me that our technologically driven system could have found a better form of contraception if it wasn't so exceedingly patriarchal. I read about a tribe in the Amazon rainforest that used herbs and ceremony to prevent unwanted pregnancies. The young women did not become pregnant until they found their mate. Unsurprisingly, that society was relatively matriarchal.

The abortion issue triggers deep emotions, similar to the topic of killing and eating animals. At the core of these moral causes, for those taking a stand against, is a lack of respect for life. Yet in my mind, it doesn't make sense to single out these topics and treat them as being separate from, and far worse than, the rest of modern civilization, which is based in long term patterns of killing and non-stop destructive behavior. I believe the question we need to ask ourselves is this: can we create a global culture that is pro-life and life-affirming on all levels and in every way?

Venereal diseases are another area of fear for most people. I first heard about AIDS from Rolando at the Pina Palmera. He called it "cita," which means appointment. He had been active in the gay scene in Mexico City and was afraid he might have it. At that time, AIDS was the equivalent of a death sentence and there was tremendous fear associated with it. The next time I remember hearing about AIDS was a year later, from an Italian woman whom I met in Guatemala.

She and I traveled together for a few weeks and one day we went on a long hike to visit an indigenous community in the mountains. I dearly love the native peoples I've interacted with over the years and have regularly threatened to go live with them in Guatemala whenever I felt too disgusted with modern society. The village we visited on that day stands out in my memory as exceptional in qualities of heart and innocence. Sadly, this innocence was in the process of being lost due to governmental death squad activities in those mountains.

On our return my knee started acting up, which slowed us down. That evening we arrived at our hospedaje well after dark, literally feeling our way down the steep mountain trail with nothing more than starlight. That powerful day led to us sharing sexually for the first time. A week later, my Italian partner said we should stop because she had genital herpes and it might break out soon and become contagious.

Several days later, I was heading back to Pina Palmera alone. I remember a night in my hotel room overcome by the fear of getting herpes. My genitals were itching from some sort of fungus, which I was convinced must be herpes. I recalled my friend's expression of gratitude concerning the fact that she at least didn't have AIDS.

As it turned out, I was grateful to not get herpes from her, only the fungus and genital warts. Frank gave me a cream that killed the fungus, but the warts were much more difficult. I had them burned off several times in the States since doctors treat them the same as warts on one's fingers. I finally got rid of them ten years later by self-prescribing very high doses of two homeopathic remedies. This resulted in a lot of emotional turmoil for a month, but the result was permanent. Without a doubt, the most difficult aspect of the warts was the integrity challenges they brought to my sex life since I didn't want to pass them on to my partners.

Although genital warts were the only venereal disease I ever contracted, this issue was very much on my mind. Spending nights with women in the nude without being sexual was one of the adjustments I made in my life. This of course also negated the possibility of an unwanted pregnancy. Furthermore, it kept the emotional intensity down to a more manageable level.

Throughout the challenges – the hurts given and received in my relationships – I continued to grow and search for greater levels of integrity within myself in relation to my sexuality. Sometimes I faltered; other times I was proud of myself. Those sex hormones are strong! Striving for both freedom and integrity in one's sexual life is extremely challenging. I suggest we all learn from our mistakes and try not to be too hard on ourselves or others.

I met Lydia in a tantric sex workshop. Her friend-lover was the instructor and she was his assistant. Lydia was the fourth woman I fell in love with. She was Jewish, petite, very upbeat, and high strung. Her precocious preteen daughter never really warmed up to me. Lydia ran a home-based public relations business that promoted cutting-edge events and authors of the early 1990s, including Louise Hay and Deepak Chopra.

We lived together for three years in Nevada City and tantric sex was an important aspect of our relationship. Working with the breath, kundalini energy flow, and ourselves as energetic beings was incredible. Although I was not able to incorporate tantra into my other relationships after Lydia and I separated, its concepts continue to inspire me with the higher possibilities and potential available to humans in our sexual activities. I left my relationship with Lydia because her lifestyle (not she) was too conventional for me and I couldn't do it anymore.

Tantra is a type of yoga; some people call it the yoga of sex. In tantra, we approach sexuality as spiritual beings who seek to celebrate our physicality through Divine union. Unsurprisingly, it is very misunderstood by mainstream society and religious institutions. My experience with it is relatively minimal, yet very powerful. Since I'm a bodyworker and do a lot of energy work with clients, I'm very attracted to the energetic aspects of tantra – so I'll share a tantric energy exercise.

A couple works with their breath, inhaling together while pulling energy up their spines from the root chakra, through the second chakra all the way up to the crown, then exhaling while they flow it back down the other side. They can pull energy up their backs and go down the front, or vice versa. This is done during intercourse while moving very slowly, if at all. Ideally the man holds off from ejaculating indefinitely in order to build and preserve as much energy as possible.

I had an experience with Lydia while practicing this exercise where there was so much energy moving through my body, I could do nothing but lay on my back in an extremely altered state of consciousness. I laid there for over half an hour experiencing myself as energy; it seemed unbelievable I actually had a physical body. An Irish man who studied tantra fairly extensively said that practicing it with a partner was the only way we can maintain a long-term committed, joyful, and fulfilling relationship. I tend to agree with him, at least for myself.

At this point in my life, I have not been sexual with a woman in over eight years. I've had to go through the fear of "not having any." I didn't choose to be celibate, but rather chose to consistently surrender to the fact that a mutual attraction with a woman has been absent for that long. I clearly wasn't meant to be in a romantic relationship. Over the past several years, it seems I've finally broken through my addiction to falling in love. It has been challenging, but I doubt if breaking out of any addiction is easy for anyone.

During most of this time, I was living with the eighth woman I fell in love with. For the last half of our relationship, we were living together as friends and learning to be loving to each other at all times no matter what the situation. I was still learning the art of love, but not the romantic sort. I must admit, romantic love is much more fun and I miss the sexual intimacy. However, I'm committed to my spiritual awakening and doing my best to find love within – which seems, at least for me, to include mastering my sexuality. Since sexuality can't be ignored, I say – master it!

Chapter 10

In the United States, and possibly worldwide, there is intense fear associated with not having enough money. If someone has plenty of money, they are usually attached to it and fear losing it. While I was living with Lydia, she promoted an author who wrote a book advocating metaphysical concepts of abundance. Financial freedom was one of the main themes.

Since the collapse of my marriage with Mia had been tied to money and my fear of not being able to succeed in society, this book resonated deeply with me. In American culture, success is more or less equated with one's ability to make money. As usual I was determined to not let this fear hold me back. I would not allow it to continue to create chaos or feed any lack of empowerment in my life.

The book Lydia promoted was based on the connection of each of us to the whole. If it's all One, everything is ours and we can simply open to and receive the abundance of the universe. I was very inspired by this philosophy and therefore extremely committed to following it to financial success. I also appreciated the author's assertion that this would enable us to fund our dreams and projects of service in the world.

I had a dream of helping to create an intentional community, one with a healing/retreat center as its main focus. I had met others in my travels who had a similar dream; finding people to be part of it would not be difficult. Having enough money to fund it was the key, so Lydia and I started a weekly group to promote the ideas in the book.

Around this time, a friend of mine named Carter brought the concept of network marketing into my life. I'm only average when it comes to words and language, but I'm a whiz when it comes to mathematics. After he showed me the numbers, I was barely able to sleep for three nights. My mind was filled with thoughts and ideas concerning this business model and how it could serve humanity when done in a higher way. It felt like this information was being downloaded into my mind.

Network marketing is a people-oriented, grass-roots system of distribution. The possibilities of financial freedom and abundance it offers the average person are very inspiring. When coupled to the distribution of health supplements, it became a focus in my life.

It took me a number of years to create a fair degree of success, but I eventually did with the *Amazon Herb Company*. They worked with indigenous communities in the Amazon rainforest of Peru. These communities sustainably harvested wild plants and herbs on their lands, which gave them an income source. The agreement our company had with the tribes went far beyond fair trade and benefited their communities in many ways. For one thing, it allowed them to protect their lands from the logging companies that were prevalent in the region.

Our company's nutritional and herbal products were made in the States and we helped distribute them. I built a significant distribution network, mainly by inspiring people to become involved with our efforts to preserve the rainforest. It became my main source of income for ten years.

Carter and I bought a motorhome in 1995 and left Nevada City to promote health products on the road. Our main focus was an arched back table that a welder had invented to heal his spine. We crisscrossed the country attending health expos, promoting our health supplements and the table for the owner of the company. During this summer tour I met the fifth woman I fell in love with.

Crystal was a massage therapist who played the Celtic harp. She was of Irish ancestry, had long blond hair, and was committed to her spiritual path with an organization named Eckankar. She happened to be playing her angelic tunes in the booth directly behind us at the Santa Fe Whole Life Expo. We invited her to a party where we were staying; Crystal and I started massaging each other in the hot tub and we barely spent a night apart for the next eighteen months. Carter decided to return to California soon after and we continued the tour. She got a gig with a flute player and the health expos turned into art fairs where she and her music partner sold their CDs.

Before we started touring, Crystal and I visited her place in western Massachusetts for about a month and packed her stuff so we could live on the road. One night, I was in a space between being awake and asleep. I had a vision of another life I had participated in with her; this was the vision connected to my core issue of abandonment. I was a wealthy merchant in a city that looked like Venice in its heyday – a major center of commerce. She was only a minor character in my life and not very relevant.

Instead my business was my life, and due to a high level of success, I decided to give a significant portion of my wealth to help the poor. The problem with this act of charity was that it came from ego; I wanted to earn people's respect by giving away money in a very public fashion. My life rapidly went downhill from that point, my business fell apart, and I ended up in debt to a money-changer. In total humiliation and utter dismay, I lost everything including my life when I was unable to repay my debts.

Not before or since have I experienced such a clear and detailed view of another life. I knew my downfall was a direct result of my ego and its desire for self-aggrandizement. It wasn't a punishment, but a lesson I was wanting to learn as a soul. My vision was truly amazing. I had probably just died, was in my energetic body reviewing my life, and thus could understand where I had gone astray. The vision may have also been a preview to an exceedingly difficult experience I endured ten years later, connected to money and business. This happened with the eighth woman I fell in love with.

Mitzi is from Hungary, and since early childhood has felt a deep connection with indigenous people from North America. She is aware of other lives as a Native American and it's on a shamanic level that we connect most strongly. Professionally, Mitzi speaks and writes five languages, most of them fluently. This allowed her to obtain a job as an interpreter for a Belgian broadcasting company in 1989, nearly a year before the Soviet Union collapsed and the Berlin wall came tumbling down.

Then she studied and taught languages and their cultural significance at the University of Bonn, Germany for ten years. After living in Australia for two more years, she came to the United States and I eventually met her in Taos, New Mexico at the Hanuman Temple on her birthday. We had an immediate and deep soul connection. Nine months later, we got married and lived together for sixteen years. She is a healer, a spiritual teacher, and a dreamer.

A year after we met, Mitzi brought home a book written by two very successful entrepreneurs who started an organization called the "Enlightened Millionaire Institute." Since she was inspired by the book, I read it as well. When she first suggested we join the Institute as students, I was completely resistant to the idea since I always did everything on my own.

Having just made more than enough money from an investment to pay for the enrollment, I changed my mind. Maybe I was being too proud and could realize my dream of a healing/retreat center with their help. So we got involved with the organization and thus began a long journey into pain and suffering.

Ironically, I had been doing well on my own with my finances and had made several smart decisions. I was still working at Ojo Caliente as a massage therapist, my business with the *Amazon Herb Company* was growing, and I had made some good investments. Yet the business was still in its early stages and growing slowly, plus I didn't know how productive my investments would turn out to be. Hearing the success of others in the Institute, I got impatient and more determined than ever to succeed. After all, twelve years had passed since Lydia and I promoted the abundance book and results had been sporadic.

Two months after we joined, Mitzi questioned our involvement in the organization and reminded me that we had a ninety-day money back guarantee. Her apprehensions arose from the fact that the people running the Millionaire Institute were certainly not "enlightened," although I'm sure they wanted to be.

One of my strengths is to consistently follow through and finish what I start. The negative side of this attribute is a tendency towards the stubborn. Mitzi follows her intuition quite effectively and I could have listened more closely to her concerns. Instead, I barely heard her and didn't seriously consider her input, much to our detriment.

Initially I was leaning towards investing in the stock market because one of the teachers had a system that seemed ingenious and had a high success rate. I was starting to practice his system while checking out other money-making strategies the organization offered. The avenue I was least interested in was real estate, but it looked promising so I was hoping Mitzi and another friend of ours would pursue it.

Soon after, I went to California to visit my family and decided to go to the Enlightened Millionaire convention in Los Angeles. I got carried away by one of the speakers, an impassioned Irish real estate investor who was making a fortune. For all of his success, he was Irish to the core and exceedingly anti-establishment. That's all it took; I was hooked.

With the Institute's assistance, I invested in three properties over the next six months with virtually no monetary output. One was in Florida and the agreement included a contract to build a four-bedroom house on the land I bought in a city that was booming. The other two were houses in Detroit. Some of the teachers were convinced Detroit would be the next large Midwest city to get revamped and experience a real estate boom.

Although I went to Detroit for a workshop beforehand, I never personally saw the properties I purchased. I did see pictures of the houses on the internet: they were very nice and inexpensive. I saw the property in Florida in person before the house was built and then pictures during construction and after it was finished. It was really beautiful.

Things started going wrong almost immediately in Detroit. I bought the first house from an investor who assisted at the workshop I had attended. After fixing it up, he asked one of the workers to live there until it sold. After I discovered the house was near an area with a lot of crime, I told the young man he could stay while we looked for a renter.

The management company I worked with proceeded to have trouble renting it and then the young man refused to leave. Although he had never paid rent, they needed to go through a formal eviction process to force him out. They finally evicted him and when the company went inside, they discovered the house was trashed. Since I was starting to make more money distributing the Amazon herbs, I decided to pay $9,000 to have the house fixed up again. While the house was being repaired, we decided to install metal bars on all the windows. In good condition, safe and secure, the house sat empty for months because the management company couldn't find a renter.

They did find someone to rent the other house, which was larger and in a better neighborhood. The renter was a single mother who received governmental assistance. A number of months after she moved in, the government agency demanded the house be repainted on the outside, so I paid $3,000 to have it done. Soon afterwards, her child started having health issues and his doctor thought the cause might be mold in the basement – so the woman and her child moved out.

While the management company was trying to rent the house again, someone broke in and stole all of the pipes in the basement in order to sell the copper. Several weeks later, it happened again after I had paid to have them replaced. They also stole the heating unit. The Millionaire Institute had, of course, promoted the positive aspects of investing in Detroit and never bothered to mention these negative possibilities.

In Florida, the property had almost doubled in value in six months, from $50,000 to $90,000. But the contract said I couldn't sell it until the house under construction was completed. They were behind schedule and all I could do was wait. With the Florida house half-finished and the Detroit property situation still in the early stages of spiraling out of control, the real estate bubble burst in the United States. Over the next several years, I watched my own perfect storm of events unfold before my eyes.

When the Florida house was finished, my management company rented it since I couldn't sell it anymore. It was already worth far less than what I owed. I made more money that year than I ever have before or since. Unfortunately, I spent the money as fast as it came in because the houses had mortgages to pay, vandalism repairs to be covered, insurance payments, etc. Damn it! My dream of financial freedom and abundance wasn't supposed to turn out like this.

Most of the time, I was strong and determined to hold it all together. Sometimes I simply collapsed in tears. At one point I was so angry at what was happening in Detroit, I seriously considered driving there with a rifle and shooting any thief who tried to vandalize the houses again. If the Detroit police couldn't do their job…. I was depressed and in general totally miserable. That may have been the lowest point in my life. One morning I told Mitzi that I was giving up and didn't want to be on this planet if I couldn't live my dreams. She called my parents for help.

Although the idea of filing for bankruptcy had come up before, I felt at the time we had too much money, viable investments, and cash flow to pursue that route. However, my *Amazon Herb* business started declining and so were the checks. I stopped making mortgage payments on the Detroit properties first, then the Florida house later. I let them all go into foreclosure.

Some months later, I was sent a letter by one of the banks notifying me of a lawsuit they had filed against me. It finally became obvious I couldn't hold things together and it was time to give up and accept total and complete failure. We called a lawyer and soon after filed for bankruptcy. Since this was the only practical thing to do by that point, I felt extreme relief during the ensuing process. At last, I was free again!

I played out some major karmic drama with this experience. After focusing on abundance for so many years, I was finally on the edge of a significant breakthrough. The Millionaire Institute showed up in my life at that time. The timing was uncanny. Soon afterwards, the Irish real estate investor reached deep inside my psyche and triggered me. He must have unconsciously reminded me of Father Davis, not to mention the fact that I have Irish ancestry and am obviously a rebel at heart. I got impatient and fanatically determined to succeed. My ego wanted to prove I could beat the system at its own game, just like the Irish investor had done.

There is heavy energy around money and that experience felt like being caught up in a karmic tornado. Ten years later, I was still processing emotions, learning, and growing from it. In the future for instance, I don't intend to push anything faster than it wants to manifest or naturally unfold. Most of us get caught up in our own timing and don't want to trust cosmic Divine timing. Learning patience is invaluable: it sure cost me a lot.

There is another important insight concerning my experience. When I began investing in the real estate deals, I completely relied on the Institute even though they encouraged us to do our own thing. In reality, I was hoping they would save me from my fears around money.

Most people live their lives hoping someone or something else will save them. Many Christians expect Jesus Christ to save them. Sick people expect the doctor and their drugs to fix them, or the healer or psychotherapist. But the fact is, we need to take responsibility for ourselves; the desire for a magic pill is a trap.

There are those who prey on this human shortcoming, such as false gurus and televangelists. Corporate advertising constantly takes advantage of this blind spot in people. It's only recently that I understood this dynamic played such an integral part in my experience with the Millionaire Institute. This realization helps me feel more compassion for those who want to be saved. We all need to ask for and receive assistance, yet we ultimately save ourselves. In the end, spiritual awakening is between oneself and Creator – no one else can do it for us.

Through my lessons in abundance, I've learned to surrender my dreams and release much of my attachment to financial freedom. The Buddha said attachment to desires is what leads to suffering. I sure got a good dose of his teaching.

I believe it's vitally important to have dreams, to have a positive and inspiring focus for one's life. Yet we can release them to a greater power and know they will manifest if it's for the higher good. If our dreams manifest, they will do so in their own timing.

I'm learning to show up for my work in the world, do my best to be of service to a higher cause, and trust the rest to the universe. Some people refer to this as: "being an instrument of Divine will" or "letting Spirit work through us." For me it's about trusting my Soul-Self and surrendering to its higher vision for my life.

Why would I want to let my ego and its desires run my life when I could let the wisest part of me do so instead? I've gradually realized that focusing on egoic desires validates and empowers the ego structure and its reality. There is nothing inherently wrong with this; it just depends on what a person wants to achieve in life.

Krishna Das, the famous mantra singer, talks about developing the "letting go muscle." He says it's especially important for Americans since many of us were conditioned to believe we should get everything we desire, which seems to be a double-edged sword. Krishna Das wanted to be a rock and roll star more than anything else. But Spirit had other plans for him. His higher path was to lead Hindu chants for others. In his surrender, he eventually found inner peace by offering up his chanting to the Divine.

Another famous person who had trouble releasing his dream was Patrick Swayze. His mother was a professional dancer and he passionately wanted the same thing for himself, but injured his knee and couldn't dance at the highest level required. Instead he went into acting and made amazing movies, including two dance films that are considered classics. He brought dance to the public through these movies in a much more powerful manner than he ever could have achieved as a dancer. Our soul knows best how we can serve the whole of Creation and might do anything required to wake us up to a higher path for our lives.

Chapter 11

A miscellaneous assortment of fears will now be addressed. Most teenagers want to fit in and be accepted by their peers in the worst way: I was no exception. For most people, this pattern continues throughout their lives. After I was fully accepted at the university in Santa Cruz, I released much of this need. I didn't want to fit into any semblance of normalcy anymore.

In my early travels, I was unconsciously running away from the traumatizing societal system I had been raised in. After living at the Pina Palmera, it became apparent I had also been searching for something. That something was spiritual and I realized it might feed me on a much deeper level than anything my culture offered.

One of the main fears travelers seem to have while searching for truth in other countries is not being able to fit in again after they return home. They are afraid of losing friends, job opportunities, and their country of origin. In essence, their fear is one of change, of changing so much, they will not be able to relate to their past.

I relentlessly left most of my past behind, yet I was always able to fit in somewhere. Although only a small percentage of humanity is striking out on its own, the total number of people doing so is rather large. Never fear – you will find like-minded people, and if you don't, look for the places where they congregate.

It is important for travelers and others on a path of truth to honor their courage. Most people don't feel the need to find their unique identity and path in life, or they are too afraid to do so, although everyone would probably benefit from the search.

Speaking in front of a crowd can be challenging! I've heard the claim that people are more afraid of public speaking than they are of dying. I find this hard to believe and question studies supporting this assertion, but I certainly agree that most of us have deep fears in this arena. I joined a Toastmasters group in Nevada City to address this and spent a year writing and making speeches in a very supportive atmosphere. I can't imagine a more direct method of initially working through this fear. Although I'm still a little nervous when I speak in front of people, my fear is nothing compared to the past.

The fear of being burned by fire is usually learned early in life. I was privileged to walk on a bed of red-hot coals two separate times when "firewalks" were popular in the '90s. The twenty-five foot bed of burning coals can reach temperatures of up to one-thousand degrees Fahrenheit.

The first time, an inexperienced couple led the walk. The coals felt hot and I got a few blisters on my feet, but it worked nonetheless. The second time, a real pro was in charge. I walked back and forth over the blazing coals several times, amazed I could barely feel the heat if I kept moving. Unable to believe what I was experiencing, I picked up coals with my hands and slowly moved them from palm to palm. It was beyond amazing – more than likely the entire group of people was in an altered state of consciousness. It was impossible to not question reality as we perceive it with our five senses in the physical realm.

Many men are afraid to commit to a relationship. I had fears committing to anything and everything. Commitment always felt like being trapped, like San Diego in my youth. While living in Taos, I worked with those difficult emotions. I made several long-term commitments: a best-friendship with Mitzi, a job at Ojo Caliente, a business with the *Amazon Herb Company*, and a property, where I developed gardens and eventually grew considerable amounts of organic produce.

Although I've made progress, freedom has always been incredibly important to me, partly because it is the natural state of our soul, which has no limitations. Yet I've discovered we can commit in life and still have complete freedom; it's only our fears that believe differently.

The fear of losing one's freedom by being thrown into jail is very real. The United States of America has a larger percentage of its population in prison than any other country; it uses this threat to instill fear in us. Innocent people are occasionally accused and incarcerated. Huge numbers of people sit in prisons for victimless crimes or because of illegal drugs. Americans are some of the least free people on our planet, although we constantly celebrate this ideal as a culture. I once heard a woman say, "Political freedom means nothing if people don't also have economic freedom."

The closest I ever came to living behind bars for an extended period of time was in Zipolite. I had been there for a week and had just started living at the Palmera. Someone at one of the cafés gave me a small bag of marijuana, which I put into my pocket. I went walking down the beach close to sunset and was stopped by a military man outside their extremely small beach-side base.

He immediately told me to empty my pockets. Out came the little baggie of pot and into the base I was escorted. They tied my hands behind my back and proceeded to tell me I would probably be in jail for the next five years. When I answered that everyone in Zipolite smoked herb, they pretended disbelief.

I soon remembered other people's experiences with Mexican cops and offered them money, but they refused. I sat in their compound for the next three hours while they let me stew in doubt and fear. After refusing a monetary offer several more times, they finally changed their minds and agreed to twenty dollars.

Since the money was in my tent, they proceeded to untie me so I could go get it. When I asked which of them was coming with me, I found out they couldn't leave the base. Needless to say, I did not return once I was free. During my ordeal, I was definitely scared and finally had to accept the reality of living in jail. It is possible I may have missed my entire Zipolite experience, not to mention my spiritual path, but I was persistent and protected and my destiny was not to be denied.

Chapter 12

It seems people have fear of the dark side on all levels. Let's first look at the darkness within each of us, and then without, in the global power structures where it appears most powerful and destructive on our planet.

I remember a yogi who stated that the battle between dark and light is not outside of ourselves, but within. I once had an experience that undeniably displayed this reality to me. I killed a mosquito with vengeance after it had stung me because I wanted revenge. Almost immediately, violence in the Middle East flashed into my mind as I remembered the Israelis and Arabs killing people on the other side in retribution for deaths on their side. I realized they probably killed with feelings of righteousness, like I did when I eradicated the mosquito. It would have been easy for me to dismiss the similarity since it was only a mosquito, but the energy and emotions with which I killed it were exactly the same as what I had experienced in Israel.

Over the years, I've become aware of how difficult it is for people to look at internal unhealed parts of themselves, the root of dark behavior patterns. They are also afraid of showing them to others. In latter chapters, we will explore the process of healing these traumatized aspects of self, but at present, simply begin to explore this subject. Considering the high level of dysfunction within humanity, few if any humans escape trauma. In modern societies, the series of events usually begins at birth.

Being born in a hospital is nearly always traumatic, although I've been told there have been some improvements. The archetypal experience of going from oneness with our mother into the world of separation triggers humanity's core issue. Emerging from the relative safety of the warm soft nurturing womb into loud noises, bright lights, and invasive machinery is a harsh beginning for the newborn. On top of this, babies are usually taken from their mother's arms, placed on a scale to be weighed, washed, etc. This tends to be extremely abusive treatment for a highly sensitive being who cannot think, only feel.

Although studies show it is best for a baby to be physically connected to its mother for the first six months to year of its life, few mothers in our busy modern world are able or willing to do this. As a baby grows and develops an ability to think, aggressive, technologically harsh societies confront a child's vulnerabilities and innocence. No matter how much a mother tries to protect her child, wounding inevitably occurs on deep energetic and psychological levels. This can lead to feeling unsafe in the world, depression, lack of empowerment, and lack of joy for life – in essence, a veritable breeding ground for psychological and physical pathology.

In indigenous and traditional cultures, children grow up with many caretakers. In the West, the nuclear family setting is the norm, with families living in separate homes and each family member commonly living separate lives. Not only is it difficult for one or two parents to raise a child, but their children often lack the deep and ongoing connections required to mature into psychologically healthy adults.

As a young adult, a person may begin to see patterns of dysfunction within their life. Romantic relationships will invariably reveal them. Family, friendships, and work relationships will show them as well. At some point a person may decide to explore their pain body to see if they can heal the root causes of their undesirable behaviors. Some of this work can be done alone, especially if guided by a book or other source of insight. Much of the deeper healing will need to be done with a therapist or healer. We need others on our healing journey because connection is integral to the healing process. These others might not be human; they may be animals or spirit beings.

It takes courage to engage one's inner pain and unhealed traumas. Often when a person does, they obsess on their past and want to share their story. This may be a helpful part of the healing process. Ideally one moves through this phase quickly; obsessing on the negative indefinitely will reinforce it through continuous focus.

Healing takes effort and commitment and can feel at times like engaging in more unnecessary suffering. I wish it could be easier than it is because more people would be willing to do their inner work. Yet we don't need to do it all at once and in fact cannot.

Using an analogy of the multiple layers of an onion, we may revisit the same issue many times in the course of our life. A person usually starts by addressing outer more psychologically oriented layers and gradually progresses to deeper ones, which are emotional and body based. The deepest layers are more metaphysical and spiritual in nature. Healing is a process with its own timing and rhythm. What is necessary is to maintain a long-term commitment. I personally believe healing is a lifetime endeavor; we are not finished until we reach a state of enlightenment.

The alternative to healing oneself is to live a life of denial and unconscious dysfunction. This may be an easier route to take at first because the initial stages of healing can be so challenging. Yet as we progress, the process gradually becomes easier by developing the ability to not take one's drama so seriously. Because of the law of attraction, people who do not heal their inner pain will create more suffering in their lives by constantly attracting new experiences that match their inner state of being.

Since unhealed wounds will re-create more of the same energetic pattern, ongoing dysfunctional activity becomes further trauma for people to hide and hold in denial. These are actions a person may feel guilty about, embarrassed of, or even afraid of being incarcerated for.

I will share several situations from my past that were shameful. By sharing, I hope to inspire others to do the same and thus release themselves from their own self-judgment. Everyone must have their own stories; they always reflect the unhealed aspects of self and the darkness within. It is vital for us to release feelings of guilt over our "sins" and instead choose self-forgiveness.

When people have NDEs, they often find themselves before a Being of Light reviewing their lives. The focus always seems to be on how loving the person was in various situations. There is no judgment towards any of their negative actions, only compassion.

Even in circumstances concerning extremely dark behavior, the perpetrator is always held in a state of unconditional love by the Being of Light!

All of my stories occurred with former girlfriends. The first happened with my first love, Lolita. She spent an entire night partying with one of our best friends and I was afraid she might be sexual with him. I was so upset the entire night she was gone, I pushed and shook her forcefully when she finally did show up in the morning. I really scared her, called her a whore, and didn't give her a chance to say anything. After sharing so much love for so long, my actions felt cruel. Since I was fairly certain she was innocent, my overreaction was terrible.

With Melinda, my second love, I also reacted somewhat aggressively after she informed me that she was pulling back sexually. My hurt and abandoned inner child freaked out, so I, as an adult male, reacted in anger. This must be an all-too-common story for men and strongly illustrates how important it is to do our inner healing work so as not to create more suffering in our world.

Years later, I spent four months in a relationship with a German woman. Soon after we became involved, I was hired at Ojo Caliente Hot Springs. The universe undoubtedly has a sense of humor with certain things. It seemed as if every time she came to visit and soak in the pools with me, I just happened to have finished massaging a very attractive woman. One way or another she always saw them. Because we had never discussed our level of commitment, she probably felt she didn't have the right to say anything. Yet her jealousy grew and became an issue, albeit one she never spoke about. We finally got into a stupid argument about my camera and I forcefully pushed her backwards over the railing onto her bed, bruising her back in the process.

In all three of those situations, after I displayed my anger in a physically hostile manner, we both knew it was over. Neither one of us was healed and mature enough to adequately address the issues in our relationship, or even to end it in a positive manner.

I don't like male aggression, whether it's my own or that of another man. To my credit, I've never hit or slapped a woman. As for men, I only engaged in two physically abusive fights with boys my age when I was young.

In one last situation, I left my girlfriend in Mexico when she was sick and in bed. She was from Bermuda and we had met at Heartwood Institute. I didn't know it at the time, but she was there to focus on her own healing and probably hoped I could help her. I was ready to leave on one of my Mexico excursions when we got involved, so I invited her to come along, which was problematic since we hardly knew anything about each other. It turned out she exemplified the Bermuda Triangle and its mysterious realities.

While traveling together, she began telling me stories about herself. When she was a child, she claimed to have had gills and was able to swim underwater for long periods of time. Her parents shipped her off to a British boarding school in England when she was young, which was very traumatizing due to her highly sensitive nature. When she came home for a visit in her mid to late teens, her parents practically forced her to go sailing with a rich man's son whom they thought would be an ideal husband for her. He proceeded to rape her on the sailboat, which was her first sexual experience. To add insult to injury, her parents were unwilling to believe her when she told them what happened. Having nearly died numerous times, I began to call her the "cat with nine lives."

Her reality began to completely dominate our trip and though I was fascinated by her, there was no room for me or us. As my resentment grew, I kept suggesting we take a break from each other, but she wouldn't hear of it. I was seriously considering leaving her when she got sick. I was positive she had unconsciously made herself sick so I couldn't leave.

Feeling manipulated and angry with the entire situation, I walked around the city of San Cristobal de las Casas, way down in the south of Mexico. I was debating with myself for hours about whether or not I could leave her when she was sick. She didn't speak Spanish, have a map, or know her way around the country.

On the other hand, she was the cat with nine lives and had always managed to survive no matter what the circumstances. Furthermore, I selfishly felt she was ruining my trip. In what may have been the cruelest thing I've ever done to another human being, I packed my things and left while she was sleeping. I found out later from my parents that she made it back to the States healthy and in a relatively sound state of mind.

Now we'll move on to the darkness within the power structures. Most people want to believe in the system, their social conditioning, and the authority figures. They can't see their lack of empowerment and have no idea they are constantly being manipulated. They also refuse to believe most of the chaos in our world is orchestrated from the top by a tiny group of power crazed individuals. They don't realize we as a species have given them so much power simply by surrendering our own. Because they refuse to see these things, they don't feel any responsibility to change the prevailing paradigm. Yet it is indeed up to us to forge a new path. We are all responsible for what is happening on our planet because we allow those in power to pursue their selfish personal agendas.

I have been reluctant to challenge the power structures in the past because I seldom saw a way to do it that resonated with me. Yet there was a situation in El Salvador in 1986 where I got involved with a group of Christians who were attempting to help several hundred El Salvadorians return to their town. Their government had created a buffer zone by removing thousands of villagers from an entire region so they could not help the guerrillas. The Christians, who were from different denominations and countries, felt they could safely escort some of these people back home in a convoy of buses.

I ran into this large group of people in San Salvador in front of the Catholic church on the main plaza while traveling with a friend. Larry and I spontaneously decided to join them and ended up on a two-hour bus ride to a small empty town of adobe buildings ravaged by war. Many of the townspeople, who had been thrown out several years prior, were in tears as they struggled with a variety of intense emotions.

After walking around for at least an hour while interacting with various people, everyone was informed that the buses were leaving to return to the capital. Since we had left all of our belongings in the hotel room in San Salvador, Larry and I decided on the outbound trip to return that afternoon rather than stay with the Christians, which we would have preferred to do.

I didn't see Larry as I boarded a bus, but there were numerous buses and people returning. After everyone disembarked at the end of the drive, Larry wasn't there and he never showed up at our hotel room. Not knowing what to do, I eventually ate dinner and fell asleep in a very uneasy state of mind.

Late the next morning, Larry finally showed up at our hotel. He related that he had been in a deep conversation with someone the previous day and didn't hear the buses leave, so he had no choice but to spend the night. As people woke up the following morning, they found the town surrounded by the El Salvadorian military. The locals were in extreme fear and so were many of those supporting them. The commander ordered the international group of Christians to leave immediately, which they refused to do.

Soon after, the military forced them to leave, giving everyone the option of first going back on a bus they were providing. Larry and a small group left at that point. Several days later, someone who followed the press told us that all of the Christians were forcibly carried off and officially deported upon arrival in the capital. We never found out what happened to the El Salvadorians, who were simply trying to go home.

Writing and publishing this book is significant for me because it threatens the global power structures by shining a light on them. The potential repercussions and backlash from doing this has forced me to deal with the fears that naturally arose. For the most part though, confronting the power structures is not something we can do alone. Humanity needs to undertake this endeavor as an entire species. Yet each of us can certainly do personal growth work with our individual fears surrounding this subject.

Most people are intensely afraid of the system collapsing, although this fear is mostly unconscious. Humanity, especially in first world countries, is in a very vulnerable state considering its extreme dependence on the system. If petroleum and/or the trucks which deliver our food were to stop, people in cities would be in a state of starvation very rapidly.

If humanity confronts the structures of world power, chaos is highly likely. Should humanity choose not to, ecological crisis and revolving systemic breakdowns are highly probable. Debt laden governments tend to spend minimally on prevention, whether it concerns infrastructure or ecological decline. Either way, it's best to deal with our deep fears concerning the potential collapse of the structures on which most people have come to depend. By doing this, we can become more proactive.

A significant percentage of the population in third world countries live on the land in a reasonably self-sufficient and sustainable manner; they could weather a systemic collapse rather well. When I travel in Latin America, I don't see poverty in rural areas, just people living simply. They don't need expensive homes in warm climates; a simple one built from local materials, an effective roof, and maybe a mosquito net over one's bed will suffice.

A proactive approach to potential systemic breakdowns is to create your home in a location with easy access to clean drinking water, and the potential to grow your own food. If possible, choose a location that is not prone to natural disasters.

Moving to a third world country, where it's much cheaper to live, is another possibility. I met a number of Americans in Ecuador who were easily living off their social security checks. Most governments in Latin America will give foreigners a permanent visa if they can prove they have a steady income or a significant amount of money in the bank. In Ecuador it was $1,000 per month or $20,000 in an account.

Dramatically simplifying your life is another proactive strategy, one that allows you to rely less on the government and corporate infrastructures. Furthermore, releasing one's focus on the corporate media frees you up from thinking solely within the narrow-minded reality system they've created. This is when real freedom can take root in your life.

Chapter 13

Now we will move on to the core fears. Let's start with that of dying. My mother once stated that I must have a death wish. I did not, yet she was not far off. I was so determined to find something new and truthful, it seemed irrelevant if I died in the process. I can understand a person's willingness to die for a cause; if your death could make a difference, one's natural fear of dying may lose its significance.

Committing suicide usually occurs when a person feels their life is intolerable. I've often felt suicide is the easy way out of a difficult situation. You take your life and immediately everything changes. It might be considered a selfish or cowardly act, but if someone has suffered for a long time and seriously contemplated their options, taking one's life could be viewed as an act of courage. It's not easy to look death in the face, to confront one's demise consciously and intentionally. Surprisingly, considering how common it is in modern societies, I have no personal experiences with suicide.

It is only more recently that I ever even contemplated killing myself in an active sort of way. As I more fully own the part of me that doesn't want to be on this planet anymore, I've been forced to consciously choose life instead. The most positive outcome of this process is that it is encouraging me to dedicate myself more fully to my spiritual awakening, to open to greater levels of joy.

I've realized a number of times that I might die in the next few minutes. Two of those situations occurred when I could barely breathe. Starting in 2008, I began waking up around three in the morning having difficulty breathing. I had no idea what was going on, having never had asthma before. Twice my breathing was so constricted, I could only focus on taking the next breath and wasn't sure I would be able to.

Each time I felt relatively peaceful and resigned knowing this might be my last breath. Although a part of me was afraid, I surrendered and let go. Another part of me didn't believe I would die and stayed focused on taking the next breath, as well as finding the best position to hold my body in order to get the excess phlegm out of my lungs. Consciously opening to one's death, to be fully present and aware, is very powerful. Try to seize the opportunity, rather than react in fear and run from it, when you are looking death in the face.

Months later, while on the East coast, I began to have difficulty breathing during the daytime as well. It got so bad, I had to call my brother who is an ER doctor. After all, it was one thing to die quietly in my bed with no one around and quite another to stop breathing in front of my friend and business associate. We immediately went to a pharmacy and picked up the prescribed medications. They worked almost instantaneously and I not only had a diagnosis, I also had my life back.

After a year or two of experimenting, I discovered the main cause of the asthma was wheat. Other grains containing gluten seem to be OK – only wheat is problematic. An informative film, *What's With Wheat?*, was recently released and is well worth watching. For various reasons, wheat is a very low-quality food. It is best to avoid it, especially if it's grown in the States. I also believe chemtrails are a major cause of asthma. Deep emotional issues are usually involved as well. As for myself, I was dealing with a real estate fiasco.

Another time I came close to dying was at Heartwood Institute. Out of nowhere, I developed an infection in my left knee, which had been injured while skiing years earlier. Despite it becoming very swollen, there were no cuts and I thought it must have something to do with the torn ligaments.

After ending up in bed with a fever, the school nurse came to check on me. When Bob and Roy suggested I be taken to the hospital, she said I didn't need to go. By the third day, I was sleeping most of the time and not very conscious when awake. In an interesting coincidence, two medical students were at the school attending a week-long massage course. They heard about my situation and came to see me. They immediately said my knee was infected and I should be taken to the hospital.

After being examined, the doctor told Bob and Roy that I was close to going into a coma and might lose part of my leg. They took me to a larger hospital an hour north, where I spent the next ten days. I didn't lose my leg, but I did need a surgery to flush antibiotics throughout the knee followed by intravenous antibiotics for the entire time I was there. It wasn't until the eighth day that my body started getting the upper hand on the infection. I found out later that the surgeon was extremely worried about me up until then. It was a Catholic hospital and the nurses who cared for me were absolutely wonderful.

The moral of this story for me was that nothing is all good or bad, black or white. As much as I disagree with the medical establishment and its absurd, invasive, and abusive way of approaching things, it has saved my life two times and helped me on several other occasions. It's extremely effective in crisis situations, although it works poorly in most others.

Because Western medicine is based in science, technology, and narrow-minded belief systems, it is limited by the physical world and its third dimensional realities. The American medical system is also dominated by corporate greed. Despite its shortcomings, there are many caring and dedicated people in the medical field.

After hitting rock bottom with the real estate deals gone awry, I began to look at the part of me that didn't want to live. We are participating in a relatively insane situation on our planet. I believe everyone has a part of themselves that doesn't want to deal with it anymore. Death is the easy way out, but most people are unable to look at this dynamic in an honest and conscious manner. Although they fear biological death, many people unconsciously live lives of self-destruction. They regularly engage in any number of negative habits and addictions and often die early deaths.

Each of us could do some soul searching around this issue. "Do I really want to live?" "Do I want to live fully, take chances, break out of my comfort zone, explore new possibilities, and challenge myself to create a meaningful and fulfilling life?" There is no right or wrong answer. Yet it is very empowering to make a clear choice. If you consciously and intentionally choose to embrace life, a deep revelation of life purpose may arise from within. More than likely, we all have a powerful mission for our life should we choose to pursue it.

After reading various stories of people who have had NDEs, virtually all of them would have preferred to stay dead. They felt so much joy and unconditional love in the higher realms, they simply did not want to return to their earthly existence. They usually came back into their bodies and lives because of others. Either their loved ones on Earth couldn't let them go and the person having the near-death experience relented, or the Being of Light told them they had to come back because they weren't finished.

It has become obvious to me that death is not something to fear; rather it is something to embrace in gratitude. It is sort of like a graduation to the next level. We leave the physical body behind and continue on in our energy bodies. The soul never loses consciousness and a sense of identity remains. Yet we tend to be freed-up from our obsessive ego-identification and the separate self it so powerfully enables.

A while back, I started to practice dying by focusing on my heart chakra and opening to my Source connection. I wish to be in a state of love and this is why. After we die and participate in the most common experience, a life review with the Being of Light, we as a soul usually go to an astral world that is in alignment with our vibratory level at death. I've heard several Hindu yogis claim that the ideal at the moment of death is to be focused on God.

Recently someone joked that if you are focused on a banana when you die, you will probably reincarnate as a monkey – point well taken! Practicing dying is an ideal way to live. Since I choose love in my heart at death, why not make this a regular life practice?

I look forward to death, yet I also embrace my life on Earth and deeply wish to fulfill its potential. The more I fulfill my potential, the sweeter the graduation and celebration will be when I do let go of this physical body. I can't help but love a good challenge and the one being presented to us humans here on Earth must be about as crazy, deep, and powerful as it gets. Dying is wonderful; it's the living that's difficult.

People's fear of death often inhibits them from taking chances and living more fully. Christianity promotes the idea of only one life, but early versions of the Bible referred to concepts of reincarnation on a regular basis. Present versions still do, but they are not obvious. A belief in one and only one human life feeds fear, plain and simple. From a purely logical perspective, why would a soul that exists for eternity only live one human life?

If one chooses to believe that we as a soul have multiple lives in a human form – not to mention animal, extraterrestrial, and multidimensional – one's reality immediately expands and we can begin to make sense of strange phenomena. How can a child of six perform complex classical music for instance? How does any child prodigy exist for that matter? From the perspective of reincarnation, another one of our lives may leak through and allow us to perform skills it took decades to learn in that life. This is one example of a way in which a new belief can help us to make sense of what we see in our world.

By believing (knowing) we have innumerable lives, one's fear of death immediately declines. It's not such a big deal if you die because you have other chances. You are also freed-up from having to be perfect your one time around since there is no eternal hell for bad souls. You can therefore live a much more creative, mistake-filled life and not fear negative religious types of repercussions.

I assure you from personal experience, it is much more exciting living this way. But don't take my word for it, explore this and find out for yourself. It is more painful and enjoyable living life on the edge since one is living much more fully. I don't know how many times I've heard quotes from someone on their deathbed saying they wish they had taken more chances in life – not played it so safe and boring.

Chapter 14

The fear of going insane is something that runs deep in the human psyche. I've come to believe it's at the root of people's resistance to fully feeling. Pent up grief, anger, and other emotions can feel like a tidal wave within when a person first catches a glimpse of them.

In sessions, most clients have a hard time surrendering to their emotions, and the more powerful they are, the more they repress them. On an unconscious level, I believe people are afraid of literally going insane if they feel their inner pain strongly enough.

What is insanity? It seems most people would agree it has something to do with losing one's mind: the conscious mind is separated from the body. I read a book written by a woman who had such an experience and it eventually became very positive. She spontaneously left her body at a bus stop and never returned.

She was able to watch, in a very detached manner, her body and ego/personality live her life. It was similar to a person having an NDE, hovering above the medical staff who are trying to revive their dead body. After going to various therapists, she found a spiritual teacher who claimed she was experiencing what many people try to achieve in meditation. He said that she had been liberated from her ego structure.

I have sat and meditated innumerable times, with mixed and mostly unfulfilling results. I've taken various types of psychedelics, maybe forty times in total. It seems to be a relatively common experience for a person to go so far "out there," they fear being permanently lost. From my experiences of spontaneously shifting into other dimensions with psychedelics, the fear of not being able to return to our consensus reality can be extremely profound. People might refer to this as a "bad trip," but I feel it's an opportunity to wrestle with our fear of going insane.

Each time I went through this type of experience, I was more confident of finding my way back due to a deeper sense of trust. I believe it's appropriate to assert that my faith in the universe, life, and the Creator was growing. When one takes enough of a psychedelic to have this experience, it becomes an invaluable lesson. The foundation of all relationships is trust. In order to have a loving, fulfilling relationship with our Source, trust is a key factor.

I've begun to realize global societies are split in a manner few people are aware of – those who have consciously experienced other dimensions and the majority who have not. This is very significant because of the potential impact it has on a person's belief system. Experiencing other dimensions makes it more difficult to accept and fit into the matrix reality system of modern society, since it's much easier to comprehend what it is and see through it.

There are highly sensitive individuals who are able to look into other dimensions fairly easily. For example, they may see fairies, spirits, ghosts, or auras. Others are able to attain this state through meditation or other spiritual practices. However, most need to use psychedelics. Simply trying to believe in other dimensional realities seems a bit ridiculous when it's so easy to experience them.

People from many cultures have historically used psychedelic plant medicines to access other realms. Helping humans wake up to their vast multidimensional selves is probably why they exist. Scientists say most people use only 5-6% of their total brain potential. I believe the majority of the other 94% is meant to interact with realities beyond the 3rd dimension.

I don't like the word "hallucinogen" because it naturally assumes that people's experiences are just hallucinations, fictitious imaginations of the mind. Yet, the other dimensions are just as real (or unreal: maya) as our five-sense reality system. They are the realms from which magic and miracles arise, the realities an advanced shaman can navigate with ease.

Since other dimensions are ethereal and empirical in nature, science has struggled in its attempts to measure and validate their existence. This speaks volumes about the limitations of the scientific establishment and nothing about the reality of other dimensions.

Have you ever asked yourself why governments make psychedelics illegal? It's not because they are dangerous: very few people die from them. Do governments want to create more fear around psychedelics because they don't want people exploring other realities? Are people who are limited to the 3rd dimension easier to control? It appears the power structures are trying to keep most people trapped in the status quo reality.

Being limited to my five-sense reality system feels exceedingly stifling to me. Exploring other realms and our greatly expanded multidimensional selves feels scary and intimidating. Yet, it also feels liberating and incredibly exciting. For these reasons, most travelers I've met have been experimenting with psychedelics.

Life can lose its magic and become boring and meaningless if there is nothing beyond the physical dimension. It's much easier to fall into obsessive and addictive patterns of behavior when limited in this fashion. People crave the magic found in other dimensional realities, yet most find it only in movies – how sad.

Exploring the nature of reality and one's fear of insanity is a Creator given right. If the majority of our brain is meant for other dimensions, then humans have a deep natural desire to regularly experience altered states of consciousness. Using psychedelics and meditation as tools for exploring the unknown simply makes sense. In a healthy society, this would be encouraged. This does not mean I advocate using psychedelics as recreational drugs.

In traditional cultures, young people always had guidance from their elders and the medicine men and women. It was unthinkable that they would begin their explorations without guidance. As with sex, the youth of today begin experimenting with psychedelics among their peer group in dramatically less than ideal situations. This is a farce! Psychedelics are incredibly powerful and the fears a person may experience when taking larger doses are extreme. I can assure you those fears go right to the core of our existence. Psychedelics are meant to be used with respect and in an honorable manner.

In my mid-twenties, I went on a backpacking trip well north of Yosemite and started hiking south. Maybe ten days into the hike, I met a man who had some LSD and he suggested we trip together at the lake we were approaching. As we set up our camp along a white sandy beach, I noticed a couple camping on our side of the lake a two-minute walk from us.

It was getting close to dark when we started coming on to the psychedelic. Sitting around our campfire, my new friend started telling me what he was up to. He had hiked into the mountains the week before with a hundred hits of acid, determined to take all of it as his method of discovering whether or not he was sane. He is the only person I've ever met who took psychedelics specifically for that reason. He said he was engaged in this process because both his mother and sister had recently gone insane. Then he informed me, with a broad smile, that he had determined himself sane. He had arrived at this conclusion after his heroic feat of taking half the hundred hits in a week. I, on the other hand, was not so sure.

Deeply ingrained fears started to emerge in my mind, instilled by the establishment of my childhood and its reaction to the Sixties culture. I started imagining my new "friend" pulling out a knife, killing me, and cutting me up into little pieces. I started panicking, all the while hoping the "lunatic" sitting at the fire across from me wasn't noticing.

At some point, I walked to the lake and kept going – over to the campsite of the couple down the beach. I filled them in concerning my situation and discovered they were teachers and very cool. They encouraged me to stay for as long as I needed, which helped me immeasurably to calm down. By the time I returned to my camp, the other man was sleeping and I did the same.

The next day I hiked by myself to Little Yosemite Valley. Not wanting to stay there, I looked at a map and located a small lake two hours distant by foot. It turned out to be little more than a large shallow pond, with plenty of privacy since no one was present.

In the middle of the night, I awoke with the feeling that something was outside my tent. Unable to sleep, I spent many hours in my sleeping bag convinced a dark spirit wanted to kill me. I was terrified; I knew beyond a shadow of a doubt there was something out there. I could feel its dark presence strongly until the light of day finally emerged. That was probably the most frightening night of my life.

Looking back, I simply didn't possess the inner tools to effectively deal with the situation. A spirit must have attached to me when I was vulnerable the previous night on acid. It took advantage of my fears and inexperience both nights. Afterwards it probably returned to my LSD acquaintance, since that is most likely where it came from.

It's common for negative entities to attach to people's auric fields, feeding off their fear and negative energy. From my experiences, most negative spirits are parasitic in nature and relatively harmless (similar to physical parasites). Still, they are draining and can create chaos in people's lives. They most easily attach to people who live self-destructive lives, especially alcoholics and drug addicts. But anyone is vulnerable when extremely imbalanced, similar to one's susceptibility to viruses, bacteria, and fungi in the physical realm.

There are many people in mental institutions who cannot control their natural ability to tap into other dimensions. They may be excruciatingly aware of the types of entities just mentioned, ones most people are completely unaware of. They are usually called psychotic and regularly drugged to control their "symptomatology." This is not only absurd, it's disgraceful.

Most likely the majority of these "psychotics" are extremely sensitive people who easily go into other dimensions without psychedelics. The problem is they can't control their abilities. Since no one acknowledges the reality of what they are experiencing, they might very well go insane out of confusion and isolation.

If we lived in a healthy society, these people would receive assistance with their "gifts" early on. They would most likely become healers or work with children and animals – or something else that utilized their high degree of sensitivity.

I used to think humanity was insane. For a number of years, I contemplated writing a book called "The Insanity of Humanity." The premise was as follows: a species that knowingly and intentionally destroys its home (and thus itself) must be insane, incredibly angry, or most likely both. But the sociologist in me eventually came to the conclusion that humanity is extremely immature, dis-empowered, and very effectively manipulated by the global power structures.

How immature are we as a species? I see humanity, when viewed as a collective, acting the age of a 13-year-old teenager. We don't want to take responsibility for our actions, are obsessed with our technological toys, constantly bicker and blame others for our problems, and expect the government and authority figures to fix everything and make it all better. On an international level, look at how our governments interact with each other: they often act like bullies and hurt children. In my final analysis concerning our sanity, humanity is an extremely traumatized species due to the effectiveness of the global power structures.

Ultimately, humanity is self-destructing because we are individually and collectively in so much pain. Feelings of separation from Source and a lack of unconditional love in our lives are at the core of our suffering. On a deeper level, we can't hardly stand it anymore. The reason this is not obvious is due to the fact that people have been taught to be so good at denying and hiding their pain. They are so adept, most don't even know they are suffering. People create excessively busy lives full of distractions in order to avoid their inner reality.

I believe this condition is the norm in modern societies and cities worldwide. If you have your doubts, I offer you a challenge. It's based on a traditional Native American vision quest, in which a person commits to being alone in nature for four days and nights. They must remain in one spot and are not allowed any distractions, food, or water. Feel free to modify this extremely challenging process in any manner you feel is necessary. Your goal is to have a meaningful and insightful experience.

Chapter 15

We will conclude this part by delving more deeply into fears intimately associated with the dark side. In the last chapter, we already began to look at dark entities. Although I've never seen dark spirits while awake, I have felt them. In the past I regularly fought with them in my dreams and they were very real in that frame of reality. They usually took form as horrible monsters. Although I've not seen dark spirits with my physical eyes, I have seen benevolent ones. Notice the similarities and differences as I recount my experiences with both light and dark energies.

Each time I saw a positive sort of spirit, it felt like a gift – a part of my awakening. In these first two experiences, no psychedelics were involved. In my early twenties, I woke up one morning and there was a spirit hovering in the air near the foot of my bed. It only had a face and there were lines flowing through it that looked like the grain pattern on a beautiful piece of wood. When I reacted in surprise and a little fright, it disappeared.

Ten years later I saw a spirit at a friend's home, but only out of the corner of my eye. When I asked if a ghost lived there, they said yes and that it tended to hang out in the exact location I had seen it. I have heard it's common for many of us to see spirits out of the corners of our eyes. Our brains want to immediately discount them though, so most people aren't even aware of what they see. I tend to laugh these days in a mix of humor and frustration because I know a spirit is most likely present, but I simply can't see it if I turn and try to focus on it.

I've taken ecstasy four times and saw spirits during two of those experiences. The first time, I went to pee and a little fairy appeared and started flowing up the stream of urine towards my penis. When I reacted, it disappeared. The other time I was with a group in Nevada City at the artist's house where I had my healing practice. I was the last person awake, alone in the hot tub. I was flowing in and out of a light sleep and each time I awoke, I saw several spirits floating in the air above the other side of the tub.

They only had heads and were misty like we imagine ghosts to be. Since I never reacted in fear, they were able to stay and each time I became conscious, they were with me. At one point, one of the spirit beings telepathically suggested I reach out to touch it. As I extended my hand, it responded in a similar fashion. Although there had not previously been a hand or arm, one appeared. We touched and I was amazed at the strength and intensity of its energy field. It almost felt solid!

There was another time I saw a spirit while high on mushrooms. I was with a friend and she pointed at a rock near a waterfall we were visiting. She didn't say anything and yet as I looked at the rock, I realized it was alive and moving. It almost looked like a giant amoeba as it slowly morphed its shape. My medicine woman friend then told me that this large stone was the master rock of the waterfall, the oldest and wisest of them all.

I've felt negative spirits many times in the past. As a child, I regularly sensed them at night under my bed or outside the window. My brother, with whom I shared a room, once confirmed their presence. I found out much later that my sister, in the next room, often felt them as well. They intimidated me and were always an unwelcome presence.

I've occasionally felt negative spirits in sessions with clients. Depending on the openness of my client to this sort of phenomenon, we either dealt with the entities or I left them alone. I may have silently asked them to leave, but acting without the knowledge of the person I'm assisting isn't very effective because the spirit will usually return.

I was happily giving a massage at Ojo Caliente in the late '90s when my therapist friend in the next room knocked on the door. I opened it to my friend's plea for help. His client was freaking out and he didn't know what to do, so he asked to trade clients with me. Although this was unprecedented, I complied.

When I went to the table and asked my new client what was happening, she tearfully told me that a spirit was present and once again terrorizing her. As she began to go into elaborate detail, I started to laugh. My laughter was totally spontaneous and as much a surprise to me as it must have been to her.

I intuitively knew she was empowering this entity by focusing so much attention on it. Before I told her this, I immediately felt the need to validate her reality by acknowledging the presence of this negative intruder. With my help, she began to realize she had a co-dependent relationship with it, one in which she played the role of enabler. She gradually began to feel more empowered, which was the key to shifting the dynamic she had been completely enmeshed in. By realizing she had some control, she could change her behavior and in this manner change the relationship.

More recently I worked with a young woman who was an empath and felt negative spirits very acutely. Her mind was constantly caught up in trying to figure out where they came from: was it the person she had just interacted with, the person she passed on the street, humanity in general, or from within herself?

I eventually told her it didn't matter where they came from, rather she needed to stop reacting so much. Since she felt a strong connection with the Divine Mother, I suggested she pray to her and ask for assistance anytime she felt her space being violated. Since her fear was the main issue, it was essential she begin to feel more safe and protected in order to change the dynamic.

In other instances, with my client's involvement, I actively focused my words and intentions towards a dark entity. I verbally ask it to leave. If I don't feel any movement, I strongly demand it leave the energy field of my client immediately. I also request help from higher beings of love and light, those who are always available to assist us should we simply ask for their help.

Very few people are asking for enough help from the higher realms, myself included. Many Christians regularly pray to God or Jesus, but they usually do so from a weak, needy, and fearful place. I suggest we request help with a much more empowered attitude and sense of equality with those in the higher realms.

Mainstream culture has communicated to us that we must struggle with our inner challenges by ourselves, especially when a particular situation or reality doesn't fit within the prevailing societal paradigm. This is simply not accurate, a terrible misconception. There are so many high spirit beings available to serve humanity in these most challenging of times. Without them, we humans would be nearly powerless when it comes to the forces of darkness. Asking for help, knowing it will come, and building trust with the forces of light is empowering. It is also essential if you are aware of negative spirits and they are affecting the quality of your life.

Humans are designed in a manner that allows spirits to enter and temporarily share our energetic bodies with us. We can serve another soul by allowing it to participate in an experience with us for a few minutes, hours, or longer. If this is all it needs for its growth, it's potentially saved from having to go through an entire incarnation. In reverse, other souls can serve us in various ways by coming into our energy field.

For instance, they can perform healing work through us, similar to My Shaman who works with me. You can also ask a high spirit being to personally heal you of any ailment you are suffering from – they can work miracles. This mechanism can be very beneficial, but the reality is it also opens the door for negative entities to enter. Therefore, it is imperative we learn to work with our boundary systems in an effective manner.

Psychologists regularly instruct people, especially women who have been sexually abused, to create strong boundaries through intention and communication. There must be entire books written on this subject alone. From my experience, any boundary strategy that is effective with humans in the physical realm also works with spirits in the non-physical.

It is important for all of us to learn to create space and autonomy by developing healthy boundary systems. "Healthy" boundaries can be lowered to allow connection when one is in a safe place. Conversely, they can be erected in an instant when needed, like a shield or cocoon. In order to become proficient, it takes practice and mindfulness. This is an extremely important skill for everyone to develop, and it's a vital component to mastering one's life.

Demonic possession has received way too much press time in Hollywood flicks. High drama sells well in the movie industry. I think the type of possession shown in films is incredibly rare. I have no personal experience with darkness on that level and do not know anyone who has. On the other hand, negative spirits are common and some can be bullies and must be treated as such. We need to stand up to them, ask for help, and be willing to fight. They retreat if we face them from a stance of fearlessness, because most of them are cowards.

When dealing with negative entities, it's not necessary to perform various types of rituals. Standing in one's power is more direct and often more effective. Real power comes through Source connection. Since very few of us are able to regularly access a powerful Source connection, we must rely on high spiritual beings who do. We must ask for, open to, and receive assistance. Although a shaman may be fearless and/or extremely powerful, he or she probably always asks for help. If not, that person may be ego driven and more than likely doesn't serve the light very effectively.

Does the Devil/Satan exist? I don't know. I assume Satan is an archetype that represents the dark side, yet I once read a channeling that talked about Lucifer and his origins. I found the story to be fascinating and worthy of being passed on.

Lucifer was the highest angelic being, the Creator's favorite. He was asked by the Creator to serve in the most difficult way imaginable, to play the part of the dark side, to be Satan. So Lucifer agreed to take on the role of the bad guy for all of eternity, in what surely must be the most profound sacrifice possible!

Do satanic cults exist? Yes they do and I personally worked with two women who were used and abused by them in their youth. I worked with the first woman in my private practice in Nevada City. She was the girlfriend of a friend of mine who was in my men's group and he asked me to work with her. "Men's groups" became popular in the '80s and '90s as a way for men to support each other in a tribal sort of manner; women had been doing this sort of thing since the '70s and men realized it might be good for them as well.

In the sessions with my client, she would remember and re-experience events from the years of abuse she had endured. The memories and images held in her subconscious mind would spontaneously arise in the safety of our sessions. She was repeatedly sexually abused as part of their rituals. She witnessed animals and human babies being ritualistically killed; their blood was an integral part of these waking nightmares. One of her worst memories was of a man putting a knife in her hand and forcing her to stab and kill a human baby.

I honestly did not know what to think of her stories and wondered if they might possibly be her imagination. I supported her the best I could, mostly by working with her energy field while she was immersed in these experiences. I was also fully present for her during and after the sessions.

Over ten years later, I became friends with a woman whom I soon discovered had also been used by a satanic group. In fact, her grandmother had been the head mistress and was able to involve her without her parent's knowledge. She was working with a therapist and had already remembered many of her repressed memories. Her stories were almost identical to those of my previous client. It became painfully obvious to me they were both telling the truth and their experiences had indeed been real.

Although she was married, her husband had not been sexual with her in five years and she knew he was playing around with other women. At one point, she told me she felt healed enough to become sexually involved with a man. She asked me to be sexual with her and told me if I wouldn't, she would find someone else. Because I was in a strong place in my life and very attracted to her on numerous levels, I agreed. The problem was that I rapidly began to fall in love.

There is another extremely interesting part of this story. She had multiple personalities, like Sybil from the famous book and movie. Sybil had sixteen distinct and separate personalities; my friend only had about half as many as far as I could discern. She fascinated me to no end as she bounced back and forth between personalities, staying in each one from several hours to several days.

Over time, I began to know when she had shifted into a new personality. Each one had a different name and some of them had different ages. The one who was present usually wanted to stay indefinitely, but sooner or later another would push their way to the forefront and take over. Our relationship came to an abrupt end because she didn't have much to give; I also discovered I was still too needy with my own abandonment issues.

I once had a client at Ojo Caliente who was a psychotherapist. She had worked with many women who had been used and abused by satanic cults. She told me it was common for them to have splintered personalities, similar to my girlfriend. She said that the abuse is so severe, their ego structures simply shatter under the pressure. The only trauma I can imagine being as painful as what these women experienced would be to grow up in a war-torn country in the midst of extreme abuse and killing.

Many years ago, I read a statistic in a newspaper that claimed two million Americans participate in satanic rituals. It is the only mainstream media article I ever read that even acknowledged the existence of such groups. From my understanding, most satanic cults and secret societies in Western countries are intimately connected to and serve the Western power structures.

It seems to me the dark side actively seeks out and attempts to convert or destroy those with psychic or similar types of abilities. I remember walking in the forest with my girlfriend who had been abused by the satanic group. All of a sudden, she stopped and started looking at something in the snow below a medium sized sage plant. When I asked her what she was looking at, she replied: "Can't you see them?" "See what?" I responded. She proceeded to describe an entire miniature sized village of fairy beings in the snow. I kept looking with intensity, but could only see snow. This was the only time she shared with me this special ability that she apparently took for granted. Since early childhood, she had also nurtured a strong Source connection. It kept her alive and sane throughout and after the abuse.

I had two good female friends who were approached early in life by the U.S. Secret Service; they were encouraged to use their psychic abilities for their country. Evidently the national testing of our youth has been used to search for those who have a lot of potential in this area.

One of these women worked on the front lines in Vietnam. The other never told me what she did, but she requested a number of healing sessions from me. She was a very strong person who lived in a fair amount of fear, probably more for her two children than herself. If I remember correctly, she terminated her job with the Secret Service and they were not very pleased with her decision.

Do black magicians (adepts of the dark occult) exist? I believe they not only exist, they play an important role in keeping the planetary power structures intact. Do we need to fear them? Not any more than anything else connected to the dark side. I feel compassion for those souls who have an incarnation such as this. They must be in extreme inner pain to cause such excessive amounts of suffering in the world.

Does hell exist? In the manner portrayed by Christianity, I certainly don't think so. Do hellish realms exist? Yes, without a doubt. I believe our emotional body is connected to the astral realms. These can be high beautiful places, but they also contain the lowest of the low. I remember one Hindu yogi who recommended we avoid the astral realms altogether. Recently I've heard several people refer to all the dimensions collectively as "the astral." This is inaccurate. The astral realm is very specific and is only one of many dimensions in existence.

It appears as if many people on our planet spend significant amounts of time in hellish realities. In a sense, hell is right here on Earth should we choose on some level to experience it. People who spend a significant amount of time in those realms obviously need help. Those who constantly obsess on the dark side or are obsessed with satanic types of images deserve our compassion, not our judgment. Whether or not they've been abused by a satanic cult, they have been gravely injured and need assistance. Ideally they would work with a shamanic healer.

Anyone can develop a relationship with the dark side and master it, but this certainly doesn't mean we want to hang out there.

The dark side of reality is not enjoyable and it does not feel good. Other than experiencing compassion for, developing an empowered relationship towards, and ultimately transforming it, I see no reason to spend more time interacting with the dark side than absolutely necessary. If you are focusing on negativity and darkness when there is not a legitimate reason, I define that as "obsessing." The shaman deals with the darker realities effectively and efficiently. He or she does not dwell in them.

Intermission #2 – South America Trip

As I write this, I'm traveling in South America. Several weeks ago, I arrived in Vilcabamba, a town in southern Ecuador. I went to visit my friend Ana, an acupuncturist from Taos, who had relocated to "Vilca" several years earlier. While en route to my destination, I was informed two separate times that people were being robbed and beaten in the Vilca area.

Upon arrival, I was rather amazed to discover that Ana was undesirably connected to these sadistic robberies and beatings. She had encouraged a close friend to live there the previous year and he was the most recent victim. He was in the hospital awaiting reconstructive surgery on his face, which had been severely battered.

Within two hours of hearing about this, we happened to run into a couple who had been attacked a month earlier. Ana knew them and the man proceeded to go into graphic detail about the psychopath who shot him in the knee; they were lucky to have escaped with their lives. After talking with the couple, we all realized they had been assaulted by the same threesome that had recently attacked Ana's friend.

Since I was writing about the dark side, it soon became obvious to me that I had attracted this situation into my life. I had never found myself in such close association with this type of violence. Within a week, the perpetrators were positively identified and soon after apprehended. The leader was an ex-cop from Quito, the capital city.

During my visit, Ana felt inspired to share an interview of John Lash concerning the Sophia Mythos. It impacted me profoundly and you will eventually discover why. After several very intense days with my friend, I went to Finca Sagrada, an intentional community in the early stages of development, located forty-five minutes into the foothills outside of Vilcabamba.

I lived at their peaceful 1,200-acre property for the next twelve days and forged a deep connection with the founders, a truly fascinating couple. Walter is Dutch, was born in Borneo, grew-up in New Zealand, studied in England, spent many years practicing biodynamic farming in the United States, and eventually relocated to Ecuador with his American wife, Susan. Walter is as mellow as Susan is high strung and dynamic. She is an idealist who dropped out of Harvard grad school and later corporate America. She eventually became a key person in helping facilitate the rise of both solar power and socially responsible investments in the States.

Within a few days of meeting Walter and Susan, I discovered they had also been robbed and physically assaulted at their home on the edge of Vilcabamba several years earlier. Evidently it had been attracting this level of violence for a number of years. American ex-pats and other foreigners have been flocking to Vilca in ever increasing numbers and it seems they had unwittingly attracted a lot of attention.

The night before I left Finca Sagrada, I was the only person staying on their isolated property. I had an experience lying in bed where I heard high pitched tones that sounded like a choir of angels. There is a good-sized river that runs along one edge of the property and my mind knew the sounds might simply be overtones produced by the current. Yet the effect was exhilarating and very well may have originated from high-vibrational beings.

Walter and Susan had actually shown me a recent photograph of what clearly appeared to be a devic nature spirit among their trees. Finca Sagrada means "Sacred Ranch/Farm/Estate" and I understood why they chose that name by the time I left.

The next day, I headed south from Vilca towards the Peruvian border, a route taken by very few travelers. The road through the Ecuadorian mountains was devoid of pavement in large sections, narrow and treacherous in numerous spots, with the bus tires occasionally tracking right on the edge of what appeared to be unstable dirt. Prior to my departure, a friend at the community had given me an I-Ching reading for my trip to Peru. The one-word outcome was "obstructions."

We reached the town of Zumba late in the afternoon – it was a surprisingly interesting place considering it was in the middle of nowhere. I spent the evening walking around town and stopped awhile to listen to a military band playing surprisingly good jazz music. I then proceeded inside the auditorium right behind them and watched a traditional dance contest.

The next morning found me on a beautiful and bumpy ninety-minute open air bus ride to the border. The subsequent border crossing was the most relaxed I've ever experienced. The customs officer on the Ecuadorian side was engaged in a photo session with three Peruvian women when I arrived. He was having so much fun, he made me wait for nearly ten minutes.

When he finally went to stamp my passport, he asked me for the date. I told him I thought it was the 5th of January and he promptly agreed. After crossing the river boundary, I found the Peruvian customs officer at his desk engaged in a deep discussion with a worker wearing a welding visor. They asked me about my travels and then jokingly accused me of coming to their country to find a Peruvian wife.

I reached the town of San Ignacio an hour later and sat in the main plaza that evening watching children play among the most amazing Christmas decorations, multi-colored lights, and music. The people here are so much more joyful and the teenagers so much softer than in the States. I was thrilled to be in Peru again, fourteen years after my last excursion into the country.

The next morning, I was enjoying a coffee and pastry when a businessman sat at the table next to mine and asked where I was from. When he found out I was traveling alone, he asked me if I was afraid of being robbed and if I had a gun. He was really indulging in fear until his meal arrived and he started eating. Feeling a bit shaken, I decided to go for a hike into the surrounding hills filled with coffee, cacao, banana, and papaya plants.

On my way out of town, I saw a young man playing really good music by a Christmas nativity scene, so I sat down and focused on working with my energy field in order to center myself. The negativity in the café and the recurring themes of robbery and danger were energies I chose to release and transform. I felt so good ten minutes later, the young man must have noticed because he came over smiling and offered me the homemade fermented soy beverage he and his family had been drinking. I accepted and we spoke about traveling and his desire to go to North America.

I hiked up a mountain road for a few hours until I spotted an unfamiliar machine near a house. It looked like a contraption I had recently been told was used for squeezing juice out of sugar cane to make liquor. I was focused on the machine and didn't notice the dogs as they approached. They began to bark and before I knew it, one of them bit me. As I confronted the two dogs they separated, with one coming towards me from the front and the other coming from behind.

To my amazement, I realized they were working together like wolves. As I loudly growled back at them and kept turning my body so they couldn't get behind me, they got more intense. Luckily two young men who lived there came and chased them away. The brothers apologized sincerely as I walked in circles calming myself. They were very kind and gave me a bottle of alcohol to apply to the bite on the back of my leg, which was deep enough to bleed profusely. As I left to continue my hike, they gave me a handful of bananas for my journey.

I followed a trail down to another dirt road, passed more houses, and once again there was a barking dog coming at me. After the owner quickly appeared, I continued on my walk feeling amazed at the intensity of my manifestation with these dogs. This was the first time in my life I had been bitten and it happened shortly after writing about that topic in this book. Furthermore, just before being bitten, I was focused on the machine and cane alcohol. Minutes later, I was asking the young man for alcohol.

Metaphysically oriented people contend these experiences are examples of manifesting our thoughts. This is certainly accurate, but it's only part of the picture since we attract with our entire energy field. I was attracting these experiences with much more than just my conscious thoughts.

As I hiked back to San Ignacio, I began to realize I was meant to write about my trip and incorporate it into this book. I wanted to start as soon as possible, but my laptop needed to be recharged and my hotel only had old fashioned two-pronged plugs. I went to the main plaza to find a three-pronged plug and eventually ended up in a modern-looking government building. Before starting to write about my South American journey, I decided to first finish writing about the chemtrails and HAARP technology in Chapter 20.

I was fully engrossed when I noticed a very conventional looking employee who seemed to be reading what I was writing. I asked if he could read English, but instead of answering he just shook his head from side to side and didn't say anything. As I went back to my writing, I saw him pick up his cell phone and begin to type out a message to someone. I immediately got paranoid because the subject matter I was writing about concerned the global power structures and it's pretty dark stuff. Closing out the page on my laptop, I got up and left the building.

Trying to keep my paranoia under control, expecting any minute for one of the cops on the plaza to walk up and confiscate my computer, I returned to my hotel. While sitting in the lobby, I was approached by a man in a leather jacket whom I had noticed earlier in the day. He started asking a lot of questions about my journey and his interest began to seem very excessive. I saw an earring in his ear and wondered if he was gay. My paranoia thought he might be an undercover cop. Going to my room, I focused once again on getting my emotions under control and soon after realized the universe was testing me.

I left San Ignacio the next day determined to regain my center. I had done really well up through the dog attack, but the paranoia that started in the government building finally got to me. I had spent much of the night wrestling with my mind and its fears. My fear wasn't so much for myself, it was more for this book you are reading. It seemed as if my entire life had culminated in this book and I desperately wanted to share it with the world – it had become my main purpose in life.

I felt like a parent wanting to protect its offspring and watch the child grow into its potential. As I struggled with fears that night, the challenge of fully practicing what I had been writing became obvious. At the core of my fears was a lack of faith, my inability to trust that both the book and myself would be protected. I only made a partial breakthrough by morning and this issue continued to arise in Peru, where the topic of robbery kept resurfacing.

My trip in South America began nearly three months ago when I flew into Bogota, Colombia. I began with almost no plans and only a general idea of where I was going. I slowly traveled south for three weeks, the last ten days with a 28-year-old spiritually aware surfer from Australia.

Jay had a manner of being that reminded me of a surfer in the movie *Point Break*, a role played by Patrick Swayze. He was blond, at least six feet tall, and good looking. He was also strong – toting around a fairly heavy backpack and two surf boards. Several days before crossing the border into Ecuador, we took ayahuasca with a taita near Mocoa, in the far south of Colombia on the edge of the Amazon rainforest.

Taita Lucho Flores was mostly indigenous, calm, and for the most part seemed highly centered. He and his wife had recently completed their fourth consecutive summer of Native American Sundances in South Dakota. His wife's name is Mercedes, the same as my grandmother. They were deeply into the "Eagle and the Condor Prophecy."

I had first heard about this prophecy from the Pachamama Alliance, maybe fifteen years earlier. It states that when the eagle from North America unites with the condor of South America, humanity will experience a dramatic shift in consciousness. The eagle and the condor represent the people from their associated continents. Taita Lucho believes the origin of the prophecy is an indigenous tribe in the Bolivian rainforest.

This was the first time I had taken ayahuasca. The taita and his brother were preparing and brewing it in huge pots over three wood fires for the entire two days we were there. They said it takes fifteen days to brew a batch. Ayahuasca is a powerful psychedelic that has traditionally been used by shamans of the Amazon.

I first heard of it in 1998 from a close friend in Santa Fe. She claimed to have seen God the first time she drank ayahuasca – that certainly got my attention! Since then, I've heard claims from other people who have also had deep spiritual experiences. The active ingredient in ayahuasca is DMT (Dimethyltryptamine). Amazingly, the human body makes DMT and produces it in the highest quantities at our birth and death.

Many years ago, I met Rick Strassman, an M.D. who wrote a book on DMT, while he was touring to promote his recent publication. His book was based on personal research at the University of New Mexico, where he injected volunteer students with pharmaceutical grade DMT. They would fill out an extensive form before and after their experience. The book is fascinating and is titled: *DMT-The Spirit Molecule*.

I knew there was a strong probability of taking ayahuasca on this trip, and even the possibility of working with a shaman. A true shaman is much more than an "ayahuascero," someone who leads ayahuasca ceremonies. In Colombia people usually call ayahuasceros "taitas." In Ecuador and Peru, they call them "shamans," but the vast majority are simply ayahuasceros with little to no formal training in shamanism. Traditional shamans drink ayahuasca for a variety of purposes and some use it more than others. Accessing spiritual realms during a healing ceremony is one of the main reasons they imbibe it.

After my time in Colombia, I visited four intentional communities in Ecuador for a total of four weeks. All of them were owned by foreigners and each was totally different and extremely interesting. The first was on the edge of the Amazon rainforest and it was owned by a British man. They are part of the ecoyogavillages.org network of Hare Krishna communities. The place was practical, the people wonderful, the food yummy, and the morning yoga a good challenge.

There were only three people living at the second community, but they had a big vision and wonderful views of the ocean. The third place was also on the edge of the Amazon basin and was run by a group of vegans devoted to regenerating the land by planting a large variety of tropical fruit trees. The last one was Finca Sagrada. I helped out at each community, offered healing sessions when appropriate, and donated enough money to more than cover my food costs. This is a really inexpensive and safe way to travel in Latin America, along with other types of work exchange situations.

I also stayed at a number of hostels, hospedajes, and hotels throughout Colombia and Ecuador. The most interesting, owned by a couple from Argentina, was in a place called Mompiche. Their beach was disappearing at an alarming rate and on monthly high tides, the ocean regularly flows into town. My favorite hostel was in Mindo, several hours west of Quito. My small room was totally open to the outdoors. I woke up to the sound of birds and sat writing on my bed while watching hummingbirds fly nearby, the rain fall a few feet away, and the fog flow along the mountain side that framed my view in the background.

I traveled through Colombia and Ecuador for a total of eleven weeks. After arriving in San Ignacio, getting bit by the dog, falling into paranoia, and spending an entire night wrestling with my fears, I traveled south to a very special mountain city.

I had heard about Chachapoyas from a traveler and knew it was a backpacker destination. I spent the first few days getting re-centered and enjoying what this medium sized city had to offer. I visited several tour agencies on the plaza and checked out maps detailing various sites of interest in the region. I never go on group tours, but decided to go to several of the places on my own.

Before leaving, I met an Italian named Matteo at my hostel. Having lived in Ireland the previous four years, he had recently graduated with a Ph.D. in neurobiology. We both wanted to hike to the Gocta waterfalls, so we went together.

After an hour in a public transport van called a "colectivo," we hitchhiked the last part and arrived in a very traditional village named San Pablo. From there, we hiked four miles uphill to the upper waterfall. There are two falls; together they total 771 meters (over 2,500 ft.), which loosely classifies them as the third longest waterfall in the world. We then hiked several miles through lush vegetation to the bottom of the lower waterfall.

Going into its dark and foreboding lagoon was a phenomenal experience. Looking up the sheer canyon wall at the water dropping 1,700 feet was indescribable. The water was cold and the energy so intense, I didn't try to contain myself, howling the entire time. From the lower falls, we still needed to hike a number of exhausting miles to reach another small town with the setting sun. During the entire day, the only people we saw on the trails were a German couple with their indigenous guide. Luckily we were able to catch two rides back to Chachapoyas, the second just after nightfall.

I left the city the following day for the "Fortaleza de Kuelap." I spent two days hiking into the ruins and back to my starting point, camping on the side of the mountain in the middle. The ruins appear to be an old fortress on the top of the mountain, built by the Chachapoyas natives 1,400 years ago. From there I took several more colectivo rides through the valley and up the side of the canyon to the town of Lamud (pronounced "Lamuk," pop. 2,000).

As I sat below the twelve-meter-high statue of Christ that overlooks the town, a young Peruvian man of twenty-eight showed up and started talking with me. Jose lived in Lima, the capital; he was visiting his brother Lauro who lived in Lamud.

Jose proceeded to show me photos and videos of the many traditional dances he studied and taught at a college. Then he spoke about the history of Peru and the many abuses to the indigenous people. We walked to Lauro's home while conversing and they invited me for a meal. I ended up spending most of the next four days with them, the last two nights at their place in my own room.

Jose and I went for long hikes on three separate days. The first was to the "Caverna Quiocta" with Lauro's friend, who was the main custodian of the cave. We left early in the morning and hiked for ninety minutes up mostly steep trails with our guide, who was simply engaged in his daily walk to work. He took us on an eighty-minute tour of the cavern, each of us with our own flashlight.

The stalactites and stalagmites were exceedingly impressive. Early on we came upon several human skulls placed on ledges along our route through the limestone, mud, and water. Our guide claimed these were skulls of children sacrificed by the natives who frequented the cave long ago. No one else came while we were there, even after washing up and eating something outside. The entire experience, including a tip and paying for Jose's entrance fee, cost me less than three dollars.

The next day, we hiked to the "Pueblo de los Muertos" archaeological site. Towards the end of the hike, we were able to see the Gocta waterfalls on the opposite side of the huge canyon, with the highway far down below. From the rim of the canyon, we proceeded to hike down a steep trail until we reached a sheer cliff.

There was no one around when we finally reached the locked gate at the entrance, but Jose was not to be thwarted in his quest to see this place and managed to make his way around the gate. I followed and we entered the remains of ancient rock and clay buildings on an outcropping situated on the edge of the cliff. "Village of the Dead" it most certainly was! Jose thought the ruins, as well as the few arm and leg bones we came across, were at least 2,000 years old.

When the cliff stopped us from proceeding further, we ate a snack and headed back towards the entrance, but Jose wasn't finished with this place. He seems to have a fascination with things from the past: traditional dances, Peruvian history, and now I was discovering, graves and bones.

From what he later told me, Jose was looking around when he saw what looked like two human skulls on a rock high above. I sat down and watched from a distance as he found a tiny trail and proceeded to make his way up a less steep part of the cliff. We had a long way to hike back and it was looking like it might rain, so I wasn't interested in following him on his new quest.

My curiosity eventually got the best of me and I walked back, found the trail, and went upwards. When I got to the end, with Jose on a ledge above me, I saw the skulls. I made my way up to him and found myself surrounded by more than a half dozen human skulls and hundreds of bones and bone fragments, some of which I couldn't help but step on. There were also several damaged above-ground oblong shaped graves about three feet tall and made of rock, clay, and some type of fibrous material.

Jose proceeded to pick up a skull and said he was going to keep the grave-robbers from stealing it. He put it under his arm and told me that he intended to bury it somewhere else. We started to leave, but before we were able to reach the main trail, he spotted another set of graves on a tiny ledge about eight feet diagonally above us in a completely inaccessible spot. They were only slightly damaged and extremely well protected from the rain and weathering. On top of the four graves were very flat faces with what looked like hats on their heads, and one appeared to be a child.

Returning to the main trail, I took the lead and we finally headed towards Lauro's home. Every time I looked back, I chuckled at Jose carrying the skull under his armpit. Because I spent time at some other ruins and he found a short cut, Jose arrived first. Lauro, who is such a caring soul, was worried sick and convinced something awful must have happened to me. I later asked Jose if he had buried the skull in a good spot; he smiled and said "Yes!"

After eleven days in the Chachapoyas area, I headed southeast into the jungle region. The Peruvian cities on the northeast side of the Andes were hot, dusty, noisy, and busy centers of commerce. Desiring to leave the city and find a quiet place, a Peruvian man at my hostel said I might be able to stay with an acquaintance of his in the village of Dos de Mayo, on the shore of Laguna Azul. Lauro had shown me some of his photos and several of them were taken at this lake, so it felt like destiny.

I arrived at the largest town on the lake in a heavy rainstorm, then caught a moto-taxi to Dos de Mayo. These motorcycle taxis, which are called a tuk-tuk or auto rickshaw in Asia, dominate some Peruvian cities, despite being a recent addition to their culture. I didn't see any in Colombia, which had lots of motorcycles, but I saw a few in Ecuador.

When we reached the village, the driver got directions to my destination. The Señora, her husband, and little girl live on the edge of this charming lake. Due to its higher altitude, it was cooler and less humid than the cities down below. When I asked how much it would cost for me to camp under one of their thatched-roof shaded areas, the Señora said I didn't need to pay anything.

As I walked around the village in the afternoon, everyone greeted me in a very friendly manner. I got in a discussion with two men and when I mentioned I was looking for some fruit to buy, one of them invited me to his home. He gave me two papayas and when I asked him how much he wanted, he said "No money."

The next day after lunch with my new family, I asked the Señora how much I should pay her. She said she didn't want to charge me for food anymore, even though her small side business was a restaurant for the Peruvian tourists. Considering her husband was sick, I felt humbled by her generosity and uncertain as to whether I should accept or decline. American cultural norms would certainly say to decline and insist she take my money.

It was only the week before that I shared a story with a fellow traveler about how I first started to occasionally smoke tobacco. During my early travels in Mexico, I had always turned down offers of cigarettes from the locals. Detecting a sadness in their faces, I soon began to accept and everything changed. The conversations became lively, even if I didn't understand much of what they said back then. When someone doesn't have much to give and you refuse their gift, you might be turning them down as well.

Just last night, I was speaking with a Peruvian man on the overnight bus from Pucallpa. He asked if I had ever drunk masato with the indigenous people in the rainforest. I replied in the affirmative, many years prior with the Shipibo and more recently in Ecuador. Masato is a fermented yuca beverage the natives make and it probably has an alcohol content similar to beer. My bus-mate then said that if you turn down their offer of masato, you will never be invited back to their home.

I did accept the Señora's generosity for several reasons, including the one just stated. Another derives from the spiritual perspective of abundance; it's vital we learn to receive from the universe, no matter how it shows up in our lives. The final reason is that I barely had enough money for this trip and was cutting corners financially whenever possible. Therefore, I genuinely appreciated her gift, but left the next morning since I didn't want to take advantage of the situation.

From Laguna Azul, I spent two wild and crazy days and nights, during the height of the full moon, heading south to the jungle city of Pucallpa, and then west back up into the Andes Mountains. Pucallpa was the only place I visited on this trip and my previous one to Peru in 2001.

This is the region from which the *Amazon Herb Company* obtained its herbs. The indigenous Shipibo communities delivered the dried plants to the city of Pucallpa. It is a major commercial center, and it hosts a very active port facility on the Rio Ucayali, the main branch of the Amazon River. It has become everything we at *Amazon Herb* tried to prevent from happening in the rainforest.

Of all the places I visited on my five-month trip, Pucallpa wins the award for being the closest thing I found to a metaphorical hell. In addition to being exceedingly hot and humid, the port area was noisy, congested, and filthy. The city had probably doubled in size since I had last visited, a boom town geared towards the exploitation of the Amazon rainforest.

In the eighteen hours I was there, I couldn't find one place where I felt comfortable. My hotel almost looked like a jail, but considering it was after midnight when I arrived, and the first hotel had been full, I chose to stay. I ended up at the city zoo in the afternoon while I waited for my bus to leave. My experience at the animal park effectively sums up the abusive vibe of Pucallpa and how it felt to me.

At the "Parque Natural de Pucallpa," it quickly became obvious that its animals had once been wild, roaming free in the surrounding jungle. I was able to walk up to many of the cages and several of the monkeys reached out and gripped my fingers. They didn't want to let go and felt very needy.

In another area, I met two large rat-like creatures who also wanted to connect. I spent time with one of them and he kept rubbing his long nose against my finger through the narrow hole in the wire cage. Since it had long sharp teeth, I tried to make sure it couldn't bite me. Yet it wasn't interested in hurting me; he only wanted some love – and desperately desired to be free again. When I backed away, it became obvious that he and the other one in the neighboring cage were literally in the process of going insane.

In the area with the large cats, a young panther who looked like a North American mountain lion kept moaning and crying out. Since the other cats were sleeping in the afternoon heat, this young one appeared to be sick and miserable. I spent much of my time connecting to the animals through eye contact, touch, or my heart – which deeply ached for the plight of these beautiful creatures.

I finally boarded my bus in the late afternoon and arrived in La Union at 3 am. A small city of about 5,000 people, it is located in a rather pretty valley and its inhabitants are nearly all indigenous. The people were very friendly, there were no foreigners, and I got an adequate room in an old hotel with nice gardens for less than three dollars per night. On the second day, I went for a long hike and burned my nose and face in the high-altitude sun. I passed empty homes, got views of snowy peaks, and met a few indigenous people walking into town or herding sheep. They were incredibly friendly and eager to speak with me.

After about two hours, I came upon the village of Lidiopampa (pop. approx. 70). Upon reaching the outskirts, I began walking with an older man and his grandson who was visiting with his parents from Lima. I got into a lively conversation with the man and then the 8-year-old boy.

I was soon invited for lunch in a small communal cook house. There were four women inside dressed in traditional clothing, plus a few of their children. They spoke Quechua, the native tongue of the Peruvian highlands. Most of the men also spoke Spanish, especially when asking me questions. I told them I was a massage therapist and also worked with herbs from the rainforest. As I explained a bit more, one of the men said I was a curandero (healer) and they all got excited upon hearing this.

It was a very special experience eating with them. They gave me space to eat and relax, occasionally including me in conversations. I don't enjoy being the center of attention for very long, therefore their high level of sensitivity worked well for me.

After lunch, I ended up chewing coca leaves with two men who were building an adobe structure. Most of the men in the mountains chew coca leaves on a regular basis, since the subtle high feels nice, similar to coffee. They are good for one's health and help our bodies cope with the high altitude.

They can also be heavily processed to produce cocaine. The 8-year-old visitor from Lima joined us, eventually asking about American dollars. He had never seen any and was extremely curious about them. One of the men said he had seen a lot of dollars while working in Pucallpa. He told us the cocaine trade in the region paid its workers in dollars, since that's what they receive. I hadn't known where Peru's coca plants were grown, but soon discovered that Pucallpa and the region I had just passed through to the north of it were prime growing grounds.

During the following day's drive through the mountains, we barely crossed the ten-degree south latitude line, the furthest point south I reached. After at least six weeks of hearing locals say the rainy season was late, it arrived with me in Huaraz. On several different mornings, when the clouds cleared a bit, I was able to see new snow at higher elevations above the city. One time, I saw a few peaks and realized the view must be absolutely spectacular when it's clear. This attractive and highly indigenous city of 120,000 people is located near the highest mountain in Peru, Huascaran (22,204 ft.).

It was easy to see why Huaraz is popular with trekkers and travelers. I spent a lot of time writing and resting in my inexpensive hostel, broken up by long walks. There was a festival happening one day and it seemed like the entire populace was out on the streets drinking beer and eating. Groups were congregating in many different locations, engaged in a variety of activities. It fortuitously did not rain that day, but it rained all of the others. Tired of the wet and cold, I took a night bus to the Pacific Ocean.

The coast of Peru is nearly all desert, which is a dramatic contrast to the Andes Mountains just to the east. I met a Swiss woman at my very cool hostel in Huanchaco and we traveled together up the coast into Ecuador. We spent ten days in four beach towns before arriving at the border. Tanya, who was thirty, was in the process of becoming a true world traveler. She had already journeyed to every continent except Antarctica, although this was her first trip to South America.

Northern Peru is a bit like the old wild west of the United States in the late 1800s. We were warned several times to not walk very far on isolated beaches or outside of town at night. In contrast to Ecuador, I never heard anyone say the thieves we were being warned about were violent. Peru tested and challenged me on many levels and I was seldom able to relax very deeply.

But even more significantly, I regularly had deep connections with the locals. Indigenous people, whether pure blooded or not, are very available to connect on a heart level. This aspect, in and of itself, made my time in Peru incredibly worthwhile, despite all of its problems. There is a beauty and sadness to Peru and its people. They seem to be struggling intensely in their attempts to integrate modern Western culture, probably because over half of the population is highly indigenous.

After crossing the border into Ecuador, Tanya and I made our way to Vilcabamba. My second two-day experience of Vilca was the exact opposite of the first: it was relaxing, rather magical, and thoroughly enjoyable. I ran into and reconnected with a 23-year-old American, someone I had met and shared powerful experiences with at the first community I visited three months earlier.

Jeffrey decided to go with me to Finca Sagrada since I was returning for another two weeks. On the day I left Vilcabamba, I ate breakfast with Ana and she told me that her friend, who had been severely beaten, was recovering nicely from both his physical and emotional wounds.

I returned to the coast and revisited friendships formed several months earlier. After eight days of mostly relaxing by the ocean, I took a night bus to Quito and some more buses back into Colombia. Ironically, over the course of my entire trip, I felt safest and most relaxed in southern Colombia.

Down to the final two weeks of my trip, I had an open date with a taita near Mocoa. Upon reaching their home, I discovered that Lucho and Mercedes were out of town until the following week. That wasn't a problem since I wanted to spend time at the magical Fin del Mundo waterfall area. I proceeded to rest and enjoy myself at the Huaca Huaca hostel, in the midst of Fin del Mundo (Edge of the World).

    I returned to take ayahuasca with Taita Lucho because I trusted him and Mercedes, their purity and intentions. During my time with them, I discovered they work with people on a deep transformational level, in conjunction with the ayahuasca. Taita Lucho told us he had learned his craft from two taitas, one of them being an old man who lived an exceedingly simple life, a three-hour trek deep into the rainforest.

    This time I drank ayahuasca on two consecutive nights. During three separate ceremonies with Taita Lucho, I occasionally struggled with thoughts that it wasn't working for me. I questioned the entire process. Despite the fact I was drinking more than most of the other people, they seemed to be having much more powerful experiences. During the final evening, I fell asleep soon after my second drink. I woke up around 4 am and did not fall back asleep. Instead I sat and meditated, focusing on embracing my last few hours with the spirit of ayahuasca.

    There seems to be very deep and knowledgeable spirit energies working with this plant medicine; it has its own unique spiritual essence and awareness. In a gradually growing realization, I began to understand that they knew exactly what I needed and was ready for. The ayahuasca was helping me open to my Source connection. I get fed on so many levels through the Creation, yet the direct Creator bond had always seemed to evade me. Taita Lucho refers to this Source connection as the Fuente Sagrada (Sacred Fountain).

    He says humanity has lost its connection to the Fuente Sagrada; this is why so many people are suffering and humanity is constantly destroying life on our planet. Taita Lucho and Mercedes are extremely focused on helping ayahuasca open our hearts to the Sacred Fountain. He says this is what it's meant for. As I sat in meditation the last morning, I felt the Fuente Sagrada as a flowing of energy into my heart chakra. I could still feel it fairly strongly for the next week.

Sort of a Shaman

By midday, I was back in Mocoa to catch a bus going north. It was four months to the day since I last left this city, to head south with Jay to the Ecuadorian border. As I stepped out of the taxi I had shared with two others from Taita Lucho's ceremonies, a bus pulled out of the terminal parking lot slowly passing right next to us. The money collector walking alongside the moving and open bus door asked if I was going to Pitalito. Yes I was, as a matter of fact. I didn't need to wait for my bus, not even one moment!

Four hours later, after my transfer in Pitalito, I was in San Agustin once again. It was here that Gustavo first told me about Taita Lucho. Someone else had claimed that this is the most spiritual area in Colombia. I joyfully returned to this small town for the last three days of my trip, to wait for my flight out of Bogota.

Within an hour, in a series of perfectly timed events, I was invited by a young Argentinian to stay at a place outside of town with about twenty other travelers. I found myself in the coolest scene of any I had experienced over the course of my entire trip. Each of us paid less than two dollars a day to stay and there was so much good music, it felt like a gathering of musicians.

There were people from all over South America and Europe. There was also a man from Turkey. I shared a really large room with three others, the Turk, a 20-year-old guitarist from Argentina, and a young woman from Chile. I slept in my sleeping bag on one of the thick pads that were provided. When I asked the Turkish man how many Americans had spent time there during his two-month stay, he said "None."

The owner of the property was a Colombian man named Christian. Along with a partially graying beard, he had long blondish brown dreads that hung down below his waist. At the age of seventy, he was an accomplished world traveler who spoke five languages. Since he journeys a lot less these days, he decided to let the travelers come to him. He has lived in the Colombian rainforest with the indigenous people for months at a time and taken on a few of their customs.

Christian tuned me in to their practice of snorting finely ground tobacco up into one's sinuses. The tobacco is called rape (pronounced rah-pay). It was exceedingly intense the first time I tried it, a little less so the second. I then followed the tobacco (male) with a spoon full of finely ground coca leaves (female) mixed with an activator plant into my mouth under the tongue. The combination offers a variety of healing properties.

The travelers stay in three houses on his steeply sloped property, which overlooks the Rio Magdelena. My room is on the second floor of the lowest building, a large three-story bamboo structure. The walls have clay in them, the floors are 1 x 12 inch boards screwed into bamboo, and the roof is made of bamboo overlaid with red clay tiles. Since bamboo is free to cheap, the house must have cost very little to build. It hosts two large wrap-around balconies overlooking a precipitously steep drop into a beautiful green canyon. The view is extremely impressive!

As I write these words, I am looking at the canyon I describe. It is late in the afternoon on the verge of darkness. Tomorrow is the full moon and a lunar eclipse – perfect synchronicity! I will leave San Agustin at 7 am and begin a ten-hour bus ride to Bogota. Late tomorrow evening, I will fly home to New Mexico.

The countries I traveled through on my trip were similar in many ways, yet each was unique. It's amazing how much difference an artificial boundary can make. A country's borders are similar in many ways to human skin, the body's boundary system. The atoms that comprise human skin are more tightly compacted than the atoms in the air outside of the skin. Yet in relative terms, the amount of space that exists in air is only slightly greater than the space within a body. It is a scientific fact that all humans are connected on the atomic level. On an energetic level, we are even more connected. Similarly, despite the cultural differences that exist within and between all of the countries on our planet, humanity is essentially one and the same.

Sort of a Shaman

Part 3

Deep and Intense

Sort of a Shaman

Chapter 16

The reasons we came to an impasse around the medicine wheel mentioned in the introduction to this book were varied, although there was a central theme. The core issue was the reluctance of some of my friends to look at and deal with the dark side of reality.

This was triggered by me spontaneously bringing a book, *Chemtrails, Haarp, and the Full Spectrum Dominance of Planet Earth*, to our full moon ceremony. It had just been published and the author was coming to speak in our town the next day. Since I had been experiencing transformation of the dark into light for many years, I wanted to bring this to our ceremonies. But I didn't realize this at first and therefore the result was unsatisfying for everyone involved.

Before we started the subsequent month's ceremony, this issue came to the forefront again because it had not been resolved. I hesitantly began to explain why I had interrupted their intentions of creating another love-and-light sort of ceremony. I spoke of things I had never put into words before as I tried to explain the transformations that occur in sessions with My Shaman.

Much to my surprise, this triggered significant revelations in my mind during the following week. Amazing realizations concerning this shamanic presence arose in a flood of possibilities, connections, and knowing.

I realized My Shaman is none other than myself in another lifetime! He lived in the Amazon rainforest and was trained in a traditional manner. The shaman who trained him came from an intact unbroken lineage of master shamans. This may have happened hundreds or thousands of years ago. Since a true shaman has transcended the limitations of time and space, it would probably be easy for him to guide and train me in the manner I've been experiencing these past several decades.

I readily admit to the possibility of being incorrect with my insights and intuitive understanding. The guidance and training I've received could be from my higher self, as two people recently suggested. Yet is there really much difference between My Shaman and my higher self? After all, he probably attained a level of consciousness in alignment with my soul. I would loosely define the term "higher self" as one's Soul-Self.

There are other possibilities as well. I've often felt My Shaman is a group, which makes sense since he probably works with his direct lineage of master shamans. Maybe he was Mayan rather than Amazonian. My Shaman might also be a different soul within my own soul family. Or maybe various healer spirit beings work with me and they rotate in and out as available. Finally, all of these scenarios put together might be the most accurate.

People in Western cultures get way too caught up in right or wrong, black or white. In Eastern traditions, duality is generally viewed along the lines of yin and yang, which is highly amorphous and malleable. I feel this is more accurate because reality doesn't fit into neat little boxes, nor is it set in stone. In the final analysis, I feel honored to be so intimately connected to a high level of consciousness, one that serves Creation in a very shamanic manner.

I've heard people complain about the overuse of the term shaman – everyone is a shaman these days. In South America, anyone who runs an ayahuasca ceremony is often called a shaman. In the States, a person who has trained with a shamanic practitioner, does some shamanic rituals, or performs healings is often referred to as a shaman. For the most part, I don't have a problem with this. Everyone has the right to call themselves whatever they want. Yet personally, I prefer not to call someone a shaman unless he or she is a real master.

Paths of mastery were historically pursued in most cultures on our planet: the Zen masters and samurai of Japan, Qi Gong and Taoist masters from China, some of the Buddhist monks and Hindu yogis from India and southeast Asia, aboriginal healers from Australia and Africa, and shamans from the Americas, Mongolia, and Siberia. The pagan mystery schools of Europe, North Africa, and the Middle East also provided paths of mastery for those who felt called.

Deep and Intense

I believe true mastery entails several traits. First and foremost, one has mastered him or her self – their fears, emotions, and thoughts. He has healed his lower three chakras and mastered the life experience as a human being. He has mastered the physical realm to a high degree. The master often works with and channels large amounts of energy (chi/prana) to heal people or perform other extraordinary practices.

A person whom I would call a master has not usually attained enlightenment. Probably only one person out of one to ten million people is a true master, which would give us only 700 – 7,000 on our planet at any given time. Maybe ten percent of those have also woken to a state of permanent enlightenment. These numbers will probably increase rapidly since the higher vibrational beings presently incarnating onto planet Earth appear to be much further along than past generations.

A master serves the Creator every moment of every day with every fiber of his being. I do not consider anything less to be a master. Anyone who serves egoic or selfish interests is not a master. A master serves the light, which always serves the whole. Purity of heart and intention are much more important than power. From a place of compassion, a master can always call on beings of vast power in service of a higher purpose.

I consider myself to be on a path of mastery, although this perspective only arose after I had the realizations concerning My Shaman. How far I've gotten is anyone's guess. I encourage everyone to pursue self-mastery, to endeavor to attain true mastery over this life experience.

Those who commit more time and energy will tend to progress further, although this is not necessarily true because earnestness is the key. A person may have attained mastery in another lifetime, one they are very connected to. This type of advantage will accelerate the process, but it still requires total and complete devotion to the chosen path.

Most people will tend to search for teachers in physical bodies to help them. I seem to prefer those who guide me from within. I feel deeply connected to an enlightened Hindu siddha, Neem Karoli

Baba, whom I often call on for help. He was Ram Dass' guru and there is a temple dedicated to him in Taos. He died over forty years ago and I never met him.

Ammachi, whom some people call the hugging saint, is also very much in my life, although I've only spent time with her in person a few times. There is another enlightened sage, Ramana Maharshi, whose message of truth I respect above all others. He died in 1950, well before I was born. His assertion to "become as you are" is gradually becoming my reality.

Ramana Maharshi was introduced to me by a friend around the year 2000 and he had a significant impact on my spiritual path. Up until then, I had been very goal oriented. A "path" implies we have somewhere to go, somewhere other than our present location. This yang type of mentality has been very prevalent in Eastern spiritual pursuits and religions.

Ramana said we are already where we want to go in our spiritual quest. Papaji, probably his most significant devotee, wrote a book: *Call Off the Search*. He says that we are One with the Creator and only need to turn away from what's obscuring this in order to realize it.

Considering this apparent truth, it becomes difficult to escape the conclusion that humans embody the Creator. In Christianity this might be considered blasphemy, despite the Bible stating that we are made in his image. Yet, it is impossible to be other than Creator if All is One.

The truth clearly appears to be: humans are both the Creator and its Creation. This seems to be another paradox. For a mind unencumbered by dogma, it is also common sense.

Paramahansa Yogananda, another Indian yogi and mystic who started SRF in the 1920s in Los Angeles, said that each of us is a drop in the ocean of Divinity: we are one and the same as the ocean. This seems to be a diplomatic perspective, one that helps us stay humble and grounded, yet still claim our Divinity.

From the perspective of already being there, spiritual awakening becomes more of a yin endeavor. Yin qualities embody:

femininity, surrender, opening, receiving, and allowing of Divine grace. As I shifted my spiritual journey in a yin direction, I started relaxing and the process became more enjoyable. I began to fully acknowledge the important inner work I had already done, which was a yang process, and to appreciate myself to a higher degree. This led to greater self-love and a sense of inner peace.

I am presently feeling guided to commit to regular meditation in order to strengthen and enrich my Source connection, to realize the depth of intimacy I've been seeking. This requires discipline, which feels very yang to me. Then again, meditation done properly incorporates the yin quality of receiving. Balance seems to be the key to everything.

As I continue to explore self-mastery and spirituality, two main approaches have revealed themselves. I most naturally align with the shamanic path of the healer, which includes the metaphysical exploration of dimensional realities. And yet, I keep getting pulled back to the approaches taken by Hindu yogis and Eastern mystics. Early Christians, those who followed in the direct footsteps of Jesus Christ, such as the desert mothers and fathers, also fall into this second category.

The first category are the indigenous shamans and traditional healers, the alchemists and metaphysical explorers. They wish to understand how the Creator and Creation inter-relate and function. They focus on mastery of Creation and duality and are equally aware of both the light and dark. Psychedelics are one of their main tools in both healing and understanding reality.

The healers need to deal with the dark side because nearly all human trauma is the result of it. To be effective in their work, they master darkness through understanding, compassion, and its inherent Oneness with the light. They gain a lot of practical wisdom in this manner, but from the photos I've seen, they aren't usually smiling or outwardly joyful.

The second category is equally complex. Meditation and contemplation are their main tools. When practiced correctly, these people deal with the dark side through an inner process. But all too often, the majority of them avoid darkness and focus on the light. Most New Age types of people do this as well.

They wish to transcend the drama of Creation, to rise above and beyond the reality of duality. This tendency to avoid the dark is usually reflected in their religious institutions. Interestingly, this helps them avoid persecution by dark power structures.

Yet the true yogi embraces Divinity on all levels. The highest state of enlightenment includes both transcendence and living fully in the world of duality, in service of one's highest destiny path. Photos of the second category of seekers often show them smiling and radiating joy from deep within themselves.

Neither category is superior and interestingly I find myself naturally bouncing back and forth between the two. The shamanic healer and spiritual warrior aspects of myself tend to become too serious and are prone to losing the joy of life. Therefore, I gravitate back in the direction of the light by opening my heart through simple, profound devotional practices. It seems the Divine Mother and unconditional love are eternally attractive.

Chapter 17

Your inner healing is a vital contribution to the most important areas of life. It can be the first step and/or ongoing component of self-mastery and spiritual awakening. I profoundly encourage everyone to commit to healing. In support of this, it's helpful to more fully understand health and sickness from a holistic perspective. This is an entirely different paradigm than the medical model most of us were indoctrinated into since childhood. Holistic refers to wholeness, the entirety of who and what we are as humans.

The system taught us we were fine until we got sick. If the sickness were physical, we would go to the doctor. If it were mental, we went to the psychiatrist or psychotherapist. If it were spiritual, to the priest. If it were emotional, we tried to ignore it. We were taught to do nothing until we broke down or went into crisis. Then we went to the specialist who tried to fix the part of us that failed. The other parts were ignored unless they happened to fail as well.

Modern cities and societies tend to be fast paced, noisy, and stressful. Digital technologies are now the norm, nature is usually the exception. Type A personalities tend to thrive in this environment, although many burn out and die young. The rest of us hang in there and do our best. When I walk into most American stores, people seldom smile or laugh; they do not appear to be happy or healthy. From my experience, people in third world countries who live simple, traditional, agriculturally-based lives are much more joyful and emotionally balanced.

From a holistic perspective, modern societies and lifestyles are inherently imbalanced. This is most obvious in their overly yang nature and their reluctance to fully value feminine attributes. Most first world countries fall into this category and some can be extremely aggressive. American culture, with its fascination and emphasis on war and violence, is a perfect example.

The left brain/right side of our body is considered masculine and the right brain/left side is feminine. People's bodies are often imbalanced between left and right, in reaction to outer stresses. There is a constant struggle within each of us to overcome the systemic yang emphasis, which takes its toll in various ways.

Dis-ease is the natural outcome of consistently living in a disharmonious manner. Generally speaking, the more extreme the imbalance, the worse the disease. Healers from most traditional cultures will agree with the following statement: if you come back into balance, the physical body will heal itself. Our bodies are the best healers. Modern medicine cannot heal a simple cut on your finger, yet the body does this with ease.

By acknowledging that modern societies lack balance, it makes sense to become proactive in our pursuit of overall health and well-being. People don't need to wait until they get cancer or have a heart attack to change their lives, or do some serious soul searching. We all draw outer situations to ourselves that reflect our inner state of being. If you don't like what your life or health looks like, this is a clear sign to make some changes.

Symptoms of disease are meant to be uncomfortable and painful; this is how our body gets our attention and encourages us to create change. Because pharmaceutical drugs are designed to address symptoms rather than cause, they curtail people's natural desire to actively engage in their personal growth process.

After a pharmaceutical alleviates one's symptomatology, a person has minimal incentive to address the cause of the disease, which is usually emotional, psychological, or spiritually based. Even in situations where bacteria or viruses are involved, there is almost always a deeper cause. One must ask the following question: why did the microorganisms proliferate so aggressively in the first place? A balanced, healthy, and effective immune system should have been able to handle them well before they got out of control.

Because the deeper reason for the disease was not addressed, symptoms connected to inner imbalances will tend to resurface over time. They are often different and labeled as a new disease, thus requiring a new set of prescriptions. People who trust and believe in the medical system often find their bodies spinning all over the place, like multi-colored balls on a pool table. The lists of extensive side-effects associated with pharmaceuticals might simply be physical manifestations of revolving imbalances on subtle levels.

A prescription drug is inherently disharmonious because it is usually a single synthetic chemical compound. In contrast, an herb is a complex and balanced array of natural components. Consider this reality – a body gets sick because of imbalances. How can a pharmaceutical bring the whole-being of a person back into balance so it can heal itself? Needless to say, it usually doesn't. On the positive side, the drug might help to keep someone alive to live another day. Then the person must focus on bringing himself back into balance in order to be healthy in the future.

As previously stated, we are physical, emotional, mental, and spiritual beings. Those four bodies make up the entirety of a human. Our emotional, mental, and soul bodies are all energetic, which is why most of us can't see them. These energy bodies exist within other dimensions, all of them being of a higher frequency than our physical body. The human auric field is one way in which they express themselves.

We can travel in our energy bodies like we can travel in our physical body. The emotional body is used to travel within the astral realms. The practice of "remote viewing" developed by the American military utilizes the mental body. Remote viewing is a method of traveling through space and time; it was utilized during the cold war to spy on the Russians. There have always been masters and gifted individuals who were able to consciously travel on mental planes of reality. Our soul body is unlimited in its ability to travel within all of Creation and is allowed direct access to our Source. The mental body is of a higher frequency than the emotional and has access to numerous dimensions. The emotional body is probably limited to the astral and physical realms.

A physical disease virtually always has its roots in our energy bodies. The more extreme the disease, the more intimate the involvement of all three bodies. Nevertheless, we can always initiate our healing by first working on the level of the physical. Healing embodies the goal of gradually creating a stronger and healthier balance in each body.

Starting with the physical body, I will briefly address each of the four bodies. The common theme inherent in the following process is to first free ourselves from the old and toxic. We release that which does not serve us anymore. This creates space, which we can begin to fill with what does serve us to become who and what we want to be.

Releasing toxins stored in our physical tissues is a fantastic first step in one's healing process. This can be achieved by fasting, juicing or eating a raw food diet for varied periods of time. To complement this, there are numerous types of colon and parasite cleanses. If a person has enough money, they can participate in a deep cleanse program run by professionals.

As cleansing progresses, it is beneficial to consume high amounts of vital nutrients. Concentrated green powder mixes can be added to smoothies for simplicity; it's worth the money to buy the best quality possible. For the long term, eating a diet with lots of locally grown produce is ideal. Know who you are buying from and how they are growing it.

Most store-bought foods, including certified organic, are usually very low in minerals and nutrients. This is due to several reasons, the most significant being the extreme depletion of the mineral base of agricultural soils. Growing as much of your own produce as possible is wonderful and working with the soil, plants, and animals can be healing on many levels. Doing this with a group of inspired people is the most ideal, as long as you can create time alone to commune with the natural environment.

The emotional body always benefits from the release of repressed emotions. Through expression, we can more fully own and make peace with them. Freeing up powerful emotions will inevitably create turmoil in a person's life. This is positive because movement is occurring. Try to flow with and not judge their emergence or your reactions. If on the other hand a person has been stuck in an over-expression of emotion(s) for an extended period of time, try to sit still and breathe deeply into them.

The ideal is to develop a mature relationship with our emotional body. As with a child, we do not want to overly control our emotions. In reverse, we don't want to allow them to run our lives and create chaos whenever they choose. There is an art to finding and maintaining a healthy emotional balance.

Connecting with higher aspects of Self will allow more joy in one's life. We all want to replace old patterns of hurt, anger, and grief with those of joy, playfulness, and love. This may be a lifelong process, so it's best to approach it as a spiritual practice. Learn to be patient and loving with yourself. Humanity is being challenged like never before, so give yourself a break and relax into our collective experience as much as possible. The ability to perceive events from a higher more spiritual perspective is an invaluable tool in managing stress and emotional reactions.

With the mental body, you must access the unconscious mind to unearth repressed thoughts and memories. Allow your dreams and any over-reaction to petty life dramas guide you in this process. Analyzing painful memories can be beneficial, but it's common for people to stay stuck and obsess for extended periods of time. It may be helpful to view your past as just a story. No matter how painful it may be, the overall objective is to create a new and healthier life.

I've found that serving others in need nearly always helped me move forward. It seems to lend perspective and helps me to not take my own pain so damn seriously. Forgiveness also helps us move on. Forgiving the person who hurt you serves the forgiver more than the forgiven. Forgiveness helps us heal on all levels.

Working with positive affirmations is a good way to start to replace old negative thought patterns with ones that can better serve. By watching your mind chatter, you can see negative thoughts as they arise and immediately replace them with something positive. Meditation is an ideal addition to mental health and also helps you find clarity with difficult life challenges.

Creating balance within the soul body is by far the most subtle work, although it can include expressions of base emotions. Ranting and raving at Creator, like I did for over a year, was my way of getting to the root of my core pain. Soul work acknowledges we are eternal beings having a temporary life within this present body.

Creating beauty and taking quiet time in nature are wonderful ways of caring for this deepest aspect of our Self. Being alone, contemplating, and meditating are all ways of honoring our depth of existence. It is common to begin to cry or even sob uncontrollably as we acknowledge our inability to be fully present with our soul. Being present is the only way to realize we haven't been. Lying on Mother Earth and offering her our pain, asking for healing, and opening to spiritual assistance is an incredible way of healing oneself on a profoundly deep level.

The four bodies we just covered interact with very specific energy systems. This happens in an unbelievably complex manner, yet the basic concepts are simple. I personally work with five energetic systems. In a sense, they are analogous to those of our physical body, such as the skeletal, circulatory and nervous systems.

The energy systems I work with are as follows: the chakra, central channel (passes in front of the spine through the middle of all seven chakras), meridian (pressing acupuncture points), reflexology (points in the hands, feet, and ears), and polarity (side to side, top to bottom). When a person has an imbalance in any of the four bodies, this creates disharmony in our energy systems. Energy slows down and stagnates.

A holistic practitioner will address this by reopening energy channels and flow. Since we are holistic beings, it is often helpful to work with multiple energy systems in the same session. This will influence one or more of the energy bodies. Sometimes all four bodies are fully activated, releasing, and integrating in order to create a new and higher vibrational balance.

As a client, it's easy to become overwhelmed in one's enthusiasm to heal. In other words, it's easy to overdo it. When this happens, people can get headaches, illness, or experience total and complete exhaustion. This is often referred to as a "healing crisis." It is our physical body's way of saying to slow down or even stop, so it can focus on balancing and healing itself. When this occurs, drink lots of water and rest. We all need to learn patience and pace ourselves. I believe true healing is a lifelong commitment, since it goes hand-in-hand with our spiritual awakening.

We will now look more deeply into the complex and difficult question of: "What exactly is healing anyways?" Medical doctors who work within the allopathic system have been taught to focus on and address symptoms of distress within the physical body. Thus, a doctor might say healing is the process of eradicating unpleasant symptoms by whatever means necessary. Most alternative health practitioners also address symptoms, partly because that is what the client usually desires. Yet those who lean in a holistic direction will always attempt to address the cause of an illness, within the scope of their training.

A healer who is completely holistic in their approach, such as a shaman, will usually ask a client about their symptoms because these are clues concerning what is happening on a deeper level. Depending on the assessment, the practitioner will approach the deeper issues from whichever angle appears to be most appropriate.

For me, healing is a continuous up and down process, where the ups gradually rise in a positive direction of overall well-being. It's best for a person to release their obsession with symptoms and stay focused on creating a meaningful, joyful, and spiritually fulfilling life. When approached in this manner, a healer might become more of a mentor. Symptoms of distress often disappear without a person hardly noticing since they aren't focused on them.

Another pertinent question concerns whether or not a person will experience permanent positive shifts in themselves and their lives after they've had a powerful transformational healing. I wish I could say yes, but an affirmative answer depends on the recipient's inner strength and desire to evolve. Therefore, the transformation isn't a cure: it's a bridge to something potentially higher.

When a person has a powerfully transformative awakening such as a near-death experience, there are profound permanent changes. A person's life perspective may change so radically, he or she may not appear to be the same person. Where they decide to go with a dramatic shift in reality such as this is their choice. In conclusion, there are innumerable variables to healing if approached from a holistic perspective, so results can be ambiguous and are unique to each person. Such is life and the human experience.

Chapter 18

I have received well over a hundred healing sessions in the past thirty years. I've experienced a wide range of alternative therapies and therapists. Depending on the modality and degree of surrender, it's common for me to drop into an altered state of consciousness. This dream state can feel like going on a journey with a psychedelic substance.

One of the most important aspects of my healing adventure has been my willingness to expose myself. I don't feel I have anything to hide, as you may have already ascertained. I will continue to share my healing process in ever more detail, offering you a real-life example of the challenges and possibilities.

For a little incentive, it feels appropriate to state that I virtually never get sick anymore, and I'm not afraid of catching anything from anybody. I attribute my strong and effective immune system to holistic healing and general self-care. No individual reason is significant enough to explain this. Resistance to disease was never a goal of mine; it seems to be a positive side-effect of my slow but steady journey of awakening.

The healing and growth I initially experienced at Heartwood Institute was only the beginning. For years, I would check in to see if I was developing my four bodies in a balanced sort of fashion. I've always been physically active, so I was constantly working with my physical body. College was very mental and Heartwood was a place where I deeply explored my emotional body.

One year after leaving Heartwood, I worked very part time as a massage therapist for a man who was a chiropractor and an acupuncturist. After receiving a treatment from him, he said my emotional body was too strong and people would have a difficult time with its intensity. He suggested I focus on further developing my mental body in order to create a better balance. It was some years before I actually accomplished this.

While living in the Taos area, I developed yang aspects of myself which had the effect of strengthening the mental body. Taos is a challenging place both physically and energetically. Not only is it a high-altitude desert on the edge of the Rocky Mountains, it is a power spot. I needed to move more fully into my maleness and strengthen myself in order to better cope with it.

I was finally ready for this after exploring and indulging my softer more feminine and emotional aspects for a number of years. It had required a lot of emotional processing to heal certain issues in my life and come to terms with the dark side within and without.

In my healing journey, I worked with my chakra system both intentionally and unconsciously. Barbara Brennan's book, *Hands of Light – A Guide to Healing Through the Human Energy Field*, made the chakra system much more real for me. She is able to see auras, chakras, and other subtle energies. I highly recommend this book to anyone who wants to understand them self as an energetic being.

Each of our chakras spins in a clockwise direction, unless compromised. Then it spins counter-clockwise or extremely slowly, if at all. The first and seventh chakras do not have a back side. All of the others do, and they are behind the front. The back sides also spin clockwise, which means they spin in the opposite direction of those in the front. Each of the chakras is a funnel shaped vortex, with the wide end pointing outwards.

Here is a brief description of each chakra and how I worked on their associated archetypal energies and psychological issues. By engaging my fears, I addressed the 1st (root) chakra, which is associated with one's foundation and survival. This chakra can be opened and healed by simply sitting on the Earth and intentionally connecting with her.

I worked with my 2nd chakra (just below the navel) by challenging my sexuality from every angle I could imagine. Since this chakra is associated with sexuality and thus reproduction, it strongly impacts our ability to create in the physical realm. By living a truly unique life, I expanded my creative potential, which probably had the effect of strengthening this chakra.

The 3rd chakra (solar plexus area) concerns one's empowerment as an individual, as well as finding one's place in the world. In some ways, this has been the most difficult chakra for me to address, yet I continue to embrace positive masculine aspects, master myself, and find inner strength. This book is part of the ongoing process of finding my niche in life.

The 4th chakra is associated with the heart and love. The many relationships of my life were all attempts at understanding the magic of love. My commitment to actualize the power-of-love, to go far beyond the romantic, is stronger than ever.

It is important to understand that the darkness with which humanity is struggling mainly resonates with and affects the lower three chakras. If they are energetically stagnant, from trauma and lack of healing, they negatively affect the heart chakra and our ability to be loving. This dynamic goes to the core of our collective challenge as a species.

The 5th chakra (throat) has to do with self-expression. Vocalizing while receiving sessions has been very healing for me. I've also released large amounts of stagnant, disharmonious, and negative emotional energy by screaming, yelling, and crying outside of sessions, often when I'm alone in nature. Not only does this chakra concern speaking out, it's also about taking in. In the physical realm, I focus on eating healthy food without being overly obsessive about what I eat. On a deeper level, I've worked on receiving universal abundance. On the deepest level, learning to receive nourishment directly from Source is my ongoing challenge.

The 6th chakra (third eye), allows us to see into other dimensions. The front is located in the middle of the forehead just above the eyebrows; the back is the occiput (the soft indentation just below the skull). Universal life force (prana) comes in through the occiput, animating our bodies and giving us life. This chakra appears to have opened on its own in conjunction with the other healing work I've done. The 7th chakra concerns our spiritual connection (the "crown" is located in the middle of the top of the head). It seems my anger towards Creator blocked this chakra for many years and had a negative influence on my Source connection.

Evidently humans have more than seven chakras, the eighth being located somewhere between three inches to two feet above our heads. It is referred to as the "soul chakra" and apparently it holds karmic residue from our other lives. There is also a ninth, which is located far off in the universe. It has been called the "spirit chakra" since it connects to our soul, and the impersonal infinite aspects of ourselves.

I highly recommend for you to regularly practice the following energy exercise. I do it fairly often, especially when I feel challenged in any manner. It can be done anywhere and requires as little as a few minutes to make a significant difference. I spontaneously created it after watching the *Thrive* movie in 2011 and it incorporates the donut-shaped Torus energy vortex.

This exercise will increase the energy flow through your central channel, which positively affects every chakra and helps to free you from their associated issues. This is the most important region in our body and auric field; maintaining a healthy energetic flow in this area will serve you in innumerable ways.

Start by focusing on your first chakra, the area called the perineum (between the anus and genitals). Slowly and deeply breathe in as you tighten your perineal muscle and pull energy up through your second chakra. Rapidly continue up the central channel, allowing the energy to flow into and above your crown chakra. Then breathe out as you imagine the energy flow moving equally downwards on all sides of yourself and ending up below your first chakra (or your feet).

Continue to repeat this process for as long as desired, working with your breath and tuning into the energy flow. When breathing out, imagine the energy flowing downwards along your Torus field (check the internet for a visual). You can expand this practice by tapping into the Torus field of our planet and thus link-up with her on a more conscious level. You can expand your energy field even further by including the Torus of our solar system – and then the Torus field of our galaxy. Now you are a galactic being!

Chapter 19

Although the shadow side of duality is within each of us, I do not believe the Christian myth that claims humanity has fallen from grace and we are born in sin. That is a bunch of crap. The real truth appears to be: we are all victims of a global system and its economic, political, and social structures of stupidity.

This system was designed by those at the top of the power pyramid. It is controlled to a high degree by the same people. The system was designed first and foremost to keep those in power in their places of privilege. It was not designed with humanity's best interests in mind. It was not designed for the well-being of animals, plants, or our Earth.

It seems most people still do not want to believe this, although the evidence is everywhere. The majority of our pain and suffering, should we choose to bring it out of the shadows of self-ignorance, is directly or indirectly due to the dysfunctional system we were raised in. It is extremely important to admit that we are all victims of dark intentions designed to keep us down, weak, sick, ignorant, and ultimately controlled.

Moving beyond denial is always the first step in the healing process. Nothing can change while a person is in a state of denial. We have all been victimized in innumerable ways; no one escapes the challenge inherent in this fact. When a person moves beyond denial and admits they are a victim, repressed emotions and memories connected to their abuse can finally arise.

When someone has experienced abuse, especially something severe like being raped, they are unable (in the moment) to express all of the emotions connected to the abuse. A child who has been sexually abused or beaten by a parent or caretaker is not able to express most of their fear, grief or anger while it is happening.

Ideally someone can help them express and process their emotions immediately after an incident, but this rarely happens.

Most of the time, abuse is heaped on abuse and the person represses all of it. Then the wounds fester within indefinitely.

Physical trauma can heal quickly since our bodies are experts at repairing it. Emotional and psychological wounds usually require outside help. This can come from human beings, animals, and spiritual beings of light.

Once a person has moved beyond denial, owned their victimhood, and processed repressed emotions and memories, it's time to shift in a new direction. At this point it's vital to release one's identification with being the victim, since that position is based in weakness. Now it's time to move forward into one's power as an infinite spiritual being. This is not as simple as it sounds and it usually takes a lot of effort.

The practical reality of healing often takes a convoluted route. It seems as soon as a person begins to move into their power, new wounds will surface and they fall back into the victim mode to process those issues. One must then work through these and commit once again to their personal empowerment. Some people get worn out by this up and down roller coaster ride, while others rise to the challenge and gradually get stronger.

Since pharmaceutical drugs are so strongly promoted as the solution to illness, most Westerners have minimal understanding regarding deeper levels of healing. Studying foundational aspects of holistic health may be extremely helpful, but nothing can replace the actual experience.

Most people must learn how to receive healing work since they are full of resistance, closed down to their emotions, and mistrustful. Learning to trust at least one person who offers help can be a doorway into more easily trusting others. Healing ultimately comes down to trust because a lack of it greatly inhibits the value of a session.

The powerful transformational experiences people had at Ojo Caliente probably occurred because they had already received a lot of healing work. In a sense, they were good at it. They intuitively sensed they could trust me and were able to have a profound experience with someone they had just met.

Let's briefly explore the concept of surrender, a primary component of an effective healing session. Learning to surrender is crucial. Surrender is about giving up all control, which can only happen if the ego structure sits in the back seat. It is a spiritual quality that requires trust and is well worth the effort to develop.

Some of my first lessons in learning to surrender occurred in the ocean, especially while being tossed about by large waves. I discovered that struggling was the quickest way to exhaust myself and ensure an early death. Psychedelics were another extreme teacher. Fighting the experience of being thrown into another dimension simply ensured that fear would dominate and lead to extreme misery. Surrendering to the experience allowed for a multitude of gifts.

In massage school, I also learned to release resistance and surrender in a profound manner, especially with deep-tissue bodywork. Actually, it was just as difficult learning to surrender to energy work because quieting the mind can be so difficult. The mind, with its strong ego attachment, always gets in the way of being present and fully in the moment.

Considering the above experiences, the ability to surrender can evidently be learned on a body/mind level. Then it can be very effectively applied to one's spiritual awakening.

Several years after I left Heartwood Institute, I received a few sessions from a man who was a professional chiropractor. He was also an ultra-marathoner. Every year he would run a race that was over a hundred miles in length. The race started in Death Valley, California in the middle of the night. The runners crossed most of the desert before it got too hot, then ran all the way to the top of Mt. Whitney. As you can imagine, this man did healing work with focus and intensity.

He never did any normal chiropractic work with me. Instead, he moved around my body pressing various seemingly unrelated points that were painful or highly sensitive. I always felt large amounts of energy running through my body and experienced various energetic shifts during and after the sessions. When your body really wants to rest afterwards, you know something very powerful is happening within.

I was exceedingly impressed with his style of work and asked him several times what he was doing. His answers were evasive and I began to feel he was mostly working intuitively. Experiencing his work seemed to give me permission to develop my own style, especially when sessions became transformational.

Over the years, my work evolved in a direction that is very free form, similar to dancers who follow their inner guidance. It also resembles the playing of an instrument. At times, I feel like I'm orchestrating a client's energy field, alternating slow and rapid movements around the person's body.

In order to work this way, I had to develop my listening skills to a high degree. Deep listening might be the most important skill a person can learn. I've discovered that listening and hearing can occur on numerous levels.

For example, I do my best to listen below the surface of people's words when they feel the need to speak and process painful experiences. I also receive guidance from My Shaman, which is a form of telepathic communication.

Another type of listening occurs through my hands since they seem to have a mind of their own. They are able to tune into a client's physical body without my brain being involved. This seems to happen on a cellular level: the cells in my hand are conscious and speak the same language as their cells. In a similar manner, my energy field appears to receive information directly from another person's energy bodies. I regularly act on this without any mental understanding or processing.

I have given many sessions for free. When asked by someone who sincerely wants to heal, money becomes a non-issue. Lack of money is not a good excuse to forestall your healing process. If you don't ask, you will probably not receive. This applies to both humans and spirit beings.

As you commit more deeply to your healing, the right people will show up to assist you. This dynamic happens on an energetic level. Try not to turn potential therapists off by obsessing on your problems. Rather, I suggest you take a proactive approach and share your insights as you grow and refine your commitment.

As a person progresses on their healing path, focusing outside of oneself becomes essential for further growth. What is your mission in life? How can you be of service in a way that inspires you to the core of your being? What is your higher destiny path?

As you heal, the natural progression is to help others, to be part of the solution. This challenges you on new levels, which facilitates more inner growth. I'm at an age when most people are focused on retirement, yet my deeper life purpose is only now revealing itself.

People often ask how to get in touch with their purpose in life. It always seems to be connected to your passion. Follow your inspiration (in <u>spirat</u> ion) and it might lead you to Spirit! Stop for a minute and ask yourself this question: "How deep is my desire to live an inspired life?"

You can use your intuition to discover your unique way of contributing to global awakening. I've recently realized the most accurate intuition comes from listening to a combination of three chakra centers.

The heart chakra is probably the most important for discerning truth. The third eye allows us to see from a place of deeper meaning, more from the soul perspective. The 2nd chakra is in the same area as the Hara, the center of our physical and energetic bodies in martial arts. I believe this area is also our emotional center and it helps us feel truth.

As you develop the ability to listen to all three centers in a balanced manner, your life lessons will tend to be deeper, yet less difficult in the physical realm. It takes practice to synthesize the information received from all three of these listening devices. Yet, intuition can be as simple as following what feels right.

For instance, if you are searching for clarity concerning one or more choices, bring your awareness into your body. If you feel yourself smiling and happy inside when you imagine being engaged in an option, this is an affirmative answer. A negative response lacks feeling and sensation or does not feel very good. If the answer isn't clear, wait until later and try again; be patient and trust this process. Sometimes I don't receive clarity until the last minute.

If a person is determined with their healing and personal growth, teachers often show up in their life to guide them. As for me, life became my teacher and guidance came from everywhere. Hindu yogis kept showing up and many of them touched me on very deep levels. Channeled beings shared their profound metaphysical wisdom, mostly in books. Nature, animals, babies, and children became my teachers. People who had been on a spiritual path much longer than myself offered insights. And of course, My Shaman was always around.

There have been too many "teachers/gurus/masters" whose upper chakras are extremely open and developed, yet their lower three are unhealed. They may have impressive gifts or be able to do amazing things. Yet they often create chaos in our world, sexually taking advantage of their followers or squashing everyone around them with their large egos. They are living proof it's best to find guidance within.

On the other hand, numerous people have benefited incredibly through their connection and devotion to a true master. Some people believe we cannot go very far on our spiritual path without direct association with some sort of guru. I completely agree considering the fact they don't need to be in a physical body to help us.

Chapter 20

Transformation is a word that is regularly used in relation to shifting or changing things for the better. But do people understand its underlying concepts and how to apply them? What follows is an exploration of our mutual desire to deal with negativity and darkness effectively, with the goal of creating something much more positive and loving.

I don't pretend to understand transformation intellectually; rather I've watched it occur with my clients and in my life for many years. Yet it has gradually become clear that Oneness is at the core of this phenomenal reality. It seems to spontaneously occur as the dark is reunited with the light.

To reiterate what was previously touched on, transforming darkness begins with moving from reaction to pro-action. In other words, you consciously choose to respond to difficult circumstances instead of unconsciously reacting to them. Reaction consists of avoidance and denial on one end of the spectrum, to obsessing on manifestations of darkness on the other extreme. Living in a proactive manner is a reflection of personal empowerment and supports a person in finding constructive ways of changing undesirable realities.

The keys to success seem to be intention, focus, and belief in a successful outcome. Overcoming doubts and fears is vital since they inhibit the process. In order to transform something, ritual and ceremony are not necessary. On the other hand, they can be helpful tools for many people. It seems to me that transformation is not something to be taught, but rather to be experienced. We all know and understand it at the deepest levels of our being.

Since most of us have been conditioned to live on the surface of life, within the physical realm, working with spiritual beings who reside in higher dimensions is often essential for effective transformation. They understand Oneness much better than we since they exist in realities where unity dominates. They are vital to this process of reuniting the dark with the light.

To access their support, simply ask for and open to assistance from any high-vibrational being of love and light. Asking is yang in nature, receiving is yin. People tend to place their emphasis on asking, not on receiving. To remedy this, open and receive with all of your heart and a passionate sense of gratitude.

Examples of high beings you can connect to are: Jesus Christ, an ascended master, an enlightened yogi, your animal guide, or even the angelic being who protects you on a daily basis. Since they are adept in the subtle realms, it makes sense to pray to them for help. This "praying" doesn't need to be religious; rather you are asking your friend(s) for help. You can ask with an open heart, request with intensity, or even respectfully demand! In case you haven't already developed a trusting relationship with a high spirit being, an ongoing mentor and ally, you've got a homework assignment.

It's important for you to have a deep and real connection with at least one ally. This relationship is ideally based in trust and love. One way to develop such a relationship is to ask for help with anything negative you are struggling with on a day-to-day basis.

You could, for example, request help with releasing negative thoughts about yourself or someone else. Ask for assistance every single time you are aware of these thoughts, which could be dozens of times per day. Asking your spirit guides for assistance, with anything and everything, is not the same as wanting to be saved. Asking for and receiving assistance is co-creative. Wanting to be saved is not.

There could be issues that arise during this process, ones you will need to address. You may not believe in spirits or you might be afraid of them. There may be issues of self-worth, feelings of not being worthy of their time and energy. Or you might not believe deeply enough in other dimensions and their proximity to our own.

Many people are afraid of attracting low-vibrational spirits who will mislead and create problems for them. The best solution for this legitimate possibility is to keep healing yourself and purifying your intentions. As you become more focused in your desire to serve the light, negative spirits will not be able to come into your energy field. You will gradually attract higher more powerful beings into your life, whether they are humans or high dimensional spirits.

Ultimately you must work through any issue that inhibits a relationship with your ally. Try asking for its name in the evening before you fall asleep. I did this several times with my angelic guide before I received an answer. It was a name I had never heard before, one I consciously forgot more than once. Over the next several weeks, whenever I asked again, the same name continued to come to me.

There are two alternatives to creating a relationship with a high spirit being. The first is to work with your higher self. The second is to open to a direct Source connection. I estimate that less than one percent of humanity can feel this connection in a deep and profound way, even though we all have it. Some of my women partners felt this connection strongly. It feeds them on deep levels and helps them in dealing with the dark side of Creation.

In the transformative experiences I've helped to serve, supplication and visualization were regularly utilized. When I saw my client going to a deeply troublesome place, I usually asked high-vibrational guides to assist us. I called out vocally for help, a request for their presence, knowledge, and power.

Not only did they serve the process, my client felt adequately supported. As I worked with a client's physical and energetic bodies, the person usually had an awareness of other light beings who were present to help them with their healing. This nearly always shifted the dynamic of the session. Because the recipient felt so much love and support, he or she was able to trust and surrender more deeply.

After being present with the memories and emotions of inner trauma for the necessary amount of time, the client often experienced a release, followed by a transformative shift. If that didn't occur, I often used visualizations to help them breakthrough.

I might ask the person to imagine him or herself floating on clouds surrounded by angelic beings. An image such as being held in the arms of the Divine Mother also worked well. Seeing oneself in a beautiful green meadow surrounded by flowers and nature spirits will most definitely create a shift towards connection. Transmutation occurs as the person releases their pain and fear while moving towards a new space of inner peace and love. Gratitude is invariably felt towards those who have assisted this sacred process.

Freeing up energy by working with a person's energy systems and contracted musculature regularly created a shift without a person acknowledging the underlying issues. Sometimes a session got really intense and I didn't have any idea what to do, so I would wait and listen. I might work on some acupuncture or reflexology points while I waited for guidance or movement. Sometimes I started working with sound, using my voice to create certain frequencies – a practice called "toning." This helped break up stagnation within the client's aura.

It seems there are two ways to look at transforming things in the outer world. If I change my relationship with something negative by changing my thoughts and/or feelings towards it, this is transformative from a subjective perspective. I've transformed my own experience and this can be very powerful in and of itself. The other way consists of transmuting darkness on the outside in an objective manner. These perspectives are not separate; quantum physics suggests that the subjective has an impact on the objective.

Since there has been so much misinformation and fear created around dark entities, we will look at this subject in a little more detail. From my experience, spirit beings are little different than the humans we encounter on a day-to-day basis. The low ones are struggling with the same sorts of issues as souls in human bodies. To transform a dark spirit's reality, you can surround it in love or send it to the light. But, if you are caught off guard or out of balance, the simplest most primal response might serve you best.

The most basic method of dealing with a negative entity is to intimidate it, as you would a dog. If you stand your ground and pick up a rock, most dogs will immediately back down. If it doesn't retreat, I slowly step back while yelling at it with intensity. I use aggressive body language and project a clear intention of fighting to the death if necessary. They will energetically feel, and therefore respond to, your intentions.

I've battled many dark entities manifesting as monsters in my dreams, mostly when I was younger. Sometimes I ferociously confronted them upon waking, a very primal response. This instantaneously evicted them from my energetic space. They have no right to be there, nor to attack me, unless I allow it!

Laughing at a dark spirit can also be effective. If you laugh with an attitude that says you don't take it seriously, it works. If you don't empower the entity, it usually can't intimidate you. Most people do this without ever thinking about it; they simply deny their existence because they don't want to believe in them.

For the other negative things we encounter in our lives, those which people are constantly reacting to, I wish to offer an ongoing spiritual practice. Ideally this is done moment by moment, as the dark shows up in your life. It can be a practice in awareness, since you will be watching your mind and emotional state.

As negative thoughts, feelings, or experiences emerge, you transform them as soon as you are aware of their existence. Positive results will follow the shift in consciousness. Through a number of examples, you will get an idea of the possibilities this practice offers.

All of us have probably had co-workers or family members who drive us crazy and it's normal to have negative thoughts towards them. Anyone with positive intentions has probably had the experience of changing the dynamic inherent in a situation such as this. After much consideration, you may have decided to stop hating this person since love is always the answer, as the Beatles so kindly reminded us. Or you may have sat down and attempted to listen to this person without judgment. As you understood their challenges, you shifted into a space of compassion. In essence, you transformed the situation into something much more loving.

Another example is to focus on finding the positive traits in someone and verbally acknowledge them on a regular basis. Previously you may have consistently focused on their negative behaviors, unconsciously sending them negative vibes. When you shifted your focus, the person began to behave in an entirely different manner.

Applying the spiritual practice I mentioned would serve to facilitate the above solutions much more quickly. As soon as you see yourself obsessing on the negative behavior of another person, you immediately choose to change your thoughts and/or actions. Your commitment is to transform dark behavior as soon as you are aware of it. You first start with your own negative thoughts and emotions. Then you attempt to transmute the outer objective reality.

Applying transformation on a much larger scale is also possible. I will address the topic of "chemtrails," to see how we might shift this negative reality into a more positive direction. A brief overview of chemtrails, as I've come to understand them, is a good place to start.

The NATO Alliance is behind their disbursal from airplanes, mostly commercial airlines at this point. They are blocking out approximately 20% of our sun's light and the U.S. government under the Obama Administration claimed that they are being used to slow global warming. This is a blatant lie. Although chemtrails reflect a significant percentage of our sunshine, during the night the chemtrail clouds keep the heat from the day close to the ground rather than let it escape to the upper atmosphere, so there is not an overall net cooling to the Earth.

Chemtrails are distributed in the atmosphere through a fine spray of metallic nano-particles consisting of aluminum, selenium, and barium. We are constantly breathing these toxic metals into our lungs. Other much more noxious substances can also be added, depending on the objective or whatever they might be experimenting with at any given time.

Their most obvious purpose is to affect weather; they are used for geo-engineering (weather modification). Scientists usually work with prevailing weather patterns and adjust them towards a desired outcome. For instance, those in charge are evidently exaggerating the drought in the southwestern United States. Instead of falling in the southwest, an over-abundance of rain falls in the

Midwest, where it creates extremely destructive storms and floods. There are various theories concerning their reasons for doing this.

A deeper more insidious purpose for chemtrails is to increase the effectiveness of HAARP technology by creating a "plasma" of ions in the lower atmosphere. The nano-particles make our planet's atmosphere super-conductive.

HAARP (High Frequency Active Auroral Research Program) is the ultimate tool and weapon developed by scientists. Its origins can be traced back to the insights of Nicola Tesla. After Tesla's reputation was ruined, his life destroyed, and his work confiscated, the Western nations began developing technology based on his concepts from as far back as the 1930s. The initial project and development site existed in Alaska and apparently it still exists. From my understanding, it is the only facility the United States government publicly acknowledges.

HAARP technology is able to access energy from the Earth's magnetic field. Since our planet has a north and south-pole, a positive and negative end, it acts like both a magnet and a battery. HAARP can collect vast amounts of energy from independent facilities and cooperatively direct it to specific locations. It seems the chemtrails allow HAARP to more effectively collect and transmit power towards targeted areas.

This energy can apparently be used to: create huge explosions, trigger earthquakes in areas prone to them, direct the path of a hurricane, and create high pressure zones where horrendous droughts follow. The Western power structure is actively bullying countries with HAARP when they don't cooperate with its agenda.

They appear to also be using it in their own countries for a variety of purposes. Evidently it can be used in mind control since the frequencies HAARP uses are very close to human brain waves. HAARP facilities are presently in many countries of the NATO Alliance. From what I read, China has also developed their own version of this technology.

In Taos, chemtrails were obvious because we had clear skies, expanded views, and were on the flight path of a large number of jets. For several years, I was hearing people around town complain about chemtrails and didn't know what to think. Similar to others, I thought atmospheric conditions might be responsible for those jet trails that took so long to dissipate.

The first time I knew they were real was around the year 2012 when I looked up and saw a jet that had just stopped spraying. Across half of the sky was a bright white chemtrail, followed by a jet that was now releasing a normal contrail, which evaporated in five to ten seconds. For the next year, I would feel angry every time I saw a chemtrail in the sky. This could and did affect the quality of my day in a negative manner.

Therefore, I began to get proactive and change the dynamic of my interaction. I started leaving the victim mode behind and became more empowered. I began to ask spirit beings to push the chemtrails out of the atmosphere and into outer space where they would do no harm. Or I simply intended with my own mind and power to send them off. Sometimes I asked higher vibrational extraterrestrials to dismantle them with their superior technology. I might visualize a dome over my property protecting my gardens, or enlarge this dome to cover the entirety of Taos. Sometimes I would pray for the people who create and implement these terrible sprays.

Whatever I did, my focus was to change the dynamic from something dis-empowering and negative to the opposite type of energy. I know my focus and intentions had an effect – how much is debatable. However, my overall objective to transform the dark nature of the chemtrails into something lighter was successful.

Even if the transformation was only subjective, it worked. I always felt lighter, happier, and more empowered after I dealt with them in a proactive manner. If tens of millions of people were to transform chemtrails similarly, I believe a major shift could occur.

Transmuting something dark into light is always the best option, but not always the easiest or most practical. Sometimes I just deal with negativity by putting it in its place. This is the angle from which I see us confronting a company such as Monsanto. If people were to organize and send large amounts of focused mental energy towards a Monsanto headquarters in a certain location, we could disrupt their computer systems. Computers are sensitive devices and this strategy would send a clear message saying that humanity will not accept companies such as theirs on our planet.

Ultimately love will become our main transformative tool. It will prove to be our most powerful approach as a species. Although love has the most potential, it may be the most difficult. In order to be effective, this approach works best if a person can hold a very high frequency.

I once had a friend with health challenges who lived off governmental support and spent most of his time isolated at home in a very rural setting. Because he didn't need to interact much with the outside world, he was able to maintain a consistently high vibration. He would occasionally watch the evening news, which I couldn't understand. When I finally asked him why, he told me that he would tune into the people and locations that oozed pain, suffering, and darkness. Then with all of his being, he would send them love. This is one way a person can transform through love. There must be an unlimited number of methods.

In the future, there will be many people teaching others how to transform darkness through love. I will probably not be one of them because I'm very eclectic in how I deal with manifestations of the dark side. I do whatever works in the moment: I'm very practical in this manner.

However there are many spiritually based people who are focused on love as their core path, and most of them are probably women. I say this because the ones I know are indeed women. They are presently developing abilities of transformation through love that will go far beyond anything I achieve in this lifetime.

One such person is Byron Katie. She wrote a book named *Loving What Is*. Many years ago, she had an enlightenment type of experience that changed her life. In a powerful revelation, she knew that if she could love whatever exists, no matter how negative, she could come to a place of inner peace with it. Her method of transforming the dark through love is in direct alignment with Christ's teaching: "Love your enemies."

I will finish by offering a transformational healing technique that you can use on anyone who is suffering. Always ask for and receive clear permission before you start. This method is similar to Reiki, which is a practice of channeling universal pranic energy into specific areas of distress in a client's body. Instead, you will focus on your heart chakra, opening to the flow of the Fuente Sagrada.

As you gradually begin to feel love flowing into your heart, visualize this love moving out through your arms and hands into the area of distress on the person you are serving. You may call on your allies to help serve this process; stay focused until you experience a shift. Your intention is to raise the vibratory level of the affliction, which might be something you either feel, see, or just know.

You may choose to visualize light shining into the focal area, or if you are patient enough, wait to see (with your third eye) if light starts shining on its own. Don't stress; just play with this, even if you are focused on helping someone with a serious affliction. If nothing else, your loving intentions will always serve the person you are attempting to help.

Chapter 21

In chapter 6, love was defined as connection and ultimately Oneness. Now we will explore the concept of love in more depth, as well as the phrase: the-power-of-love. In one of the *Anastasia* books, which came out of Russia, Anastasia says love is more powerful than any weapon on Earth. She claims love is more powerful than all the hydrogen explosions that power our sun.

Paramahansa Yogananda states very similar perspectives in both his book "Autobiography of a Yogi" and his meditation lessons. He also quotes at least one reference in the Bible that supports this reality. In light of this, it seems sensible for us to access the power-of-love to create the lives and world we desire.

When the word love is used, most people think of the romantic idea of falling in love. This is such an amazing experience, it appears as if a lot of people besides myself have fallen to its addictive tendencies. Fortunately, romantic love also taught me some things about love as a state of consciousness and being.

As you are aware, I've been exploring altered states of consciousness for a long time. Our body's biochemistry responds strongly to falling in love, with the release of endorphins and other "love chemicals." I remember having trouble staying grounded and functional when I fell in love. My heart would open and inexpressible levels of joy would arise. Feelings that might be described as ecstasy would surface. My insides felt like they were smiling. Life felt good and a deep gratitude for the life experience would fill my being. As I went through my days, a part of me was somewhere else connecting to my lover. The bond was strong and the desire to be together in the physical even stronger.

Yet, it has become apparent that going beyond the falling in love stage to experience love on deeper levels is arduous. The difficulty of holding relationships together is a testament to the challenge of taking romantic love to another level. From what I'm able to ascertain, this requires a commitment to consistently deepen the connection. More than likely, the couple must evolve their relationship into a spiritual practice.

An invaluable practice is that of "living" Oneness on a day-to-day basis. In order to accomplish this, we must go beyond the belief or even the knowing that everything is all One. From the perspective of living Oneness, the well-being of every other person – not to mention plants, animals, and other beings – is just as important to me as my own.

Sometimes I prioritize others, which is commonly referred to as service. Other times I prioritize myself. If I don't prioritize myself when I need or deserve it, then what I give in service may not be energetically sound, high-vibrational, or loving. Living Oneness is the ultimate challenge to our ego structure because the ego is like a child who always wants to be the most important.

In order to give you a better idea of how incredibly connected we are as humans, it's helpful to dive more fully into how we are designed. On the physical level, we embody the lower three dimensions of the mineral, plant, and animal kingdoms. We are made of minerals and plants often form vitally important synergistic relationships with our bodies. In addition, our DNA is at least 99% the same as other mammals.

On the emotional level, we are incredibly interconnected with unlimited worlds through the astral plane of existence. Our psychic and telepathic abilities are a byproduct of this.

Our mental capabilities encompass multiple dimensions. Our brain, neurons, and nervous system could be compared to the hardware of a computer and they exist in the 3rd dimension. Our astral (4th), etheric (5th), and causal (6th) bodies all have mental components to them. Our chattering mind, which never wants to shut up, probably exists in the astral realm. Love and compassion are highly associated with our etheric body. The 6th dimensional causal plane is a reality of pure thought and concepts and it contains the Akashic records of all soul incarnations.

As spiritual beings, we are interconnected within even more dimensional realities. According to written material I highly respect, we as an individual soul exist in the 7th dimension. Beyond this we are connected through what are often called "soul families" and could also be thought of as "soul groupings." They exist all the way from the 8th through the 12th dimensions.

The original Soul, which is our Source, transcends all twelve dimensions. From pure Being-ness, it manifested into twelve soul groupings within the 12th dimension. Each one of those split into twelve more, which fell into the 11th dimension. This process continued all the way down to the 7th where we manifested as individualized souls.

I don't believe for a moment that the scenario just described is exactly what happened, but it is a model that gives our minds something to work with when trying to conceptualize these levels of reality within Creation. The Hindu Vedas and Upanishads, ancient scriptural writings of India that go back at least 5-10,000 years, have names for various levels of consciousness attained through samadhi. These levels correspond surprisingly well with the channeled material presented in the previous paragraph, concerning varying degrees of consciousness within dimensions 8 – 12.

Several years ago, I had an extremely powerful experience on psychedelic mushrooms while living for a month in the Sacred Valley of Peru. I found a secluded meadow in a side canyon between two waterfalls and a young American couple journeyed with me.

At some point, I received a communication concerning souls within Creation: we are never lost. There is always a way back home for us through our soul lineage, from soul family to family to Source. The degree of love and compassion I felt during this experience was profound.

Paramahansa Yogananda, who refers to the Hindu Vedas regularly, states that the ultimate goal of meditation is samadhi, total immersion in the Infinite. Yogis in samadhi often stop breathing and their hearts stop beating. They can remain in this state of suspended animation for days at a time and then return and reanimate an apparently dead body when complete with their experience. It is only through the deepest states of meditation that we can access ourselves as expanded soul families.

Deep and Intense

I recently saw the movies: "Samadhi" Part 1 & 2. They were released in 2017 & 2018. They are free on YouTube, although Part 3 wasn't available yet. They are beyond amazing and may be the most important films ever made. If anything represents the new paradigm for humanity, they do.

Here are several quotes from Part 1: "Samadhi is awakening from the dream of the separate self or the egoic construct." "Samadhi is awakening from identification with the prison that I call me." "Enlightenment is the merging of the primordial spiral, the ever-changing manifested world or lotus in which time unfolds, with your timeless being."

The mind and ego structure are intertwined and the combination is what comes between us and samadhi, which can only be experienced beyond the thinking mind. Our ego structure wants a clear path to samadhi and easily becomes attached to definable results, which usually brings on self-condemnation and suffering. Furthermore, the ego wants to control the process of awakening, which of course is a trap. Fully surrendering and trusting is the only solution!

Because our mental bodies encompass several dimensions, our minds are very powerful and more than ever dominate people's realities. Out of balance modern societies are way too mental. This is partly due to the extreme complexity of our technologically driven lifestyles and our mind's desire to manage the onslaught of details associated with simply living a normal life. People are also living in their mental body as a convenient way to escape excessive pain in their physical and emotional bodies.

Most people are unconsciously stuck in their lower chattering mind and ego structure. This is a form of resistance, to living in the present moment, and to living life consciously, intentionally, and deeply. Samadhi is about dropping all resistance, to pain and outer stimuli. Resistance to pain creates suffering. Embracing what is, in each and every moment, offers complete freedom from suffering.

Four months ago, I started working with Yogananda's written lessons on meditation and self-realization. They embody discipline, consistency, devotion, and a focus on God throughout the day.

Meditation is a gradual process of letting go more and more deeply into the unknown within. Most techniques promote watching and/or releasing thoughts and emotions. Yogananda prefers to focus the mind on the Divine and its highest manifestations.

Meditation within our stressed out, hyper-rapid, modern digital reality is incredibly challenging for most of us. Many sincere people will not devote themselves to a committed practice because they feel it's not possible for them to succeed.

Consider being creative; tune into your own guidance and intuition. Most people seem to want a prepackaged formula, a spiritual practice done exactly the same way every time. Yet some of us find this to be boring. The artist in all of us desires to pursue creative challenges. Although I have appreciated all of the spiritual practices that came into my life, most were not creative and I always had trouble staying committed to them. Creativity keeps things interesting and brings us more fully into the moment.

A friend of mine engages in a practice of seeing the Creator in every person he meets. I suggest we take this one step further and focus on seeing this presence in everything our eyesight beholds. Then take it even further and practice unity with everything we cannot see, throughout all dimensions. This works best when you focus on your heart chakra or third eye while doing it.

I intuited the practice of constantly transforming darkness, the negative into something vibrationally higher, moment by moment as it shows up in my life. This can be adapted to a person's personal preferences since there are unlimited ways of transforming darkness. I believe both of these practices will help us access the power-of-love.

It appears the power-of-love comes through an awareness of connection, achieved one way or another. Yogananda says unlimited power comes through self-realization – the ultimate experience of connection. As we realize and experience our Oneness with Creator/Creation on deeper levels, our desire and ability to serve the whole increases. As we are able to be trusted with power, Divine grace allows us access to more of it.

In contrast, various esoteric methods teach the initiate how to gain power through rituals or realizations concerning how to manipulate Creation interdimensionally. This is not as pure a path and is susceptible to controlling influences by the dark side. People who gain power in this fashion are limited in the amount they are able to access.

By focusing on Oneness, we create connection within our lives – through which the love vibration can flourish. It appears vital we engage in some sort of spiritual practice that serves a growing awareness of connection, one that gradually becomes more continuous. In this manner we nurture the power-of-love.

As we better understand this power, we use it for our mutual benefit. As more of us practice the power-of-love, we transform our species and our collective experience.

I'm gradually understanding Love as the multidimensional reality it is. The power-of-love comes through Unity consciousness. If we could consistently feel connection with Creator and all of its Creation, from the highest to the lowest dimensions, the potential power must be truly unlimited.

It slowly begins to be more obvious why the power-of-love is so much greater than anything stuck in and limited to the physical dimension. I'm beginning to understand how we can transform our world with it!

Chapter 22

Does humanity need to confront the global power structures that are guiding us in exceedingly dysfunctional directions? Our species is destroying the ecosystems on which all life on Earth depends. What if we feel guided from within to take a stand for ourselves, our community, or our planet? Rather than give in to my inner warrior and advocate outright revolution, I prefer to create a dialogue concerning this most important of questions.

Violence can never create permanent positive change. This has been proven time and again over thousands of years of patriarchal warmongering. On the other hand, Martin Luther King, Mahatma Gandhi, and Nelson Mandela have shown us that positive foundational change can be forged through non-violent means.

They have shown us at least part of the path we need to pursue. Yet to make significant progress towards our evolutionary potential, many of us must develop new skills of transformation and learn how to effectively access the power-of-love.

The depths of darkness that exist within the global power structures is truly staggering. For the most part, humanity has been completely incapable of dealing with the dark forces on this level. The power structures remain intact, their degrading and destructive behaviors continue more or less unimpeded. Because most individuals are unable to effectively and consistently transform darkness within themselves and their lives, the collective shares the same shortcoming.

Christianity has taught Westerners that the dark side is evil, the stuff of Satan. It has painted a horrible image of the shadow side of reality, a graphic picture and cultural mindset that is unavoidable from the day we are born.

A tremendous amount of fear, most of it unconscious, is associated with these beliefs, including the fear of being tortured should we confront the power structures (Christ crucified and bleeding on the cross). So unsurprisingly, people tend to avoid interactions with darker realities, and/or constantly obsess about how difficult and unfair life is because of them.

From the Christian perspective, no structure exists to facilitate any type of meaningful relationship with the dark side. This leads to fear, judgment, and separation. The shaman, conversely, has mastered his fears of darkness and developed a relationship with it. He is able to proactively deal with the dark forces in whatever way is most appropriate. It seems to me the shaman has shown us the underlying strategy needed to deal with the global power structures.

Information is leaking out everywhere concerning the power structures and their agendas. People who have worked for the "secret government" have been speaking out for several decades. They have risked their lives and the well-being of their families because they evidently came to the point where they couldn't live with themselves and the secrets they were sworn to hide. There are numerous people exposing and discussing these topics on radio stations, in books, and on the internet. Since there is also a glut of misinformation, a classic power structure strategy, I feel compelled to recommend several sources I've been exposed to.

The first is the movie *Thrive*. From a completely different background than myself, a highly educated Ph.D. scientist and heir to the Proctor and Gamble fortune, Foster Gamble arrived at the same conclusions as I did concerning the Western power structure. It seems his most difficult realization was that this power structure is actively engaged in an extermination program directed at humanity. This film is one of the most important ever made.

Why in the World are They Spraying? is a film about chemtrails. At the time I saw it, two more were being made as part of a series. For a much deeper analysis, read: *Chemtrails, Haarp, and the Full Spectrum Dominance of Planet Earth*, by Elana Freeland. Professionally, she is a historical researcher. Elana shares information she gathered without drawing conclusions. Concerning chemtrails, the first people to start noticing them were former military and airline pilots, due to the fact they were constantly looking up at jets flying across the sky. A chilling revelation concerns the expression "full spectrum dominance," which originated within the American military.

Freeland's book is emotionally difficult to read, seeing how blatantly our governments work against and even attack us.

A book I found in Ecuador, *Transylvanian Sunrise*, written by Radu Cinamar, was originally published in Romanian under the title: *The Enemy Within: In the Secret Corridors of Power*. In this book, the most important figure, a highly evolved man who was the head of Romania's paranormal phenomenon agency, became the object of the Illuminati's desires to recruit him. This occurred soon after the discovery of a phenomenal underground facility created by advanced extraterrestrials tens of thousands of years ago. In his recruitment attempts, a high member of the Illuminati shared various details about how they operate; he claimed they have most successfully implemented their strategies in the USA.

I also recommend the *Anastasia* books. I read the first three and know several people who deeply appreciated all nine books in the series. Anastasia, a modern-day shaman from the Siberian Taiga, became the center of a huge movement in Russia, as well as an international phenomenon.

Destined to become classics of our times, read the Pleiadian channelings by Barbara Marciniak: *Bringers of the Dawn* and *Earth*. As far as I know, the term "lightworker" originated in these books. The Pleiadians claim things were, and still are, so bad on our planet, the Galactic Federation had to quarantine our solar system from the rest of the galaxy. These books woke me up to a galactic consciousness. Although I read them many years ago, they are incredibly relevant to our present and future.

Another amazing source of pertinent information is the insights of John Lamb Lash. There are interviews of him by Lisa Harrison available on YouTube. He is American and she is an Australian radio host. The two interviews I heard explore the *Sophia Mythos* and its relevance to the power structures. John Lash is also the main contributor to the www.metahistory.org website.

I recently read Lash's book: *Not in His Image*. Since it's a challenging read on numerous levels, I doubt if many people will read it. Yet it is truly paradigm shifting and due to its importance, I will offer a brief synopsis. At the core of the book are the findings of the Nag Hammadi codices, discovered in an Egyptian cave in 1945. These texts presented amazing information, including the *Sophia Mythos*, a story previously lost in history, yet one that existed at the core of the pagan culture of pre-Christian Europe.

The pagans were the indigenous people of Europe and their cultures extended into North Africa and the Middle East all the way to western India. Pagan cultures were life affirming, Earth and Spirit based, and equally balanced between the masculine and feminine polarities. They lasted until at least 400 C.E. (A.D.).

The Gnostics were the mystics of the pagan world and their roots reached deep into pre-historic shamanism. They were also the educated class and they managed an extensive and thriving mystery school network. The Mysteries were taught in a university system that encompassed: vocational training of all types, subjects taught in colleges today, and training in shamanic and spiritual principles for those who were so inclined.

Each school was unique to a fair degree and had its own library, those of Alexandria, Egypt being the most famous. Socrates and other historical figures less famous taught within the framework of these institutions. For over a thousand years, so much literature existed within pagan cultures, it appears as if most of the populace was literate.

The pagan world was torn apart by the Christian-Roman alliance and all evidence of its high culture was meticulously destroyed. The Dark Ages in Europe resulted from the destruction of pagan cultures. John Lash clearly states that the European power structures wiped out their own indigenous populations many centuries prior to doing the same thing in the Americas and most of the other continents.

Over the next 1,500 years, paganism was consistently discredited and demonized. This resulted in an extreme amount of negativity being directed towards a truly incredible time period in Western history. But the truth is that our indigenous pagan heritage is something to be proud of. We can certainly use it as a foundation from which to create a positive future.

I've been watching this type of information come out into the public realm for three decades. It started slowly at first and now it's like a flood in comparison to the trickle it once was. I have not indulged in most of the dark ugly details because they pull me down too far when I focus on them. Then I need to work on integrating the information and pulling my frequency back up.

I approach these types of materials with the clear intention of developing a general understanding of what is going on behind the scenes on our planet. I've been focused on understanding the underlying causes of humanity's pain and why our species creates so much suffering in the world.

In contrast, the media obsesses on what the power structures want us to focus on – symptoms and dysfunction. Modern medicine does the same. This approach keeps people and governments in poor health and a state of perpetual crisis and division.

I've come to the conclusion that there is a concerted effort within factions of the global power structures to ravage the heart of humanity and destroy the best of what it means to be human. In a sense, there is a battle raging on planet Earth for the soul of humanity. The global power structures are controlled by "families of power." I've never heard that term before, but it perfectly describes what I see.

Some families of power go back hundreds or even thousands of years. Think of monarchies, dynasties, adepts and manipulators of commerce. They reside most strongly in countries with a long history of continuous civilization.

For instance, in China there are probably families who have managed to maintain power and control for at least 2,000-4,000 years. These families are the real powers on our third dimensional planet, not the governments, militaries, and corporations they mostly control. From what I can tell, the darkest and most powerful group of families control the countries of the NATO Alliance.

Over the past decade, I've repeatedly heard this group referred to as the "Cabal." They seem to be focused on maintaining and gaining power at all costs. Some of them created the Western banking system and for all intents and purposes, they own it. This helps them maintain control over the countries that use their currencies. For some history on this subject, watch the film: *The Money Masters – How International Bankers Gained Control of America*. You can watch it on www.freedocumentaries.org

American, European, and third world governments all owe their debts to some of these people. The money these governments borrowed (and their citizens supposedly owe) was literally created out of thin air. The fact that these bankers don't show up on the highly publicized lists of the richest people in the world simply means they are clever at hiding their wealth and/or have total control over whomever creates those lists. They probably also consider themselves to be beyond such a meaningless classification, since they actually control the creation of money.

Most people are quick to discount such talk with the magic words "conspiracy theory." Not too long ago, the way to discredit contentious and progressive ideas was to call someone a "communist." Calling an intentional community a "cult," network marketing a "pyramid scheme," or a black person a "nigger" were effective ways of silencing and degrading people who did not fit within the accepted societal norm. These types of derogatory terms have been extremely effective in maintaining the power structures of the elite and ultimately inhibiting change.

All of the power structures we see in our world are top-down pyramid shaped organizations. Governments, corporations, and militaries are all run in this manner. To deny that there may be a covert and organizing top-down power structure behind these overt organizations is rather naive. It is almost the same as denying one's pain body, originating from a severe trauma, even as it creates total chaos in one's life.

There might be only one or two individuals in each family of power who negotiate with their counterparts. Upon retirement, they either pass on control to the oldest male, similar to monarchies, or hand pick their heir, similar to the mafia. The patriarchs from each family probably do their best to cooperate, but most likely end up competing across cultural lines.

There may not be more than a hundred individuals who pull the strings and orchestrate most of the pain and suffering on our planet. Yet all humans are responsible for their actions and we have minimal right to lay all of the blame at their feet. We as a species are giving away our power to these select few individuals and we must all be held accountable for their actions. This is a classic codependent relationship occurring on a global scale.

Families of power use their immense influence to consistently resist all positive change in our world. Instead, they are guiding us down a path of technological slavery through New World Order dictatorships. While this occurs, environmental self-destruction becomes more real and immanent. Many people believe technology will save us, but the fact is they control the best technology. The power structures, for instance, have managed to keep "free energy" devices out of the marketplace for many years now.

Most of these devices use Tesla's concepts to tap into the Earth's magnetic field (or other energy fields) in much the same way HAARP technology does. Consensus reality claims perpetual motion machines are not possible, yet these free energy systems continuously produce clean electricity and do not require batteries for storage. I have a friend who has seen one working and Foster Gamble, from the *Thrive* movie, claims to have seen many functioning models. They have the potential to transform everything in our world!

Free energy devices are not large or expensive to build, from my understanding. Every house, building, or block on our planet could have one, leading the way to a non-toxic world. We could run our electric cars with them as well, charging them in our own homes. Incredibly, we could get rid of all nuclear power, stop drilling for petroleum, stop using coal, tear down most of the hydroelectric dams, get rid of all those ugly and inefficient power lines, and stop paying energy bills.

The energy industry is the largest and most toxic on our planet. Militaries and their ridiculous wars are not far behind, but they are often motivated by the energy industry. Humanity has free energy technology, yet we are not being allowed to use it. People are not able to get patents and probably have their facilities destroyed if they do apply for a patent. Keeping this technology out of the marketplace must be one of the FBI and CIA's top priorities.

All of this information is extremely difficult for people to ingest, digest, and cope with. I believe it is especially difficult to deal with one's emotional reactions. It can be difficult to mentally wrap one's head around these realities, but that doesn't compare to the emotional impact of what we are up against as a species.

I've been processing intense emotions for several decades around the darkness prevalent in the power structures. Sometimes I've felt as if I'm doing this type of inner work for millions of people who don't seem to be able to.

During my last two days in Mocoa, at Taita Lucho's ayahuasca ceremonies, a young Norwegian woman of twenty-two asked me if I believe evil exists. I had just finished a relatively long healing session with her. She told me she had been contemplating this question for quite some time. It had also come up in her first ayahuasca experience two nights earlier. I replied that my dad had asked me the same question some years earlier. After talking around the subject, I said that ultimately "No, I don't think evil exists."

Several days ago, a realization flashed in my mind concerning this subject. It seems to me, the word "evil," by definition, means there is no hope for redemption. Yet the yin/yang symbol suggests there is always a little light in the dark; nothing in Creation is beyond redemption. As for Lucifer, he agreed, from a stance of unconditional love and service, to play the part of darkness for all eternity. That does not seem very evil to me.

The word evil is "live" spelled backwards, which lacks the extremely judgmental philosophy of Christianity. I believe its original meaning was in alignment with how I view the dark side. Steeped in profound levels of suffering, manifestations of darkness on our planet can't help but project their inner pain outwards in the form of destructive and anti-life behavior patterns.

Chapter 23

Is there any question concerning the need for a revolution on our planet, the question of evil notwithstanding? One must consider the fact that the forces of light do not engage in battle with the forces of darkness. Rather the light embraces them in love to bring them back home. The inherent challenge presented to humanity is that most people are not even close to being able to accomplish this in an effective manner.

It seems as if most of the transformational work, past and present, is being accomplished by people on an individual basis. Inner healing, spiritual practices, and living in joy are raising people's vibrations.

However, in the future, progressives must learn to work together more effectively. Since the '60s, this has challenged those who managed to break away from the status quo reality, because it was their individualistic drive that encouraged them to follow their hearts on a path less traveled. Learning to co-create in a powerfully positive manner will be the next major breakthrough for many of these people, as well as our species as a whole.

As far as confronting the power structures on an individual basis, please do so when guided. A very Buddhist way of living says to sit back and watch the movie of life. There is ultimately nothing wrong, from a spiritually transcendent perspective. However, Buddhism also promotes action, when a person feels guided from within to do something – out of a sense of compassion or for any other reason. The Bhagavad Gita from the Hindu Vedas also recommends action, to fulfill your duty, your role or destiny in life.

It's important for every conscious person to work on the highest level they can, each and every day, to transform darkness on our planet. Some people are much further along in their spiritual development than others. In any given moment or day, one's vibration may shift up or down; each person will need to transform negativity from wherever they are at. If we each strive to work from the highest level possible each and every day, this is a beautiful contribution. We are personally rewarded for our efforts by attracting experiences that are in alignment with our frequency. The higher we vibrate, the higher our experiences.

We cannot effectively challenge their New World Order by staying stuck in third dimensional reality. The global families of power effectively control this dimension and it would be absurd to try to beat them at their own game. In a manner of speaking, they have all the guns. As more people continue to wake up, it's important to do interdimensional work, such as the healing and transformational practices I've recommended.

In our history, there were many who worked for the light on these levels, but the European power structures killed most of them in their centuries of conquest. They murdered the "witches" in Europe and America, women who were often healers with psychic and paranormal abilities. Then they wiped out most of the native peoples in the Americas, and along with them their shamans. Indigenous cultures all over our planet were compromised in much the same manner. The power structures did their best to destroy their competition, with Christian churches often leading the way.

The metaphysical movement started in the late 1800s by Madam Blavatsky and others in England, followed by the New Age movement in the States, helped keep ancient traditions of the light alive in the West. They offer modern teachings of the masters; some of them serve us very effectively in doing interdimensional work.

On the physical plane of reality, we can forge forward with practical steps such as building community locally, growing healthy food, and implementing sustainable technologies whenever possible. Living a proactive life can occur on different levels. Here are a few examples from my own life.

I recently grew large amounts of high-quality organic produce and sold most of it locally, over a five-year period. Rather than complain about the medical establishment, I heal myself and help to heal others. Instead of obsessing on ignorant bosses and corporate backstabbing, I am an entrepreneur who occasionally works as an employee for small businesses. Instead of complaining about the corporate media, I ignore it and focus on understanding the nature of reality. My entire focus in life is on creating a positive new future for humanity, one that honors individuality and communal sharing of resources and love.

We are certainly living in a time of extremes. The light and dark are both increasing their efforts and humanity seems to be caught in the middle. Since the light is based in the truth of Oneness and the dark in the illusion of separation, I choose to believe humanity will succeed, despite present circumstances. Once again, we can all choose to believe whatever we want to believe.

I do not accept failure; I do not accept the New World Order the Western power structure is focused on implementing. I do not accept their warped vision of a mechanized, digitalized, emotionally compromised and spiritually retarded humanity. Instead, I choose to believe in the potential and beauty of my species. This is what inspires me!

If I am not able to live an inspired life on our Earth, I choose not to live here at all. I am not willing to compromise my personal quest for deeply fulfilling meaning, honorable service, inner peace, and joy.

Chapter 24

It is important for us to assimilate and process these difficult questions: who is at the apex of the Western power structure and how do they operate? There appears to be two main branches at the very top, although it's unclear whether or not they presently work together, and if so, how effectively. They almost certainly cooperated closely in the past, and more than likely they've had a tumultuous relationship at times.

The Cabal emphasize the practical-physical aspects of ruling and the Illuminati focus more on the mystical-occult. The "Illuminati" must be the ultimate secret society. John Lash claims their roots reach all the way back into the pagan world. They were Gnostics who turned to the dark side when they realized they could use core mystical methodology to control others and rule.

Although some members of the Cabal are almost certainly American, the majority are European. The reality is that Europe never gave up its power base. There is no evidence to suggest that the families and organizations who gained the most from the European conquest and colonization of much of our planet over the past millennia ever lost their power.

The families who gained the greatest power and managed to hold on to it simply changed how things look on the surface. They got a lot smarter and more deceitful; they learned to hide and play their world domination chess games in the shadows.

The Illuminati and Cabal are experts at manipulation and are subtle enough that most people have no idea it's happening. They are exceedingly organized, assuming their overt organizations are a fair indication of their abilities in this area of expertise. They are also very patient.

Although I disagree with everything they represent, I don't blame them for wanting to keep and consolidate their power. It's what they know; it's what they've been doing for generations and generations. If humanity wants to play a game of denial, fear, and dis-empowerment, why shouldn't they take what they want?

The Cabal's main strategy on all levels is to "divide and conquer," which of course taps into the energy of separation. They are experts at getting people to point their fingers at each other, blaming others for their problems. This occurs in marriages, politics, between countries and cultures, and almost everywhere we look.

The organizations they control are often run on a need-to-know basis; the people on each level only share information with those below if they need-to-know. The Cabal gain the cooperation of others by finding out what an individual wants intensely enough that he or she will sell out their integrity. On the upper levels, this is usually power and control, large amounts of money or resources.

What does the ego structure of a person want badly enough: beautiful women, fancy cars and houses, security? On the lowest levels, most people just want a job so they can eat, raise a family, and pay the bills. As a person loses faith in life and the system, believing in what he or she does to earn a living is not very high on their priority list.

All global families of power use deception to influence and control the people of their countries. With advances in technology, this is being honed to a fine art. Recently, I've come to believe that all digital technologies are frequency control devices; they affect the user's state of consciousness in a negative manner.

Our brains and energy fields naturally align with outer stimuli, especially light and sound technologies. Televisions have been used in this manner for many decades. Mechanical motors and machines are less sophisticated, but they are similar because the EMF waves they emit have an adverse impact on human energy fields.

Up until recently, terrorism was the Cabal's main weapon of deception and it is obvious the Western power structure was behind the 9/11 destruction of the Twin Towers in New York City. The U.S. government cooperated with their agenda, as it always seems to do. I believe the main reasons they masterminded it are as follows:

1. With China embracing capitalism and the collapse of the Soviet Union, the "failure/defeat" of communism was final. The Western nations needed a new enemy! There must be an "us" and a "them." The new enemy was terrorism, which is hidden and feeds fear exceptionally well. The main terrorists were Muslims, the centuries-old enemy of Christianity.
2. This gave the NATO Alliance the excuse it needed to enhance and maintain control of the Middle East, starting with the American invasion of Iraq. They wanted to control the oil and other resources, but its strategic location bordering Russia, China, and India was potentially more important.
3. This allowed the United States to continue to spend profane amounts of money on its military, with other militarily-advanced countries in NATO doing the same. All of this created more separation and tension between the world powers, feeding more fear and uncertainty globally.
4. The constant stress inherent in these dynamics serves the Cabal by allowing them to covertly compensate many of their supporters through international corporate and governmental structures. This happens by graft and deception on every level, which creates a constant downward force on the level of integrity within these institutions. A culture of "kick-backs" has become the norm in Western politics.
5. This creates innumerable distractions for the corporate media to focus on, allowing the Western power structure to negotiate and bully all rivals into submission both publicly and behind the scenes.

It is impossible to know who funded extremist Arab organizations, but I would be very surprised if the Cabal didn't channel significant amounts of resources towards at least some of them. The dynamic was too perfect for their strategies of deceit and manipulation of mass consciousness. As fundamentalist Christians battled fundamentalist Arabs, the Western power structure hid behind the chaos. In the media, "terrorists" became anyone who challenged the system controlled by the power elite. Limitations on freedom were legislated in the name of protecting the people from an illusive enemy.

Much more recently, the coronavirus pandemic replaced terrorism as the new instrument of manipulation. Statistics showing that the Covid-19 threat is much less severe than the media makes it out to be are common. There are many reasons people are sick and dying and Covid is only one of the causes.

For instance, the 5G digital technology is one hundred times more powerful than 4G and many people in Taos expressed deep concern shortly before it was implemented. When a strong enough energy field disrupts our body's energy systems, it throws them dramatically out of balance and physical illness is often the result. Unsurprisingly, 5G towers and technologies were implemented at nearly the exact same time the Covid epidemic began.

Instead of helping people improve their health by supporting them in building strong immune systems, the vast majority of governments reacted by creating fear and separation. Separation even became the norm with the concept of "social distancing." Global lockdowns were the equivalent of martial law in many countries. Vaccines were promoted and often required to maintain one's freedom of movement.

Similar to terrorism, the virus is hidden and feeds people's fears and uncertainty extremely effectively. In fact, there appears to be a clear pattern of control, separation, and fear that goes backwards from this pandemic: terrorism, communism, the cold war, nuclear weapons, and world wars 1 & 2 in the first half of the twentieth century.

I recently watched the British film "The New Normal." It questions the real agenda behind the Covid pandemic, the safety of the vaccines, and whether it was planned beforehand. Implementation of sophisticated technologies was at the heart of the documentary with artificial intelligence (AI), 5G, enhanced surveillance and personal tracking leading the way. The film shows the potential for (what I can't help but view as) an antiseptic high-tech hell in the very near future.

I believe the global power structures are preparing us for much worse epidemics in the near future, laying the foundation for concerted systemic reactions and restrictions by governments. They are getting people acclimated to the new rules of their game and finding out just how far they can push us in different parts of the world before we rebel.

Along the same lines, the global power structures have created a system that subjugates, confuses, and demoralizes people everywhere. Even worse, they viciously protect this system, which is slowly and methodically destroying people, plants, animals, and everything it touches – if not physically, then spiritually. None of this happens by chance, although the system would have you believe differently. Everything in Creation has intention, along with mental and/or emotional energy behind its existence.

Let's look at some of the worst practices within their system of deceit. I will focus on the United States of America, whose culture is dominated by the corporate media and mentality. In the States, most people are in debt and live their lives little different than the serfs in middle age Europe. The majority work at monotonous jobs they neither enjoy nor believe in. They live to work long hours each week, work to pay bills, and use vast quantities of caffeine, alcohol, legal and illegal drugs just to cope with their reality.

Speaking of drugs, medical doctors are highly respected members of our society and the majority earn large pay checks. Yet most have been gradually coerced into becoming little more than legalized drug pushers for the pharmaceutical industry. On the other hand, illegal drug pushers are considered to be the lowest scum of our society and thrown into jail for years if they are caught.

Yet the statistics state that hundreds of times more people die from legal drugs than from illegal ones. Obviously, the distinction between legal and illegal is only minimally due to their safety. Evidently most people die from pharmaceuticals when they become desperate (because they aren't getting better) and start mixing prescriptions that shouldn't be taken together.

The two main treatments for cancer, other than surgically removing it, are chemotherapy and radiation. Considering the fact that chemicals and radiation are the most common causes of cancer, modern medicine's "cures" are counter-intuitive and absurd – unless the intention is to create repeat customers, which is simply "good" business.

These procedures might temporarily eradicate tumors, but doctors expect them to return. They usually inform their patients how long they can expect to be "cancer free." Years ago, I read two books about the medical establishment's active suppression of effective non-toxic cancer cures. One was a Native American herbal formula called Essiac and the other was Royal Rife's frequency generator machine.

One last extreme example from our system of hypocrisy also concerns the subject of killing people. If you kill someone for your own personal reasons, you have committed a "mortal sin" and are looking at a lifetime jail sentence or possibly execution if you did it in the wrong state. If you kill someone for the military, you may receive medals and become a hero. Militaries serve their governments and most (if not all) governments in the NATO Alliance serve the Western power structure.

This all sounds like a good (or bad) movie plot, which of course it is. Humans seem to love drama and we certainly have a great one unfolding before us, with constant CNN updates no less. However, the wise old yogis of yore constantly suggested that we not take any of this (maya) too seriously. As we look at this reality from a more transcendent perspective, we can see the humor/tragedy/perfection in it. It's good theater, a wild and crazy experience for Creator!

Then my human part, the aspect most strongly participating in this extreme duality reality, says "This is all a bad joke – hasn't it been told enough times already?" People are suffering. I've personally been "privileged" to experience high levels of suffering in many of my clients over the years. All life on Earth is suffering. This is so unnecessary. For the humans, and probably all mammals, their suffering is real because they are experiencing it as real. I feel great compassion and I want to do something to help. Isn't it time we get our act together, change the channel, and put on a new movie?

We keep hearing we are powerful beings, more than we know or can believe. Even science says our minds are incredibly powerful – and we are so much more than our minds! More and more of us are saying, "It's time to create a new movie," or as a shaman might say, "Let's dream a new dream!"

I personally want to live in a Garden of Eden. I don't believe humanity ever fell from grace. Rather, we are mostly pure of heart, extremely naïve, and gullible. There is simply a part of us, a part of Creation, which is dark and destructive, stuck in pain and suffering. So let's embrace the hurt child in all of us and love him or her back into the light.

Chapter 25

Spiritually inclined individuals have spoken to me of the "hundredth monkey effect." They say humanity can create massive change even if only a small percentage of people change. There is scientific evidence to back this theory. Although I believe a small number of highly conscious people can make a dramatic impact on humanity's collective destiny, I don't believe this will be enough to save us from an exceedingly difficult transition period in our very near future.

Almost everyone, from Born Again Christians to New Agers to Techies are hoping we will somehow be saved. The unconscious sentiment seems to be that if there is a God, surely he will take pity on us and save us from ourselves! The realist in me says: "I don't think so." Where is the learning and spiritual growth in being saved?

Even the more highly evolved evangelical Christians contend that we need to do more than give lip service to Christ in order to be saved. The practical reality appears to be: a much higher percentage of humanity needs to do the real day-to-day work and commit to love, self-mastery, and spiritual awakening.

In order to receive what we seem to collectively desire – the peaceful world the vast majority of people want to live in, the higher dimensional reality it has been prophesied we will shift to, the "golden age" some channeled beings and mystics say we are destined to go – we cannot avoid a full-fledged healing crisis. We will go through an extreme cleansing of that which does not serve us as a species. I simply don't see any other way for positive, foundational, systemic change to occur.

I sense humanity as a whole will eventually come together in a unified field of power. This process will entail rapid unrest growing on a global scale, which will eventually lead to revolution occurring in many countries more or less simultaneously. A spiritual shift in consciousness will not occur without a revolution in the physical realm preceding and leading up to it. That is part of the process of building enough psychic energy to create profound transformation.

I had a vision many years ago of people around the world on their knees praying together. They were praying in humility and with intensity. They were asking for help from the forces of light, as each person understands this in his or her own belief system. Humanity will eventually realize its unified power and affirm: "We will not let you control and dehumanize us through your hi-tech dictatorships. This is our planet and we are not going to let you destroy it – or us!"

Despite this positive outcome, I doubt if the power structures will go meekly or quietly. Since they control the banking systems, they create economic chaos whenever and wherever they need to. An older man who formerly had a high clearance in the American military wrote that when the global elite feel exceedingly threatened, they will create a fake UFO invasion to distract humanity and get people focused against a common extraterrestrial enemy. It seems the power brokers have plans within plans.

Thus, the ensuing process will probably be one of high drama and intensity and may take many years to unfold. It is likely our survival instincts as a species will kick in and influence the outcome. In the end, I believe we will not only succeed, but do so from a place of love.

I read a science fiction book that takes place on a galactic scale. The humans swept the rulers out of power and imprisoned them on their own planet with full freedom of movement. I felt this was a brilliant solution. We could do the same with those in the higher positions of power on our planet, only we would place them on an island. We don't need to give them a particularly nice or large island, but they would be free to compete, cooperate, or power trip among themselves. This would be a compassionate solution, devoid of revenge. Yet it would serve the purpose of getting those people out of the picture so we can make significant changes as a species.

I would not want to be involved with deciding who gets to stay (for a second chance) and who needs to go to the island. I prefer to leave that job to the younger more highly evolved souls who are presently incarnating onto our planet. They will not have suffered very long under the old system, nor do they believe in it. They could bring the appropriate level of wisdom and detachment to the "judgment" process. Maybe this is the final judgment referred to in Revelations.

Although I trust we will succeed, I believe at least half of the human population on our planet will die in the process of reaching a massive collective shift. I heard a Native American prophecy that predicts two-thirds of our species will die in the transition. Apparently, the power structures want to cull the human population down to 500 million, presumably because that is the number of people they think they can effectively manage and control. That would be more than a 90% reduction. From a biological perspective, any species that grows at an exponential rate, such as humanity has done for over a thousand years, can expect to experience a die off of up to 99% at some point. All of a sudden, half of the population dying doesn't sound so extreme.

There are reasons why I am willing to give humanity the benefit of the doubt. One of them is that despite our dysfunctional state, I experience humanity as an incredibly good-hearted species. The vast majority of people desire to do good all of the time. The fact that we don't consistently act in a loving manner is due to inner pain and suffering, not bad intentions. In general, people everywhere regularly participate in loving acts of kindness. This has earned us an abundance of Divine grace and continues to do so.

As for the system, the matrix, it's difficult to say how much of it is salvageable. The system is designed "wrong." It was conceived from a consciousness of separation and constructed on a similar foundation: it's upside down and inside out. Because of this, it constantly pulls us away, on multiple levels, from experiencing our Source connection. As for me, personally, I simply know that the more involved I am in the system, and the less space I have from it, the more dysfunctional I tend to become.

Do we really even need the global system and all the irrelevant things it offers? Did indigenous populations all over the globe need it? Even democracy is a joke, since it's so easy to manipulate people with the media propaganda machine – or make the computers spit out the desired results. The best things in life are free and independent of the system. Nature, intimacy, touch, sex, and love are but a few examples.

Many of the people who die in the coming transition period will succumb to epidemics since modern medicine, vaccines, stress, poor nutrition, and an increasingly toxic environment are ruining people's immune systems. Unsurprisingly, some of the worst diseases of recent times are well documented to have been created by governments and corporations in their laboratories. Although I've not read them, I was told about a book written on AIDS and another on Lyme disease.

The deaths of over three billion people will be a necessary component to the process of pushing humanity through a collective transformation. In a sense, it will take that many deaths to wake people up. The higher we vibrate as a species, the less deaths will need to occur, whereas a lower vibration will result in more deaths. Those who vibrate at low frequencies will tend to be the ones dying, since they will attract negative and chaotic experiences into their lives. People who live in a higher consciousness will tend to be the ones ushering in the new reality. This is my sense of what is coming, yet no one knows for sure.

I have seen an underlying perfection concerning the scenario just presented. From my personal experiences, I estimate over 95% of people unconsciously resist change. They resist what they don't know or understand. Most individuals claim to want change, but they don't work very hard for it. They aren't willing to do their deeper healing work, to give up their pride and beliefs, their sense of control and security, or sacrifice their comforts and possessions. Since most will not consider gut-wrenching foundational change until their lives fall into chaos, humanity is in the process of creating a significant global crisis in order to give ourselves enough incentive to make radical changes.

Without extreme crisis, I doubt we will be able to make the necessary shifts. This is due to our immaturity and lack of empowerment as a species. From the perspective of a healing crisis, turmoil, death, and destruction can all be seen as positive signs of imminent change. For the sake of inner peace, it's vital to release the natural desire to judge them as bad. It's all simply part of the process. We must constantly remember we are Spirit; we as eternal souls cannot possibly die.

For hundreds and even thousands of years, prophecies have come forth concerning our present time frame. Generally speaking, they say humanity succeeds in its quest, despite the hardship. I agree with Christians who believe we are in the time of the apocalypse. However, I don't usually agree with their interpretations or most of their conclusions.

Violence will inevitably be part of the coming revolution, but it will become more peaceful as it progresses. If you don't want to be around violence, choose to live in a more peaceful location or culture. Don't go to demonstrations; others can play that part. Serve change by following your inner guidance and doing what feels appropriate. Raising frequencies individually and collectively in communities will help keep violence at a distance: you will not attract that type of activity.

I don't think the global systems, man-made or environmental, will collapse. Most people tend to think in extremes, emotionally over-reacting to their fears. They believe the system will only go through minor hi-tech types of change or it will completely disintegrate. It seems to me the future will be something in between those polar extremes.

As a global revolution builds, shortages and periodic or long-term breakdowns in distribution and services will become more and more common. The internet is a sensitive digital construct that functions within the electrical grid. I believe it is extremely vulnerable to intense solar activity and powerful cosmic energies. Consider the snowball effect of change that will occur if the internet is highly compromised.

Since people will not be able to rely on the system, they will need to rely on each other and the Earth. By sharing mutually intense experiences, people will begin to have real, meaningful, and more deeply fulfilling relationships!

The transition period may be similar to life in Europe during World War II, but for a much longer time period. Some people in rural Europe barely noticed the war, while others, especially those in cities, had their lives completely dominated by it.

I am reluctant to discuss the subject of time because almost everyone is wrong when they try to predict time frames. But I've felt guided to do so anyways. I think the transition period began to intensify dramatically with our Earth's 2012 alignment with the galactic center. Climate changes are accelerating: these are symptoms of imbalance within the global body. Our planet will help force the change that wants to happen. The global power structures will also force change by compromising economic structures when they feel threatened. The system could start to unravel at any time. By the year 2040, massive change will have occurred on all levels.

People tend to respond to these types of predictions with fear; their endocrine system produces adrenaline and they go into fight or flight survival mode. I feel it's vital to address our fears on emotional, psychological, and spiritual levels before making dramatic physical realm preparations. In my opinion, it's not worth surviving if our actions are primarily driven by fear. Moving forward with an attitude of adventure and service is obviously preferable.

Once you've made sufficient inner breakthroughs concerning your survival fears, you might choose to focus outwards and create a lifestyle of sustainability. This is an inspiring way to live and it will ease the difficulties inherent in the transition period. I suggest people with land suitable for growing food look for others whom they naturally align with, in order to co-create intentional community. Those without land can engage in a similar process, and the sooner you start, the more freedom you will have in choosing where to live.

I've always found the passage from the Bible "The meek shall inherit the Earth" to be fascinating. It seems the most technologically advanced societies will suffer the most during the transition. Yet Russia does not fit into that mold. Anastasia spoke extensively about the dacha movement in Russia and the *Anastasia* books impacted many of the dachniks profoundly.

"Dachniks" is a term for the cottage-gardeners of Russia, the recipients of free land given to them by the Russian government a number of decades ago. In the year 2000, 35 million families (71% of the population) produced approximately 50% of the country's food, probably the most extensive microscale food production practice of any industrially developed nation at that time. The president who gave a parcel of land to each family must have seen extreme chaos in the future, and acted out of a sense of compassion for his people.

I believe the overview I've presented, concerning an extremely tumultuous transition, is the highest probability for our future. From my perspective, this is the future we are presently co-creating. My love-and-light friends will probably be angry with me; most of them seem to believe that by putting out these thought forms, I am actively creating them. I disagree with their assessment.

The vast majority of people constantly exude profound and mostly unconscious fear concerning the compromise and potential collapse of the system. I believe they will collectively manifest those fears, despite their positive thoughts, desires, and intentions.

Only as more people own, engage, and overcome their fears on an individual basis can we collectively avoid so much death and destruction. I am willing to hold space for a much more graceful process than the one I've just presented. That is what I do in the love-and-light ceremonies I've attended. This book was written for the same reason. As more individuals devote themselves to a path of mastery and commit to their spiritual awakening, this affects the collective and allows for a more positive transition.

Chapter 26

As an individual, claiming a positive vision for your future is an essential aspect of your healing. When you let go of the old, you will want to replace it with something new. This may include healthier foods, beliefs, and potential scenarios in which you serve something much greater than your egoic-self.

This is an integral aspect of the healing process because it can inspire you to move forward with clarity, enthusiasm, and purpose. That which serves the individual can also be applied to the collective. As a species, it's important for us to claim a positive new future for ourselves.

The future unfolds through a mosaic of possibilities and probabilities. It is highly probable people will start moving away from cities, since metropolitan areas are the most vulnerable to systemic breakdowns and the spread of disease. People who survive the transition will do so by learning to work together and protect each other. This will occur in both cities and rural areas.

People who choose to stay in cities will face unique challenges, ones I cannot begin to imagine. Dark karmic dramas will probably be all too common. It's extremely possible that city life will be the most difficult and unpleasant alternative.

Those who migrate to rural and equatorial regions will tend to create intentional communities and villages. Through cooperation and developing deep relationships of trust, some communities will thrive. They will blossom as their inspired inhabitants explore the vast possibilities of human potential.

As more people go back to the land, they will learn to grow food in a sustainable manner. Everything in the future will move towards sustainability out of common sense and necessity. Suppressed technologies will emerge and be developed in areas where there is enough infrastructure to allow their production. As societies rebuild in a sustainable manner, beneficial technologies that serve the whole will expand.

Local economies will tend to fall back towards the practicality of trading and/or localized monetary systems. Life will become simpler and people will return to cyclical time patterns dictated by the natural rhythms of the seasons, the sun and the moon. In many ways, we will live like our ancestors and yet have access to some of the best technologies from modern life.

People will eat much simpler and healthier, more raw fruits and vegetables. They will mostly stop killing animals and each other. When plants are harvested and animals eaten, it will be done with respect and gratitude for what they offer us, in a manner similar to the indigenous people of North America.

The raising of our children will occur within community and education will completely transform; it will be unrecognizable from its present form. It will be holistic and focused on how everything connects; it will also be inspiring!

Music and the arts will flourish. Music will draw people together in regular and spontaneous expressions of joy, movement, and a profound gratitude for life. Creativity will replace humanity's present obsession with money, things, and technology.

Energetic healing will become the norm, whether it occurs through people or machines. Illness will become less common as people begin to live more harmoniously. Traditional tribal values will re-emerge because they are effective, having evolved through hundreds of thousands of years of human experience.

Women will play an integral role throughout the transition period and their deeply intuitive manner of living will guide communities in new directions. Feminine values will prevail in a general backlash against past patriarchal abuses. Noisy, aggressive, yang types of machinery will be outlawed and a quiet softness will emerge in human societies. Eventually a healthy balance of yin and yang will emerge.

Communication between dimensions will become increasingly easier and more natural for people as they raise their frequencies. Psychic and telepathic communication will reach new levels of importance, serving us in innumerable ways.

Short periods of enlightenment and bliss consciousness will become more common. People's values will shift in a more spiritual direction as a natural outcome of this. Respect and integrity will arise naturally out of awareness of the Oneness of everything. Love will become more of the norm, fear and feelings of separation will gradually fall away.

Humans will learn to become more fully present for experiences, as opposed to constantly doing and serving their egoic selves. Higher creativity will serve people by showing them the Creator aspects of themselves. This will serve to heighten their Source connection.

Although some people may have trouble dropping their cynicism as they attempt to embrace such a scenario, we are already seeing these types of changes on a grassroots level. Without the power structures to hold us back, the natural evolution of our ideals will occur rapidly. The deaths of so many family and community members will give the survivors a lot of incentive to pursue radical new directions. The collective will choose to honor them by creating a positive new future for humanity.

The vast potential inherent in these types of possibilities offer us a powerful incentive to heal and stay healthy, in order to participate in this awakening. I think we will see much of the future I've just described manifest by the years 2050 – 2080.

It could be quicker since everything is accelerating so rapidly, but I doubt it because change keeps happening more slowly than I expect. It may require more than 100 years. I once read a channeling that predicted it will take 500 – 1,000 years for the golden age to fully materialize. Whatever the time frames end up being, it will inevitably require tremendous patience, persistence, and faith to co-create a higher vision for ourselves.

Chapter 27

It's highly possible the human form is an apex achievement within Creation. The seven chakras within our bodies represent archetypes that cover the spectrum from the lowest to the highest. Our lower three chakras embody the physical realm and allow us to fully engage in an animal type of existence. The upper three correspond to higher aspects of ourselves, our spiritual nature. In the middle is the heart chakra, connecting the extremes from a place of love.

The human form allows us to fully and consciously experience any and all aspects of Creator/Creation. Human beings are also designed with high creative capacity. In other words, we strongly embody the Creator itself. The human form has enormous potential; some people assert it's unlimited!

In a very real manner, humans have the essence of duality built into their chakra systems. Because of this, I've recently begun to believe our species can't help but draw challenges to itself.

Individually and collectively, we tend to attract problems and tension disputes between the light and dark. Maybe this apparent drawback balances our vast potential as a species. It certainly gives souls a perfect platform to work out karmic issues.

Shamans are often adept at a practice called "soul retrieval." This is a process of calling in, of reclaiming, lost "soul parts." Soul loss has been described as a spiritual illness that can create emotional and physical disease. Trauma in this life and others may cause the soul to splinter and lose pieces of itself, negatively impacting our life force and vitality. Shamanic practices of healing may include any number of possibilities, depending on training and the practitioner's insights into what is necessary.

In the book *Soul Integration* by Sal Rachele, he calls these parts "soul fragments." He says that although the soul is a sovereign entity, it fragments in different ways for a variety of reasons (including denial). Evidently the soul regularly fragments for reasons unrelated to trauma, such as a desire to have more experiences within the same time/space continuum.

At Heartwood, I experienced two sessions from a person practicing a technique called "alchemical hypnotherapy." It was packaged in psychological jargon, for better or worse. The objective of this work is to align the different parts of oneself so they can cooperate much more effectively. The process is as follows.

First the therapist helps the client get in touch with various personalities, while in a state of deep relaxation. Either they themselves tell us their names or they are given names. Common ones are the: inner child, warrior, saboteur, and domineering father or mother. The next step is to create a discussion, allowing them to express their grievances, frustrations, desires, and gratitude – like a family would ideally do.

When all of this was explained to me by my student therapist, I was highly skeptical of not only the process, but also my ability to connect to these phantom subdivisions of myself. Yet I proceeded to experience more or less exactly what was just described, much to my amazement.

It seems as if Sybil and my girlfriend with the multiple personalities are not such strange phenomena. We all have different aspects within our being. I believe these personalities are soul parts and fragments.

In some ways, I prefer another term that recently came to me: "soul energies." Along with it came insights concerning the reality that we may not be individualized souls at all. Rather, each of us might be a collective of soul energies. This is in alignment with and mirrors the fact that humans are a collective of trillions of cells, multiple physical systems, and various energy bodies and systems.

There is probably a primary soul energy that our ego structure is built around. It certainly makes sense to align our various soul fragments and get them on the same page. Less obvious is the possibility of attracting higher ones, such as My Shaman. The inspiring possibility is that these highly conscious soul parts can help us access much more of our human potential.

Soul energies travel on various planes of reality and some are looking for a home, especially those who are stuck in separation and desire connection. If we are in a low-vibrational energy pattern, we might attract negative entities. If we vibrate on a high level, we can attract or intentionally call-in high spirit beings. If we can keep our frequency high enough, they may choose to stay with us.

These soul energies are parts of our larger selves, ones we co-create with in other lives and dimensions. They are members of our soul-family. We become more powerful as we gain more of them. We attain self-realization more easily and serve the light more effectively as we attract higher ones.

I've come to believe the transition periods in between the three stages of my life were times when at least one new soul energy came to me and I began to integrate it into my energy field. In a very real sense, each successive stage became a new life because the core of my being had expanded and evolved.

I was able to unconsciously attract these higher soul energies through my openness, intense desire for something new, and lack of resistance to change. I believed my life could only change for the better, so my faith was rewarded accordingly.

I have seen that souls who work together in the physical realm for an inspired purpose also work together in higher dimensions to achieve their goal. The higher aspects of human beings work in teams with others in their soul families. As they organize energetics from various dimensions, pieces of the puzzle gradually come together on various levels.

If people in the 3rd dimension need to supply vital ingredients for the success of a project, they may receive an inner prompting to act. Since humans have free will, they need to choose to act on this guidance. If a person is not willing to take action, the next one might. "Divine timing" may very well be linked to, and depend upon, a practical and potentially lengthy process such as this.

Now let's look more deeply at the multidimensional nature of humans, as well as our planet Gaia. Shamans say our waking life is only one of our many ongoing dreams. At night we regularly access our other lives in other dimensions and parallel realities. This occurs on an unconscious level for most of us, most of the time.

However, human beings have the potential to consciously connect with any life in any dimension within and beyond time and space. So what do these other dimensions look like anyways? I have a theory: we are constantly being told and shown. The other dimensions, especially the astral realm, are like science fiction and fantasy novels and movies – plus anything else you can imagine.

Telepathy seems to be the universal form of communication within Creation. From my personal experiences, I receive messages as thought forms and concepts. My brain is able to translate these into the English language if needed, in order to better understand or remember the message. I also receive images that I pick up with my third eye. Once again, my brain may or may not choose to decipher an image in more detail by grabbing on to it.

I first began to be aware of these communications in my twenties while spending time alone in nature. Since it was such a gradual process, I didn't realize it was happening, especially because we've all been conditioned to believe our thoughts always originate in our own brains.

Over the years, I've received messages from trees, animals, our Earth, sun, moon, and spirit beings both seen and unseen. Yet it was through the guidance I experienced while giving healing sessions that telepathy became a regular occurrence in my life. This was also the manner in which telepathy became more valid and real for me, because I knew beyond a shadow of a doubt this guidance was not originating in my own mind. The clarity and wisdom went way beyond my ego and training.

Artists and highly sensitive people receive telepathic communications much more easily than the general population. I believe people who create science fiction and fantasy often receive their ideas and images from other dimensions. This is how much of the book you are reading came to me, through thought forms and visuals. Communications might come from one's soul parts, higher self, or less connected spirits and soul energies. These could be devas, ghosts, extraterrestrials, and much more.

Mother Gaia is a multidimensional being who is, I have little doubt, fully enlightened. What she contains within her energy field on an interdimensional level must be astounding! Shambala, the fabled city of higher consciousness, must exist in the Himalayas on another dimension.

I once heard about a high-vibrational human civilization living inside a mountain near Santa Fe, New Mexico. In the Romanian book mentioned in Chapter 22, the protagonist met with an advanced human civilization deep inside our planet. Stories such as these are not uncommon in Western cultures. Rock and molten lava are different in other dimensions or they don't exist.

A friend of mine, who was raised locally, told me about a pyramid of gold inside Taos Mountain, which is sacred to the Taos Pueblo native people and still on their land. Many years later, another person said she had met someone who was mapping mineral deposits from an airplane using cutting edge technology. The largest concentration of gold they were able to find in the United States is below that exact same mountain!

There must be a Galactic Federation. It's highly doubtful they are third dimensional, due to their higher consciousness and the difficulty of long-distance space travel in the physical realm. The concepts of warping time and space or traveling through worm holes are certainly interdimensional in nature.

All extraterrestrials who visit our planet probably have the ability to shift between dimensions. That is how UFOs are able to disappear in an instant, something many people have seen. Their interdimensional capabilities require advanced technology or a higher consciousness.

I know a Cherokee medicine woman in Taos, Nancy Red Star, who wrote a book called *Star Ancestors*. She interviewed elders from tribes all over North America, ones who were old enough to have heard some of the stories passed down over many generations. They consistently said humanity comes from the stars.

Over the years, the most common star systems mentioned in this manner have been the Pleiades, Orion, Sirius, Arcturus, and Andromeda. If there is a Galactic Federation, they are deeply involved in humanity's process here on Earth. Because of karmic implications, they are reluctant to intervene further without being invited. The more we ask for help, and open to receive it, the more they will assist us.

I'm convinced our Sun and Earth are in full support of humanity's efforts. There are reasons the ancients often thought of them as our father and mother. In the past few years, I've experimented with "sun gazing" and feel it may be extremely important. One Hindu mystic spent many years researching this topic. He says that by following his regimen, we can go without food and will never get sick. You can find his website at: www.solarhealing.com

We call our Earth "Gaia" and she is also known as "Sophia." Mother Gaia can assist us in many ways. When I am struggling with disharmonious energies, I often place my hands on the bare ground and ask her to receive and transform the darkness. She has a virtually unlimited capacity to serve us in this manner.

Once when I was in fear concerning the future, I received a crystal-clear thought form from Gaia; she communicated that she would carry me through the coming turmoil if I physically connect with and trust her. My cats and other animals understand this much better than humans – they are constantly rolling around in the dirt! Several years ago, I heard a wise being give a beautiful answer when asked what we can do for our Earth: "Just love her; all she needs from you is for you to express your love to her."

Our transformation as a species is the Holy Grail we seek. It's impossible to know how it will appear, if and when it occurs. People within the New Age community tend to believe humanity will shift to a higher dimension along with our planet Gaia. However, this possibility tends to discount our multidimensional nature, since we already exist in higher dimensions.

I have another theory. Each of us will continue to attract experiences that are in alignment with our personal energy field. People who believe in the system and don't feel they can live without it, will die along with it.

Those who vibrate high enough and desire to leave their physical body may rise to a higher dimension, possibly joining advanced civilizations of human beings and/or light-beings who already exist within and around our planet. They will probably retain their ego structures, as well as their emotional bodies. Others will ascend, with or without a physical and emotional body, to even higher dimensions.

There will also be another option and it's the one I'm signing up for. We stay in our physical bodies and gain much easier access to our multidimensional selves. This option allows us to realize the full potential of our human design.

Chapter 28

We are all actors in an incredible drama being played out on planet Earth. Each of us has the ability to choose our part in this dramatic movie we find ourselves engaged in. You can choose to be a major actor or hide in the shadows and play a minor role. You can choose to transmute darkness into light or passively follow the lead of dark power structures who only have their own best interests in mind. You can live in fear or pursue courageous new directions.

The more I view life in this manner, the more excited I am to be here in these most challenging of times. It is virtually impossible to imagine a more interesting movie than the one occurring on our planet. No one knows exactly how this will play out, since it's a moment-by-moment multidimensional co-creation of innumerable forces. I wish to acknowledge Creator for its courage in allowing wild and crazy experiments such as this. I used to be angry at such audacity, but now I'm in awe.

I believe life is meant to be lived fully. We are meant to take chances, to experience the highs and lows. The intense emotions associated with an experience such as falling in love and losing it are vital aspects of the dance of life. Experiencing other cultures, other dimensions, new ideas and realities is what makes life fascinating and eternally fresh.

I believe humanity is on Earth to experience extremes, to get thrown off balance, to always endeavor to return to center, to enjoy our experiences as much as possible, and to always remember our Oneness with all that is. Let us embrace the extremes of our times and the incredible challenges we face individually and collectively. Let's see if we can find inner peace and joy, despite the chaos, by breaking through all pain and fear.

By embracing the dark as well as the light, we can ultimately reunite them. By choosing compassion over judgment, we will see the healing we desire in our world. By taking a stand for our highest ideals, we will be able to realize them!

Epilogue

Writing this book has been an incredible experience, and it was also extremely challenging. In fact, writing and self-publishing it ended up being the most challenging thing I've ever done. I followed inner guidance the entire time and at some point it became obvious that My Shaman and those who assist me in sessions were intimately involved. In reality, it is their book and I simply played my part in its amazing co-creation.

The telepathic and other abilities I've opened to over the years were often gifts from Spirit: they arose as I healed and purified my intentions. The frequency of our planet (Schumann resonance) has been rising for a number of years and the scientist Gregg Braden has written and spoken extensively about this. People within the New Age community believe the rising frequencies will enable our multidimensional gifts to come forth on a large scale.

Please resist the temptation to put me or anyone else on a pedestal; instead stay focused on opening to your own abilities. I believe they will naturally arise for you, as they did for me, if you are committed to your healing and in service to life on Mother Earth.

Towards the end of 2017, David Icke's recent book, *Phantom Self (And How to Find the Real One)*, spontaneously appeared in my life. Although I had never read any of his books, I knew he was British, extremely controversial, and claimed to have evidence of a sentient reptilian race involved with the global power structures. When I read the first chapter of his book, I was surprised at how similar it was to what I've been writing. Then I skipped to Chapter 4 to see what he had to say about the reptilians.

I first heard about these reptiles in 1992 in the *Bringers of the Dawn* book. The Pleiadians, such as those who channel through Barbara Marciniak, have similar DNA to Earth humans. They also have a wonderful sense of humor and refer to the reptilians as "lizzies." Humor seems to be an essential ingredient to staying sane in the realities we are dealing with.

Epilogue

We've been hearing rumors for years that the U.S. government, as well as others, have been interacting and cooperating with at least two extraterrestrial races. The phenomenal technological revolution we've been experiencing is evidently one result of those interactions.

Marciniak's Pleiadians claim that the reptilians are not only technologically advanced, they have also been manipulating human affairs on our planet for hundreds of thousands, if not millions of years. Another source said these reptilians feed off human fear, anger, and other low-vibrational energies. Long ago they altered our genetics in a manner that ensures a regular food supply.

I've never knowingly seen an ET and can't personally vouch for their existence, yet I've believed for many years they exist. The plethora of abduction stories, cattle mutilations, crop circles, and UFO sightings were more than enough evidence. By the way, I don't seek out information about aliens or the families of power. It just comes to me, similar to yogic masters and psychedelics. I don't take any of them lightly; they are all powerful forms of medicine.

I didn't need to read beyond Chapter 4 in David Icke's book because it contained the information I needed. Similar to myself, Icke has been committed to understanding what is happening on our planet. He obsesses a lot on the dark side, but that was his mission in life and he deserves our respect. Through extensive research, he discovered that many ancient cultures revered and often worshiped reptilian "gods."

To put this phenomenon into context, there is a reptilian component to all humans. The "reptilian brain" is at the core of the human brain and it runs some of our most basic behaviors. Quoting David Icke: *"Mainstream science says the reptilian part of our brains is responsible for the following behaviour traits: cold-blooded behaviour and 'territoriality' - this is mine; a desire to control; an obsession with hierarchical structures of power, reputation, superiority, intellectual pre-eminence and can also lead to acquiescence to hierarchy and authority."*

Furthermore, in the early stages of fetal development, the human embryo goes through a "reptilian phase." The reality is that "reptilian genes" are foundational building blocks of human DNA.

All mammals have genetics strongly associated with reptiles; it's how we were designed.

David Icke says that the global families of power have a higher percentage of reptilian genes in their DNA than normal humans. The reptilians, who mostly exist in another dimension, infused certain individuals – think GMO – with some of their genes several thousand years ago. These hybrids then migrated from the region of Babylon to other continents, always being careful to practice inbreeding with their own kind in order to ensure minimal dilution of their DNA. They eventually became the pharaohs of Egypt, emperors of Rome and China, royalty of Europe, and rulers of various other civilizations.

Twenty years ago, I heard about experiments in an underground base; it may have been Area 51 in Nevada. A person who had worked at the base went public. Apparently, there were wild genetic experiments taking place on the lowest two floors – creatures being created by mixing human genes with those of other species. At the time, I had no idea what to think about those claims.

At this point, it appears to me that the Centaurs of Greek "mythology" were real. The many "gods" of Egyptian mythology, such as Horus and others with human bodies and animal heads, also existed in physical bodies. The Hindu god Ganesha, with its elephant head, human body and multiple arms is another example. Apparently, the reptilians have been doing this type of DNA gene splicing for a long time.

I finally have a context in which to place the story my girlfriend from Bermuda told me in 1989. She was the person whom I left in Mexico when she was sick because I felt trapped and thought she was ruining my trip. Maybe the real reason I left was – she was freaking me out. She told me the most outrageous things, stuff that sounded like pure fantasy.

Most of us seem to have selective memories and I must have blocked out a lot because I can't remember most of what she said. Yet I was certainly listening at the time; I constantly asked her questions to see if I could trip her up. I distinctly remember never being able to prove she was lying because her stories were consistent and held together. One of them was of her having gills (similar to fish) when she was a child, which receded and went away as she matured. Was someone in her ancestral lineage a result of genetic experiments? She often had a vacant look to her, as if no one was home.

It is clear that things are not what they seem to be on the surface, here on planet Earth. It's clear the power structures constantly mislead and lie to us. It appears as if Monsanto is only the tip of the iceberg concerning the GMO reality. It seems to me, whatever is going on behind the scenes must be incredible because the situation we find ourselves in is so extreme – to the degree that some of us have regularly questioned humanity's sanity.

Whatever the reality may be, the fact remains: humanity is in a terrible mess, one we are co-creating with whomever and whatever. We can only remedy this through massive change on all levels, no matter who the culprit is or what their DNA looks like.

I can't help but laugh at the cosmic perfection concerning the lizzies. The reptilian traits represent the lower aspects of humanity and correspond to the third chakra. Humanity is so judgmental of our animal nature and the shadow side of ourselves, so reluctant to look at and heal the darkness within – we've collectively attracted what we resist and deny – in the form of bestial power structures that seek to control and dominate us.

The most positive aspect of this dynamic is that we are being forced to perfect ourselves as a species. The dark side serves Creation most effectively in this manner. It acts as a constant irritant, prodding soul energies and their various manifestations towards the comfort of higher dimensions and Oneness. A spiritual teacher once said that the dark side constantly forces us to hone the edge of our metaphorical sword.

David Icke gets a significant piece of his information from the Nag Hammadi codices. John Lamb Lash spent decades studying and interpreting these old Gnostic texts, which were buried in approximately 400 AD. The *Sophia Mythos* they contain has been systematically repressed for 1,600 years; he calls it the original story of our species. When I first heard Lisa Harrison's interview of John

Lash in Ecuador, the tears came to my eyes and wouldn't stop because I felt the truth of this story in my heart and throughout my entire being.

Sophia was one of the creator beings who reside at the center of the Milky Way. They design and create virtually everything in our galaxy. The Gnostics called them "Aeons" and the Pleiadians refer to them as "Creator Gods." Sophia and her Aeonic partner, Christos, designed the human species genome. They designed humanity with a variety of extreme traits.

The Aeons love creating living experiments; then they watch to see what happens. But Sophia became emotionally invested in our species and eventually realized what humanity needed in order to succeed. In an act of great love, she left the galactic center and physically manifested as our planet. She embodied herself, possibly unintentionally, in order to support our success.

However, her action created a karmic reaction, which took form as the "Archons." They are the opposite of Sophia's love and their agenda is the opposite of her desire to nurture our success – they actively promote our failure. The Archons are at the core of the global power structures!

Archons are an interdimensional force/energetic. They can manifest in a variety of physical forms, including Reptilian and Grey extraterrestrials. Gnostics described them as "messengers of deception," as well as the rulers and controllers. They have very little, if any, creative potential and abilities. From my understanding, the Archons also lack an emotional body; because of these deficiencies they are envious of humanity.

It appears the satanic cults worship their leader, the "Lord Archon," who is also called the "Demiurge." They worship him as the Christian God of the Bible because that is evidently who he claims to be. John Lash says the Gnostics describe him in the Nag Hammadi material as having a lion-like body and a reptilian type of head. Although androgynous, he strongly displays a masculine and macho attitude and posture.

From what he has pieced together, Lash believes the fates of humanity and Gaia-Sophia are deeply intertwined and humans are connected to her memory in a vitally important manner. It seems that as we remember our Divinity, Sophia is liberated along with us. It appears she can also lose herself in the physical realm and forget she is a Galactic Goddess.

John Lash believes our Earth is the tenth planet where humans have manifested in our galaxy. The other nine, who manifested in various star systems, all self-destructed. Frank, the founder of Pina Palmera, told me in 1987 that our present civilization is the seventh – the other six failed. I'm fairly certain the ones he was referring to were Atlantis and others even earlier in our planet's history. Frank said our present civilization is the one destined to finally succeed, yet present circumstances tend to point, once again, towards self-destruction.

I venture to say the human species has a propensity towards this type of behavior. According to Lash, our species has not been able to handle its extreme and vast potential. Wouldn't it be incredible to play a significant role in humanity finally succeeding?

The information presented by David Icke and John Lash is the stuff of science fiction and fantasy, but they appear to have done extensive scholarly research on these subjects. As you can see, I have personally come across similar information from various sources over the past thirty years. I am initially skeptical when I come across information such as this, but I also keep an open mind. After hearing something more than once or twice, I accept it as highly probable if I respect the sources. It then becomes a part of my reality system.

Over time, I feel and process all of the emotions that are triggered by difficult information. I suggest you do the same, although admittedly it's not easy. Here are some helpful tips. Honor all of yourself, your four bodies. Regularly engage in some type of physical activity to help process your emotional reactions. If necessary, do more research in order to satisfy your mind. Since the internet is more controlled and biased than most people want to believe, pursue a variety of sources. Possibly most important of all, especially when you are struggling, view everything from a more transcendent perspective – connect to your higher self.

No matter what the story is concerning our predicament, the solution is the same. More of us will commit to self-mastery and master this life experience. Many will begin by facing their fears and starting to heal. As darkness shows up within and without, we transform it into higher vibrational realities. If for no other reason, we do this because the high ones feel so much better than those that are low.

Since we find ourselves in a human body in this extreme duality reality, let's choose to honor Creator/Creation by embracing the experience. Commit to nurturing as much joy and inner peace as possible in these very unique times. When that isn't working and you are in a negative space, call on your allies for assistance. Always remember to practice Oneness. Finally, we can transform darkness and/or we can choose to surrender. Nurturing a sense of trust in this entire process is essential to one's state of well-being. I'll finish with a quote by Ammachi: "Real faith is the faith in one's own Self."

Special Features

These extra pieces are all connected to South America. I was deeply moved by the "Eagle and the Condor Prophecy" when I first heard about it. While on my trip, I was inspired by the possibility of helping to serve its full manifestation.

Sort of a Shaman

Special Features

Traveling in Latin America

I encourage everyone to travel in Latin America. I have always been strongly attracted to indigenous people, even if their cultures only impact the local regions indirectly and in a diluted manner.

Traditional indigenous cultures are most prevalent in southern Mexico, Guatemala, Peru, and Bolivia. These regions are the least developed and most third world. Although indigenous communities and values are under assault, they continue to persevere and are strongest and most intact in South America. And although it requires imagination and effort to find the most traditional people, it is so incredibly worth the effort. In general, all Latin cultures are more relaxed and humane on core levels than Western countries and cultures. They feel better to most sensitive people!

In South America, the system is minimally invasive of people's personal space. It feels freer and less regulated. People are building all types of interesting and inexpensive homes, since most regions are warm year around. It's easier to create intentional communities because building codes and zoning restrictions are more relaxed or even nonexistent in rural areas. There are less digital and frequency control technologies messing with one's mind and energy field. I never saw any chemtrails in South America and very few, if any, in Central America. Their absence is significant and enough of a reason for some people to consider living there.

Although I prefer South to Central America, it is rougher and the types of people creating intentional communities in S. America are pioneers. I went on two more trips to S. America after the one I wrote about in Intermission #2. On the second trip, I spent six weeks in northern Columbia before going north by boat into Panama, where I spent two more weeks. Then I lived in Costa Rica for four months and spent a majority of the time in three intentional communities. They were extremely inspiring and more spiritually based than the ones I've experienced in South America. For various reasons, Costa Rica is drawing a different quality of people. The Covid pandemic began while I was living at the second community. I eventually invested in the third one and plan on living there part time in the near future. Their website is: www.purafruta.org

Connecting with international travelers from any country is a joy for me. In so many ways, I've always deeply identified with them. During my most recent trips, they treated me as an equal even though I was 25 – 35 years older than most of them.

I've met numerous South Americans traveling outside their countries of origin over the years. Ever since I started meeting them in Central America in the 1980s, they've always felt different than Americans and Europeans. They often express a quality of being and appearance I find to be unusual and fascinating. These qualities are so subtle and unique, I am unable to be more specific.

Fears of robberies and violence in Latin America are valid, so I act accordingly. Since the largest cities, harbor areas/cities, and the main tourist locations attract problems, I avoid them as much as possible. I rely on my intuition and challenge myself to stay present and aware. I don't hang out in bars and nightclubs. When I do venture out in the evenings, I usually go with other backpack travelers or stay around the central plaza where it is safest. A simple rule of thumb in Latin America is: if there are women and children on the streets, you can relax. Small towns, villages, and rural areas are usually safe and friendly.

The police seem trustworthy, at least that is my experience in the types of places I prefer. I virtually never heard emergency vehicle sirens in South America, although I occasionally saw them with their lights flashing. The sirens in the United States are twenty decibels above the level that causes damage to our ears. They are stressful, extremely disharmonious, and definitely affect our energy fields in a negative manner. They are also part of the crisis mentality conditioning sold to the American public.

For those who wish to travel in Latin America, I feel guided to offer assistance in choosing what to carry in your backpack – as well as a few other tips.

A List of What to Pack

1. Money belt
2. Small day pack
3. Sleeping bag
4. Bed sheet
5. Backpacking mattress
6. Plastic ground cover
7. 2-3 sets of clothes
8. Long-sleeve shirt and a sweatshirt
9. Swimsuit and short pants
10. Raingear
11. Sun hat that folds up and a warm cap
12. Light boots and sandals
13. Health products and/or medicines
14. Personal care products (toothbrush, etc.)
15. Insect repellent
16. Flashlight
17. Phone and/or laptop
18. Several pens and a small writing pad
19. Rubber bands and tape
20. Padlock (for lockers in hostel dorm rooms)

I recommend using an older backpack since new ones draw more attention; you don't want it stolen. Bringing a separate day pack allows you to put your most valuable items inside. With buses and vans, your large backpack is usually stowed outside, but you can keep your day pack with you.

I use a money belt that wraps around my waist against my skin. I keep my passport, credit card, and the majority of my money in it. I have a wallet in my pocket for day-to-day monetary needs. At night, I sleep with my money belt on my waist or in bed with me if

I'm in a dorm room. I am more careful with it than most backpack travelers; having it stolen would be very problematic.

There is always a shortage of small monetary notes in rural areas and small towns, so hold on to them whenever possible. Banks, hotels, large stores, and bus stations are the best places to spend large bills or exchange them for small ones.

Bringing a sleeping bag allows you to be flexible. I also like to have a sheet for areas where the sleeping bag is much too hot, especially early in the evening. I will lie on top of my sleeping bag and cover myself with the sheet. As it cools down at night, I begin to go inside my sleeping bag.

Although I've brought a tent on trips, I suggest leaving it behind if you are alone. In general, I don't use it often enough. On the other hand, if there are two or more people traveling together to share the weight, it's great to have a tent for keeping the rain, mosquitoes, and biting flies at bay. It also allows for maximum flexibility, especially if you want to go backpacking in the mountains. In mountaineering towns, it is often possible to rent tents, heavy boots, and thick sleeping bags.

Packing minimal clothes keeps your backpack light. You need to wash more often, but many hostels have an area to wash and hang clothes to dry. When it's very cold, I wear my raingear for extra warmth. You can always buy a sweater if that is not enough. I often wear a light pair of pants and long sleeve shirt to protect myself from mosquitoes and biting flies, which are abundant in the jungle and some beach areas. The flies can be especially vicious and their welts can last for up to two weeks, depending on the species.

I took some health and herbal products with me. I never carry a first aid kit while traveling or backpacking and never seem to need one. As a compromise, I suggest taking homeopathic arnica (pills and a multi-herbal cream), and tea tree oil (to soothe bug bites and as an antibiotic for infections).

If you have the time and freedom to travel extensively in South America, I highly recommend buying a one-way ticket to Bogota and traveling south with total flexibility as to when and where you will return. Bogota is not a safe city, but the area where most of the hostels are located is fine. Tickets to Bogota are usually cheaper than those to any other city in S. America. Colombian customs officials don't seem to care if you only have a one-way flight into their country; Ecuador and Peru are similarly lax concerning one-way flights.

I spent $11/day on the trip I wrote about in Intermission #2. On the following trip, I lived at an intentional community in northern Chile for two weeks and traveled around southern Peru for over three months, spending an average of only $9 per day. I traveled with the smallest backpack ever and loved traveling lighter. In stark contrast to my previous trip, I never heard anyone talk about people being robbed in Peru.

Amazon Herb Company

The story of Amazon Herb and its founder is remarkable.

In September of 2000, I joined the *Amazon Herb Company*. A year later, I went on an all-expense paid trip to Peru with John Easterling and a group of *Amazon Herb* distributors. It was only the second time John had taken key distributors and employees to the rainforest to meet the Shipibo people who harvested the plants from which our products were made.

The story of the company starts with John having a near-death experience in a hospital in North Carolina. The combination of Rocky-Mountain-Spotted-Fever and hepatitis nearly killed him and afterwards left him in a state of chronic fatigue. Nonetheless, he began traveling to South America, inspired by the lost cities of gold mentioned in the books of his youth. He was convinced there were still treasures in the Andes and Amazon rainforest. John would buy precious stones, pre-Colombian artifacts, pottery, clothes and almost anything he could resell in the States to fund his next trip to South America, approximately 200 in total.

Ten years after his NDE, he became very sick while visiting an indigenous village in the rainforest. They gave him a combination of medicinal herbs, and after ten days, he was the healthiest he had been at any time since his illness. In fact, John said he felt more alive than ever before in his entire life. Soon after, he met Nicole Maxwell, a professional dancer and self-made ethnobotanist who had spent decades studying herbs with native herbalists and shamans in the rainforest. Before she died in 1998, Nicole left him volumes of notes on Amazonian herbs. Her book, "Witch Doctor's Apprentice," is fascinating.

John finally realized the treasure he had been seeking was the rainforest itself. He founded the *Amazon Herb Company* and began working with several holistic health practitioners to develop formulas based on indigenous wisdom dating back millennia. The company originally sold its products direct to health practitioners. Eventually so many clients wanted to bypass their practitioners, the company decided to sell direct to the public through the network marketing business model.

On the other end, John worked out agreements in Peru with about ten communities who harvested the herbs on their own lands in a traditional and sustainable manner. John was once asked if he was paying the Shipibo a fair price for the herbs. His reply was simple and straightforward. He said that after speaking with community leaders, they agreed on prices everyone was happy with. Then he asked us if this seemed like a fair price. If the entire global economy were to move in the direction of this type of win-win philosophy, things would be much different.

John further empowered the tribes by helping them obtain titles to their ancestral lands. He worked with several lawyers in Lima to accomplish this. After one of the tribes gained legal rights to their lands, a company started logging on their property. When the tribe confronted them, the loggers refused to go. So the native people got their bows and arrows and ordered them to leave. The loggers left their equipment and went to the authorities to complain. The case went to court and the tribe won.

Along with paying the communities for dried herbs, the *Amazon Herb Company* gave them water filtration systems, radio equipment, machetes, rubber boots, etc. When we visited several of their communities during our company trip in 2001, it was obvious the Shipibo loved and trusted John. By then he was called "Amazon John" by almost everyone. The indigenous people gave us an exceedingly warm welcome; their villages were as primitive as any I've experienced in my many years of travel in Latin America.

The *Amazon Herb Company* grew steadily up until the real estate crash in the States, at which point the economy started going downhill and so did our company. Nevertheless, we reveled in our confidence and determination to preserve the Amazon with our progressive business model. If destruction of the rainforest were to stop, its medicinal and nutritional plants could be sustainably harvested indefinitely for all of humanity. The Amazon rainforest is the most impressive ecosystem on our planet. It boasts an incredibly high level of plant and animal biodiversity, staggering quantities of fresh water, and significant amounts of oxygen production.

Our yearly *Amazon Herb* conventions up through 2009 were amazing and inspiring. At the breaks, the company served us large amounts of tinctures, herbal capsules, teas, powders, and our marvelous marble sized chocolate power balls. Some of us consumed so much "herbage" we were practically flying, especially since the products vibrate at such a high level.

In 2008, John Easterling married Olivia Newton John, the famous actress-singer from Australia. Despite the fact they were both in their late fifties at the time of their marriage, they were a very attractive couple. John looked like Harrison Ford in his Indiana Jones movies, especially when he wore a similar looking hat. Olivia had her eternally girlish good looks and appeared twenty years younger than her age.

At one of our conventions, Olivia told us the story of the first time John saw her in the movie *Grease*. This was the movie that skyrocketed her and John Travolta to international fame. Having spent so much time in South America, John had not seen it at the time of their marriage. Olivia Newton John told this to John Travolta, who then invited her and John Easterling to see the movie on his private jet.

Around the year 2012, Amazon John finally gave in and merged with a much larger company named Trivita. We had not been able to right the floundering ship of our gradually declining situation. It's only now that I understand what must have happened. After the real estate crash and the corporate banking bailouts, I believe the American public lost a lot of faith in the system, resulting in both anger and depression. *Amazon Herb* was the most idealistic company I've ever experienced and it had grown on optimism. It simply wasn't able to recover and neither did a lot of people in the United States. Trivita still distributes their formulas and John continues to be involved.

Ayahuasca Journeys in Colombia

This is the full story of my ayahuasca experiences in Mocoa. The account begins in San Agustin.

The cook who told me about Taita Lucho was a Colombian man named Gustavo. I spent five days getting to know and like him. He was a long-haired, lovable character who had depth beneath his happy-go-lucky facade. Gustavo would chide me about working too much and say I needed to relax more. After telling him I was writing a book and his hostel was a perfect place to write, he wanted to know its name. I told him, to which he responded: "I know of a good taita in Mocoa who I've worked with one on one. He doesn't do what he does for money." This immediately piqued my interest because I knew many ayahuasceros only held ceremonies with larger groups and were definitely into the monetary aspect of the business.

Jay and I had just spoken the previous day about taking ayahuasca. With this plant medicine, I knew it was best if events unfolded in an obvious and effortless manner. In contrast, while traveling in Peru several months later, I met three travelers who signed up for a ten-day ayahuasca retreat through the internet and it did not go well.

Gustavo didn't have Mercedes' phone number, so he drew a map. He said we could just show up at Taita Lucho's and he was right, although we did catch them off guard. Mercedes even got a bit impatient with me because my Spanish was still extremely rusty, having barely spoken in over five years.

As she began to tell me the details, Jay kept asking for translations. Only half present, I was still tuning into the situation – were we really supposed to be there? Mercedes shifted gears and fed us, everything slowed down, and Taita Lucho came over to talk with us. When we met the men preparing and brewing the ayahuasca, the rightness of it all suddenly became self-evident.

Lucho took us on a half-hour walk the next morning, from his home to a large waterfall. We were definitely in the jungle, albeit on the edge of the Amazon. Jay and I proceeded to swim in the cool water while Taita Lucho watched silently.

In the evening, Mercedes joined us for the opening ceremony, but not with the ayahuasca. A young Colombian, who appeared to be studying with Lucho, did join us. We drank one small bowl each of the molasses-sweetened, rather strong but relatively pleasant tasting substance. We drummed and chanted and then the young man and Lucho played guitars and sang.

In less than an hour, I started feeling the psychedelic. I threw up a half-hour later despite not feeling nauseous until the previous moment. As with peyote, most people go through a cleansing process. Ideally a person eats fruit or fasts for days to weeks beforehand. This helps a person avoid getting sick and also enables a deeper more powerful experience. I was not able to cleanse myself in this manner and neither are most people. Therefore, the ayahuasca does it for us.

It was relatively cold that night, so Jay snuggled up in his sleeping bag. I walked around under the stars and eventually asked the taita if we could drink another bowl since I still wasn't feeling very much. As I waited for the second serving to kick in, I started to get cold and this coerced me into my sleeping bag as well. Maybe an hour later, I awoke from a deep sleep. I immediately realized the ayahuasca had arrived because I was seeing patterns moving around on the backs of my eyelids. I opened my eyes and looked around as the designs faded.

Sensing another vomiting episode, I quickly put on my t-shirt and stumbled out of the maloka (a circular ceremonial structure). Afterwards, Mercedes walked up in her warm Andean cap. She was glowing and so was everything else. She looked incredibly indigenous, like another person from another life. She just stood there smiling at me. I mumbled some words in Spanish trying to tell her I was all right, but I was a bit overwhelmed by the experience of suddenly waking up in this altered reality.

The plants around me were exuding an incredible amount of energy; they shined a bright phosphorescent green. As I continued to look at the glowing plants with total fascination, the young Colombian came and helped me to my feet. Since I was starting to shiver, he guided me to my sleeping bag. I quickly warmed up and immediately went outside, but the plants had lost their vibrant glow.

I wandered around the property and ended up at the huge pots of brewing ayahuasca. I was sitting there alone wondering what had happened to my magical experience when the young man walked up. He told me Taita Lucho had gone to sleep, having been extremely busy the previous week.

We began to speak about ayahuasca, which he used for his spiritual path. He warned me to be careful on my journey to Peru if I planned on using it there because some ayahuasceros were mixing the wrong types of plants and sometimes taking advantage of the high foreigners. It was at this low point in the conversation that I had to vomit again. Since it was cold and the magic was over, I went back to my sleeping bag and fell asleep.

The following morning, Jay told me that he had experienced all sorts of altered dimensional realities and wasn't very aware of the physical most of the time. He never felt sick, nor did he vomit. Jay is a vegan and had been eating a very clean diet, mostly raw foods.

After Mercedes made us breakfast, she tied bracelets on our wrists, we paid our modest fees and said our goodbyes. I told her of my intention to return since I had only experienced a taste of what ayahuasca offered and it was positive.

When I returned, I stayed at the Huaca Huaca hostel. I had met Janneth, the attractive 40-year-old owner, on my first visit to the area. Her extended family owns all of the land in and around Fin del Mundo, a beautiful, magical spot in the jungle with a number of waterfalls and large pools in which to swim and play.

At the hostel, we cooked our food on a wood fire and went to bed early since there was no electricity. It had simple, decorative rooms, good mattresses, and cold showers, plus colorful birds and miko monkeys in the neighboring trees. It was the perfect place to rest and wait for Taita Lucho and Mercedes to return from their trip. I was the only guest for the first few days, until two 25-year-old Colombians arrived. Javier was from Medellin and Santiago from Bogota. Similar to myself, they had also come to Mocoa for the waterfalls and ayahuasca.

They had never taken ayahuasca, but Javier had an intense desire to "heal his soul." He had been living in Los Angeles, California for the previous four years. He went there to study diplomacy, yet realized he wanted to follow his heart and was instead making music in his own studio.

Javier didn't warm to me at first and started asking pointed questions. He asked me about Taita Lucho's ceremonies and mystical powers. I didn't offer very good answers, nor did he like them. When Santiago told him to back off, Javier said my Spanish was terrible and I was no better. Since Javier had said he needed help with his soul, I wasn't surprised by his behavior.

Several minutes later, I realized I needed to tell them something. I went to their door and said that power is overrated; rather purity of heart and intention are most important. It is vital for the taita to be trustworthy and hold a clear space for the ayahuasca, since the plants do most of the work.

The next morning, they told me that they were interested in a taita in Sebondoy, a town in the mountains nearly three hours west of Mocoa. They wanted to do two ayahuasca ceremonies over the next three days. I told them I had gone through Sebondoy on my way to Mocoa several days earlier. I didn't tell them the rocky dirt road they needed to travel was long, windy, and a bit extreme. Before they left, I gave Santiago the cell number for Mercedes.

They left for Sebondoy early in the afternoon and were back the afternoon of the following day. The first thing Javier half-jokingly said to me was that I was a "mean person." They had taken a colectivo to the town as planned, but it was raining and the unpaved road was treacherous, much worse than the dry one I had traveled. The narrow mountain road had large roaring streams crossing it, in place of the small ones I had experienced.

On the way back, they spotted a truck that had gone over the edge, probably killing its occupants. I finally understood why that road had several hundred white crosses along its banks, each one signifying the death of a loved one. I couldn't help but laugh as Javier and Santiago related how frightened they had been for much of the trip. It appeared as if a significant aspect of their journey was about deeply feeling their fears.

Santiago had experienced a wonderful ayahuasca journey in Sebondoy, but Javier had not felt much of anything. Not wanting to give up, he was pro-active and had spoken with Mercedes. There would be a ceremony the following evening and the three of us decided to go together.

There were eight people who participated: five Europeans, my two Colombian friends, and myself. We started around 10 pm and several hours later I drank a second cup. I vomited one to two hours after each serving, more than long enough to get the ayahuasca into my system. Compared to the first time four months earlier, my experience was even less eventful and I couldn't help but feel disappointed. I fell asleep around 3 or 4 am and only slept for a few hours.

Upon awakening, I discovered an extremely excited Javier. He had experienced the healing he had hoped for – and even more. He was extremely grateful and completely filled with joy, all the while thanking me profusely. Lucho brought us all together, offered some words of wisdom, and then asked if anyone wanted to share their experience. Javier was the first to speak and I was the last. They left soon after breakfast since Javier needed to fly back to Los Angeles, but everyone else stayed for the coming evening's ceremony.

Starting late in the afternoon, Mercedes led the group in constructing a large, colorful, and incredibly beautiful mandala in the center of the maloka to honor the spring equinox. Thirteen Colombians and eight Europeans joined me in the ceremony that evening. I found the presence of the Colombians to be most interesting. Some were alternative, but the majority seemed relatively conventional and consisted of a wide range of ages. This was a strong sign of how deeply the people in the Mocoa area have opened to this traditional plant medicine.

At around 5 am, I finally knew the ayahuasca was helping to heal my heart on a level so deep, I could hardly tell anything was happening. Up until then, it seemed as if it wasn't meant to be part of my spiritual journey. Like so many people who questioned the effectiveness of the Amazonian herbs I had distributed, I desired obvious quantifiable results such as visual effects, strong emotional reactions, profoundly deep mental understandings and beautiful heart openings. Those were the types of experiences other people were having and I had expected.

Instead, I got deep subtle help from the Spirit realms in the area I desired and needed it most, that of feeling my Source connection. This realization was strongly validated by the incredible ease and grace with which the rest of the day unfolded after leaving the taita's place.

Ayahuasca is an herbal mixture and Lucho's recipe utilizes male and female vines. Since herbs work in cooperation with our bodies, it can take time for them to have the desired effect. When taking plants as medicine, people tend to desire rapid results since that's what they often experience with pharmaceutical drugs. The reality is that it might take weeks or months to obtain the desired outcome. Herbs work on such deep systemic and holistic levels, it simply takes time for our bodies to respond and make adjustments. However, the results are usually long lasting, if not permanent.

Taita Lucho says there is a lot of confusion around ayahuasca. There also appears to be regular debate and some controversy about what constitutes legitimate ayahuasca. More than likely, shamans from various regions have traditionally used different plants in their mixtures to produce a variety of effects.

Lucho said that some ayahuasceros are mixing the male ayahuasca vine with the tree, "chacruna." They mix it with chacruna partly because it makes the brew more visual and psychedelic. People might have powerful experiences, but they are not drinking what he considers to be real ayahuasca since the chacruna is replacing the female vine. Taita Lucho claims that ayahuasca requires the feminine component to effectively do the deeper work of opening our hearts to the Fuente Sagrada.

A friend of mine recently put together some magical words. She addresses the need on our planet for an empowered feminine awakening: *The feeling life of the feminine connects us in a way that cannot be experienced with masculine intellect; this connection allows us to live in a more peaceful, compassionate, and loving manner. The inner realms that have been buried, the shadows that hold treasures, and the places inaccessible to the rational mind must be accessed, faced, and integrated as we evolve. The impulses to find balance and evolve are inherent in the design of Creation. May you continue to follow this impulse, climb the volcanoes of your fears, and find surrender in your eternal Source connection!*

www.ingramcontent.com/pod-product-compliance
Lightning Source LLC
Chambersburg PA
CBHW031412290426
44110CB00011B/345